Red Hat® Linux® 7

FOR

DUMMIES®

Red Hat® Linux® 7 FOR DUMMIES®

by Jon "maddog" Hall
and Paul G. Sery

Hungry Minds™

HUNGRY MINDS, INC.

New York, NY ◆ Cleveland, OH ◆ Indianapolis, IN

Red Hat ® Linux ® 7 For Dummies ®

Published by
Hungry Minds, Inc.
909 Third Avenue
New York, NY 10022
www.hungryminds.com
www.dummies.com

Copyright © 2001 Hungry Minds, Inc. All rights reserved. No part of this book, including interior design, cover design, and icons, may be reproduced or transmitted in any form, by any means (electronic, photocopying, recording, or otherwise) without the prior written permission of the publisher.

Library of Congress Control Number: 00-108205

ISBN: 0-7645-0795-8

Printed in the United States of America

10 9 8 7 6 5 4 3 2

1B/QZ/QU/QR/IN

Distributed in the United States by Hungry Minds, Inc.

Distributed by CDG Books Canada Inc. for Canada; by Transworld Publishers Limited in the United Kingdom; by IDG Norge Books for Norway; by IDG Sweden Books for Sweden; by IDG Books Australia Publishing Corporation Pty. Ltd. for Australia and New Zealand; by TransQuest Publishers Pte Ltd. for Singapore, Malaysia, Thailand, Indonesia, and Hong Kong; by Gotop Information Inc. for Taiwan; by ICG Muse, Inc. for Japan; by Intersoft for South Africa; by Eyrolles for France; by International Thomson Publishing for Germany, Austria and Switzerland; by Distribuidora Cuspide for Argentina; by LR International for Brazil; by Galileo Libros for Chile; by Ediciones ZETA S.C.R. Ltda. for Peru; by WS Computer Publishing Corporation, Inc., for the Philippines; by Contemporanea de Ediciones for Venezuela; by Express Computer Distributors for the Caribbean and West Indies; by Micronesia Media Distributor, Inc. for Micronesia; by Chips Computadoras S.A. de C.V. for Mexico; by Editorial Norma de Panama S.A. for Panama; by American Bookshops for Finland.

For general information on Hungry Minds' products and services please contact our Customer Care Department within the U.S. at 800-762-2974, outside the U.S. at 317-572-3993 or fax 317-572-4002.

For sales inquiries and reseller information, including discounts, premium and bulk quantity sales, and foreign-language translations, please contact our Customer Care Department at 800-434-3422, fax 317-572-4002, or write to Hungry Minds, Inc., Attn: Customer Care Department, 10475 Crosspoint Boulevard, Indianapolis, IN 46256.

For information on licensing foreign or domestic rights, please contact our Sub-Rights Customer Care Department at 212-884-5000.

For authorization to photocopy items for corporate, personal, or educational use, please contact Copyright Clearance Center, 222 Rosewood Drive, Danvers, MA 01923, or fax 978-750-4470.

For information on using Hungry Minds' products and services in the classroom or for ordering examination copies, please contact our Educational Sales Department at 800-434-2086 or fax 317-572-4005.

Please contact our Public Relations Department at 212-884-5163 for press review copies or 212-884-5000 for author interviews and other publicity information or fax 212-884-5400.

Hungry Minds™ is a trademark of Hungry Minds, Inc.

About the Author

Jon "maddog" Hall is the Executive Director of Linux International, a vendor organization dedicated to promoting the use of the Linux Operating System. He has been in the computer industry for over a quarter of a century (somehow that sounds more impressive than just "25 years"), the past 18 years of which have been spent using, programming, and admiring the UNIX Operating System. Currently, Jon works for Compaq Computer Corporation, where he is helping to shape Compaq's strategy with respect to Linux. Previously, Jon was the Department Head of Computer Science at Hartford State Technical College, where his students lovingly (he hopes) gave him the nickname "maddog" as he tried to teach them operating system design, compiler theory, and how to live an honorable life.

While working for Digital Equipment Corporation in May of 1994, maddog met Linus Torvalds, and was intelligent enough (his critics say maddog was just lucky) to recognize the potential of the Linux Operating System. Linux changed his life, mostly by providing him with 22-hour workdays. Since maddog has started working with Linux, however, he has also started meeting more girls (in particular, his two godchildren). You can usually find Jon speaking at various Linux conferences and events (maddog just barks), and he has also been known to travel long distances to speak to local Linux user groups.

Paul G. Sery Paul works for Sandia National Laboratories in Albuquerque, NM, USA. He is a member of the Computer Service Unit, Special Projects which specializes in managing and troubleshooting UNIX and Linux systems.

When he is not beating his head against systems administration problems, he and his wife Lidia enjoy riding their tandem through the bosque in the Rio Grande valley. They also enjoy traveling throughout Mexico. Paul is the author of Red Hat LINUX Network Toolkit, IDG Books Worldwide, 2000 and has a bachelor's degree in Electrical Engineering from the University of New Mexico.

Dedication

Jon "maddog" Hall: To Mom & Pop (TM), whose aversion to things electronic is well known, and who can still call their son Jon rather than maddog.

Paul G. Sery: To my wife, Lidia Maura Vazquez de Sery.

Author's Acknowledgments

I want to thank my wife, Lidia, for her patience, support and good advice that made writing this book possible. Without her, I would not have been able to start, much less finish the project.

I would also like to thank Laura Lewin, who gave me the chance to help write this book. She showed great confidence and patience in me. I am very grateful and wish her success in her new venture. Thanks also to Greg Croy for doing a great job managing the project to its conclusion.

And, of course, I'd like to thank the staff at IDG Books Worldwide who provided considerable and essential help too. I owe the Development Editor James Russell a six pack of Guinness (at least!). He worked tirelessly to keep the book on track in spite of many unanticipated problems; his advice and assistance was absolutely essential. Thanks also to Jeremy Zucker and Drew Michaels for their vital advice and assistance.

I'd also like to acknowledge a total lack of assistance in writing this book from my dog, the infamous Oso maloso; eater of many things that should have ended his career early, including but not limited to: ant poison, advil, many pounds of tootsie rolls one halloween, several bags of chicken bones one party, beer and other assorted items; escaper of many fences and gates; and friend of Paunchy (whose name you'll see throughout this book) and local bitches.

How useful was Oso? Well, one night while working on this book I got a call. Leaving my apple pie behind next to the keyboard, I went upstairs to answer the phone. I should have known something was up because he had a cell phone with him and no one answered when I picked up to take the call. I went down the stairs while he went up. The apple pie was gone. Oso 1, human 0.

— *Paul G. Sery*

Publisher's Acknowledgments

We're proud of this book; please send us your comments through our Online Registration Form located at www.dummies.com.

Some of the people who helped bring this book to market include the following:

Acquisitions, Editorial, and Media Development

Associate Project Editor: James H. Russell

Previous Project Editor: Jade Williams

Acquisitions Manager: Gregory S. Croy

Copy Editor: Jeremy Zucker

Previous Copy Editor: Kim Darosett

Proof Editor: Teresa Artman

Technical Editor: Drew Michaels

Permissions Editor: Laura Moss

Media Development Specialist: Gregory Stephens

Media Development Coordinator: Marisa E. Pearman

Editorial Manager: Kyle Looper

Media Development Manager: Laura Carpenter

Media Development Supervisor: Richard Graves

Editorial Assistant: Sarah Shupert

Production

Project Coordinator: Emily Wichlinski

Layout and Graphics: Beth Brooks, Jacque Schneider, Jeremey Unger

Proofreaders: Corey Bowen, Karl Brandt, Nancy Price, Charles Spencer, York Production Services, Inc.

Indexer: York Production Services, Inc.

General and Administrative

Hungry Minds, Inc.: John Kilcullen, CEO; Bill Barry, President and COO; John Ball, Executive VP, Operations & Administration; John Harris, CFO

Hungry Minds Technology Publishing Group: Richard Swadley, Senior Vice President and Publisher; Mary Bednarek, Vice President and Publisher, Networking and Certification; Walter R. Bruce III, Vice President and Publisher, General User and Design Professional; Joseph Wikert, Vice President and Publisher, Programming; Mary C. Corder, Editorial Director, Branded Technology Editorial; Andy Cummings, Publishing Director, General User and Design Professional; Barry Pruett, Publishing Director, Visual

Hungry Minds Manufacturing: Ivor Parker, Vice President, Manufacturing

Hungry Minds Marketing: John Helmus, Assistant Vice President, Director of Marketing

Hungry Minds Production for Branded Press: Debbie Stailey, Production Director

Hungry Minds Sales: Roland Elgey, Senior Vice President, Sales and Marketing; Michael Violano, Vice President, International Sales and Sub Rights

◆

The publisher would like to give special thanks to Patrick J. McGovern, without whom this book would not have been possible.

◆

Contents at a Glance

Cartoons at a Glance

By Rich Tennant

page 59

"Think of our relationship as the latest version of Red Hat Linux— I will not share a directory on the love-branch of your life."

page 309

page 327

"When we started the company, we weren't going to call it 'Red Hat'. But eventually we decided it sounded better than 'Beard of Bees Linux'."

page 9

page 199

"I'M GONNA HAVE A LITTLE TROUBLE WITH THIS 'FULL MOON' ICON ON OUR GRAPHICAL USERS INTERFACE."

page 115

Fax: 978-546-7747
E-mail: richtennant@the5thwave.com
World Wide Web: www.the5thwave.com

Table of Contents

Introduction

• •

*R*ed Hat Linux 7 For Dummies is designed to help you get Red Hat Linux working quickly and efficiently. This book shows you how to do fun and interesting — to say nothing of useful — things with Red Hat Linux. The book is also designed to be an effective doorstop or coffee coaster. Whatever you use it for, we hope that you have fun.

About This Book

This book is designed to be a helping-hands tutorial. It provides a place to turn to for help and solace in those moments when, after two hours of trying to get your network connection working, your five-year-old tells you that you need to use the `eth0` and not the `eth1` Ethernet interface.

We tried our hardest to fill up this book with the things you need to know about, such as:

- ✔ Installing Red Hat Linux
- ✔ Getting connected to the Internet
- ✔ Getting connected to your local network
- ✔ Building a simple firewall
- ✔ Using Red Hat Linux to do useful things, such as playing CDs, MP3s, and listening to the world's radio stations
- ✔ Understanding the GNOME desktop manager
- ✔ Using useful and usable applications, such as the StarOffice desktop productivity suite from Sun Microsystems, Inc. and RealPlayer from RealAudio, Inc.
- ✔ Working with the StarOffice desktop productivity suite to satisfy your word processing, calculating, and presentation needs
- ✔ Knowing where to go for help
- ✔ Managing your Red Hat Linux workstation

You'll see troubleshooting tips throughout the book (there's even a chapter devoted to the subject). It's not that Red Hat Linux is all that much trouble, but we want you to be prepared in case you run into bad luck.

Foolish Assumptions

You know what they say about people who make assumptions, but this book would never have been written if we didn't make a few. This book is for you if:

- ✔ You want to find out about the Linux operating system. Surprise — Red Hat Linux 7 is included with this book.
- ✔ You have a computer.
- ✔ You want to put the Red Hat Linux operating system and the computer together, and using duct tape hasn't worked.
- ✔ You don't need to become a Red Hat Linux guru — at least not yet.

Conventions Used in This Book

At computer conventions, thousands of computer people get together and talk about deep technical issues such as:

- ✔ What is the best hardware for running Red Hat Linux?
- ✔ Is Coke better than Pepsi?
- ✔ Could Superman beat Batman?

But these aren't the types of conventions we're talking about here. Our conventions are shorthand ways of designating specific information, such as what is and isn't a command or the meaning of certain funny-looking symbols.

Typing code

Commands in the text are shown `like this`. Commands not shown in the text, but set off on lines by themselves, look like this:

```
[lidia@veracruz lidia]$pwd
/home/lidia
```

Note: See the `[lidia@veracruz lidia]` in the preceding? You won't necessarily see that on your system, unless you happen to be my wife's mirror image who also likes Veracruz, Mexico very much. But you will see something similar depending on what your computer and username are. The first name — `lidia` — is replaced by whatever your user name is. The second name is your computer name. The final one is the directory that you are working from, which in this case is `lidia`'s home directory. Therefore, if your user name is `zoot` and computer name is `wishbone`, then your prompt is:

```
[zoot@wishbone zoot]$.
```

When you see stuff in boldface, it means it's something you should type. For example:

Type **man chown** at the command prompt and press Enter.

If we tell you to type something in a bolded step, the text you type won't be bold. As in:

   1. Type man chown **at the command prompt and press Enter.**

Here's a rundown of the command syntax in Linux:

- ✔ Text *not* surrounded by [ ] or { } brackets must be typed exactly as shown.
- ✔ Text that is italicized must be replaced with appropriate text.
- ✔ Text inside brackets [ ] is optional.
- ✔ Text in *italics* must be replaced with appropriate text.
- ✔ Text inside braces { } indicates that you must choose one of the values that are inside the braces and separated by the | sign.
- ✔ An ellipsis (. . .) means *and so on* or to repeat the preceding command line as needed.

Don't concern yourself with this too much now. For most of the book, you don't need to know these particulars. And when you do need to know something about a particular syntax, come back here for a refresher course.

Keystrokes and such

Keystrokes are shown with a plus sign between the keys. For example, Ctrl+Alt+Delete means you should press the Ctrl key, Alt key, and Delete key all at the same time. (No, we don't make you press any more than three keys at the same time.)

Most of the applications and utilities that we describe in this book use graphical user interfaces (GUI) such as GNOME, which allow you to control your computer by pointing and clicking with your mouse. Occasionally, however, we give non-graphical instructions that require pressing keys on your keyboard. In those situations, we often simplify the instructions by saying, "select OK". That generally means that you press the Tab key, which moves the cursor to the OK button, and then press the Enter key. That two-step process is equivalent to clicking an OK button in a GUI.

How This Book Is Organized

Like all proper *For Dummies* books, this book is organized into independent parts. You can read the parts in any order. Heck, try reading them backwards for a real challenge. This book is not meant to be read from front cover to back; rather, it was meant to be a reference book that helps you find what you're looking for when you're looking for it. Between the Contents at a Glance page, the Table of Contents, and the Index, you should have no problem finding what you need.

If you do read the book in order, you encounter the useful and interesting things first and the more technical items last. For instance, after installing Red Hat Linux in Part I, you may want to immediately proceed to Part II to see how to connect Linux to the Internet or your local network. From there you can use your new workstation to surf the Internet and use e-mail.

The following sections describe each part.

Part I: Installing Red Hat Linux

In Part I, you find out what Linux is and how to prepare your computer to install Red Hat Linux. We then walk you through installation and show you the basics of working with Red Hat Linux.

Part II: Got Net?

In Part II, you find out about connecting to the Internet and local networks. You see how to jump on the Internet with your everyday modem as well as how to join an existing network. If that local network has a high-speed Internet connection, then you can use it as your portal to the wonderful world of surfing. The Internet can be dangerous, so we include instructions on creating your own firewall. Finally, we show you how to use Netscape to satisfy your browsing and e-mail needs.

Part III: Linux, Huh! What Is It Good For? Absolutely Everything!

Part III guides you through the glorious particulars of actually doing something with Red Hat Linux. You are introduced to the GNOME desktop window environment. You are taken through its paces, by moving, resizing, hiding, closing windows, using the file manager, and much more. Two chapters are devoted to using Red Hat Linux's multimedia capabilities. You can listen to CDs and MP3s, as well as rip and record them. The world's radio stations are now available to you with streaming data technology. The full-featured StarOffice desktop productivity suite is described in some detail. You can use StarOffice with your Red Hat Linux machine to do all your writing and other work-related functions. You can even write a book with it! Finally, you see how to use your PalmPilot with Red Hat Linux.

Part IV: Revenge of the Nerds

In Part IV, you are guided through the processes necessary to care for and feed your new Linux computer. It's real nerd city but fun in its own way. Topics such as file management, script writing, and so on are introduced. We also introduce the software package management system — called RPM. We devote an entire chapter to the art of troubleshooting and take you through the process of configuring the X Window System, which is the basis for all Linux graphics.

Part V: The Part of Tens

A *For Dummies* book just isn't complete without a Part of Tens, where you can find ten all-important resources and answers to the ten most bothersome questions people have after installing Red Hat Linux. (The folks at Red Hat Software provided these questions.)

Part VI: Appendixes

Finally, the appendixes. Appendix A describes how to find out about the details of your computer's individual pieces of hardware; this is sometimes helpful when installing Red Hat Linux. Appendix A revisits the Red Hat Linux installation system using the *Text* mode. The nongraphical installation system — known as the Text mode — is described there in case the installation system cannot use your graphics driver. In Appendix C, instructions are given for using the de facto Linux text editor vi. In Appendix D, you find out all you need to know about the Linux man pages. Appendix E finishes by describing what you can find on the companion CD-ROMs.

Other uses for CD-ROMs

Where computers and computer programmers abound, lots of CD-ROMs arrive in the mail or as part of the software that someone bought. Eventually these CD-ROMs become obsolete or are never installed — that's the case with software products that arrive as unwanted advertising. What can ecologically minded programmers do with these CDs so that they don't fill up landfills?

One group of programmers we know uses them as coasters for drinks. Another group makes mobiles out of them. (The sun shining off the CD-ROMs makes wonderful rainbows on the wall.) Still others use the CD-ROMs as clocks, by purchasing inexpensive quartz-crystal clock motors (complete with hands) and using the CD-ROM as the face of the clock. I have four

of these clocks made out of Windows NT CD-ROMs — hey, can you imagine a better use for them?

More exotic uses require high heat to melt the CD-ROMs around the base of a water tumbler, creating either a nice flowerpot or, with the hole plugged, an ashtray. As you can imagine, this causes some consternation among management at these facilities, particularly after they find out that one of the more expensive programs they've purchased has ended up at the bottom of a flowerpot.

For now, please keep your *Red Hat Linux 7 For Dummies* CD-ROM in a safe place, such as the sleeve in the back of the book, when you are not using it.

What You're Not to Read

Heck, you don't have to read any of the book if you don't want to, but why did you buy it? (Not that we're complaining.) Part I has background information. If you don't want it, don't read it. Also, text in sidebars is optional, although often helpful. If you're on the fast track to using Linux, you could skip the sidebars and the text with a technical stuff icon. But we suggest instead that you slow down a bit and enjoy the experience.

Icons in This Book

Nifty little shortcuts and timesavers. Red Hat Linux is a powerful operating system, and you can save unbelievable amounts of time and energy by utilizing its tools and programs. We hope our tips show you how.

Don't let this happen to you! We hope that our experiences with Red Hat Linux will help you avoid the mistakes we made.

Recall information that is given here for later use.

 This is particularly nerdy, technical information. You may skip it, but you may find it interesting if you're of a geekier bent.

 This icon flags discussions that relate to the CD-ROM. The CD-ROM is a copy of the Red Hat Linux 7.0, the latest distribution available at publishing time.

 This icon points out new features in the Red Hat Linux 7 distribution.

Where to Go from Here

You are about to join the legions of people who have been using and developing Linux. We've found Red Hat Linux to be a flexible, powerful operating system, capable of solving most problems even without a large set of commercial software. The future of the Linux, and Red Hat Linux in particular, operating system is bright. The time and energy you expend in becoming familiar with it will be worthwhile. Carpe Linuxum.

Part I
Installing Red Hat Linux

The 5th Wave   By Rich Tennant

"When we started the company, we weren't going to call it 'Red Hat'. But eventually we decided it sounded better than 'Beard of Bees Linux'."

In this part . . .

You're about to embark on a journey through the Red Hat Linux installation program. Perhaps you know nothing about setting up the operating system on your computer. That's okay. The Red Hat Linux installation system is savvy and helpful. Plus, we will help guide you.

In Chapter 1, you begin to discover what Red Hat Linux is all about and what it can do for you. Chapter 2 helps you to get ready to install Red Hat Linux. The real fun begins in Chapter 3 when you install your own Penguin. Finally, Chapter 4 gives you a brief, but important, introduction to working with Red Hat Linux.

Chapter 1

And in the Opposite Corner . . . a Penguin?

In This Chapter

▶ Napping through a bit o' Linux history

▶ Finding out what Red Hat Linux can do

▶ Checking out how you can use Red Hat Linux

*W*e see a penguin in your future. He's an unassuming fellow who is taking on a rather big foe — Microsoft's Windows operating systems — in the battle is for computer users. Red Hat Linux, with its splashy brand and the notorious logo, is undeniably one of the most popular distribution of Linux, if not the most popular.

This chapter introduces you to the latest and greatest Red Hat release: Red Hat Linux 7. This book covers all the bases — well, a good number of bases at least — including how to use Red Hat Linux as a desktop productivity tool, Internet portal, and multimedia workstation. You can do lots of things with Red Hat Linux, and this chapter gives you a good overview of the possibilities, as well as a brief look at the history of Linux.

After you get the hang of Linux, you can use your Linux system in the ways described in this chapter; or you can invent new and creative ways to use it! That's the power of the penguin — it's up to you.

History of the World (Err, Linux) Part 2

In the beginning of computerdom (said in a booming, thunderous voice) the world was filled with hulking mainframes that got so hot that they required chilled water to cool them down. These slothful beasts lumbered through large corporations, required a special priesthood of ultra-nerds to herd them, and ate up huge chunks of space and power — and money. Then came the IBM PC and Windows, and the world changed. Power to the people — sort of.

Then in 1991, a student at the University of Helsinki named Linus Torvalds found himself dissatisfied with his current operating system. Torvalds thought that the Unix operating system may be better suited to help him accomplish his task, but Unix was very expensive and so he began writing his own version of Unix. After formulating the basic parts himself, Torvalds recruited a team of talented programmers and together they created a new operating system, or *kernel,* now called Linux.

One of the most important decisions that Torvalds made in the early days of Linux was to freely distribute the Linux kernel code for anyone to do with as they wish. These free distributions were and still are available in several forms: from the Internet, on CD-ROMs and floppy disks, from software publishers (who charge a distribution fee), or bundled with other programs (which organizations can charge for). The only restriction: If you distributed the modified code, you couldn't prevent anyone from using, modifying, and distributing — freely or for profit — it. We can't overstress the importance of making operating-system source code freely available; this method has resulted in a Linux operating system that continues to improve rapidly — even organically.

By the early spring of 1994, the first real version of Linux (Version 1.0) was available for public use. Even then it was an impressive operating system, including features found in operating systems that cost hundreds of dollars and running smartly on computers with less than 2MB of RAM and a simple 386 microprocessor. By the summer of 2000, the number of estimated Linux users sat at something like 15 million (because no licenses are issued to individual users, a more precise number can't be determined), proving pretty decisively that Linux is here to stay.

By the way, if you're wondering about the whole penguin thing, the answer is actually disappointingly simple. Linus Torvalds, the inventor of the Linux operating system, loves penguins. Thus, the friendly penguin is the natural symbol of the Linux world. Some mystery, eh?

Knowing What You Can Do with Red Hat Linux

Linux is free and the source code for the entire operating system is easily available. Red Hat Linux is an *integrated product,* meaning that Red Hat, Inc. combines the basic Linux operating system with software (some made by others, some made by Red Hat) to produce a package whose value is greater than the sum of its parts. That combination is known as a *distribution* of Linux.

Linux everywhere (Multiplatform, buuuuddy)

The Linux operating system has been *ported* (or converted) from the 32-bit Intel architecture to a number of other architectures, including Alpha, MIPS, PowerPC, and SPARC, giving users a choice of hardware manufacturers and keeping the Linux kernel flexible for new processors. Linux now handles *symmetric multiprocessing* (more than one CPU or mathematical and logical programming unit per system box). In addition, projects are in the works to provide sophisticated processing capabilities, such as:

✔ **Real-time programming:** Controlling machinery or testing equipment.

✔ **High availability:** Running a reliable computer all the time.

✔ **Scalability:** Boosting computer power by adding more system boxes rather than faster CPUs.

This last capability — known as Extreme Linux systems — enables research organizations to create machines of supercomputer capabilities at a fraction of the price of supercomputers. In certain cases, Extreme Linux systems have been made from obsolete PCs, costing the organizations that make them nothing in material costs.

So that you can get up and running with Red Hat Linux 7 as quickly as possible, we've been sweet enough to include the operating system on CD-ROM with this book. See Chapters 2 and 3 if you're chomping at the bit to install the new version.

Initially the sole domain of business and university servers, Red Hat Linux is now used by businesses, individuals, and governments to cut costs, improve performance, and just plain get work done. You can use Red Hat Linux as a desktop workstation, a server system, an Internet gateway, a firewall, the basis of an embedded system (such as a smart VCR or a robot), or even as a supercomputer. And thanks to the thousands of people working on different parts of Linux, Red Hat Linux becomes more flexible and capable with each release.

The following list includes some of the cooler features of Red Hat Linux:

✔ **Fully-protected multitasking:** System tasks are automatically prevented from interferring with each other, which allows more than one program to run at a time without your system crashing every five minutes. This feature prevents problems such as the dreaded Windows *Blue Screen of Death* (where Windows tells you it's messed up and that you'll have to reboot and like it, basically). Fully-protected multitasking also means that multiple people can access a Red Hat Linux computer at one time.

✔ **Large file support:** Red Hat Linux can handle very large files and programs. In fact, the Intel Pentium processor can handle files as large as
2GB. If you are the type of person who works with large databases, for
example, you can store them on your own workstation if you have a
large enough hard drive.

✔ **Graphical user interface (GUI):** Red Hat Linux includes a sophisticated
windowing system called the X Window System, also known as X, and
the GNOME desktop manager (and even KDE if you want to use it
instead of or in addition to GNOME). Together, X and GNOME give you
a powerful and very stable graphical workstation.

✔ **File sharing:** Red Hat Linux can share files with Windows, OS/2,
Macintosh, most other distributions of Linux, and of course Unix computers, showing just how flexible its networking capabilities are. For
example, if you run both Red Hat Linux and Windows on the same computer, you can retrieve Microsoft Word files from your Windows partition so you can read them with StarOffice.

Boosting your personal workstation

With Red Hat Linux you can easily create a powerful personal workstation,
with Linux providing the platform for all the applications that you need to get
your work done. Many applications come bundled with Red Hat Linux, such as
the Netscape Communicator Web browser, address books, editors, and database engines. You can also download products such as Sun Microsystems'
StarOffice office productivity suite to satisfy your word-processing, spread-
sheet-editing, and other desktop publishing needs.

The following list describes just a few of the major categories of free software
that are available for Linux, along with some examples of popular programs.

Not all of the software listed below is included on the CDs with this book.
StarOffice, for instance, is only available for download over the Internet or
on CD.

✔ **Automated network backup systems:** Commercial backup systems
that can automatically back up your workstation, can back up other
computers on a network, and can dictate exactly which systems get
backed up, when, and how the backup is performed. Knox Software's
Arkeia (`www.arkeia.com`) and Enchanced Software Technologies' BRU
(`www.bru.com`) are two examples. Both provide free demonstration systems that you can use for testing purposes.

✔ **Compilers:** Used to convert the source code of a program into a form
that your computer can understand and execute. Red Hat Linux provides several source code compilers, including compilers for languages
such as C, C++, and Fortran.

✓ **Freely distributable and freeware programs:** Programs that can be downloaded from the Internet and used without paying to register the product. Literally dozens of software packages are available on the CDs that come with this book, including (but by no means limited to) the `pine` text-based e-mail reader, the zip (that compresses files using the same format as WinZip) data compression program, the Gimp graphics manipulation program, and the gedit text editor.

✓ **Office suites:** Complete desktop productivity suites such as StarOffice and Applixware offer packages that include word processors, HTML editors, spreadsheet editors, and graphics editors; or you can go with straight, no-frills word processing with the well-known WordPerfect word processor. For more information on office productivity applications, see Chapter 12.

✓ **Web browsers:** Netscape Communicator 4.75 is included with Red Hat Linux 7. Red Hat Linux also provides the `lynx` and `links` text-based Web browsers, which do not show graphics but are otherwise fully functional Web browsers. The text-based Web browsers come in handy when using an older, slower modem because they do not require as much speed as Netscape Communicator does. For more info on Netscape Communicator, see Chapter 7.

Accessing Internet/intranet services

Many capabilities of the Internet (outside of a single business) and intranets (internal to a single business) are possible because of HTML and the Web. Unix systems were at the forefront of these developments, and Linux shares many benefits of that heritage. Both the Internet and intranets require similar services, such as the following:

✓ **Firewalls:** A system that controls access to your private network from any outside network (in this case, the Internet) and to control access from your private network to the outside world. To keep the bad guys out, Red Hat Linux provides protection by giving you the tools to build your own firewall. Red Hat Linux is very flexible in this regard and many software packages are available, including the popular and simple to use `ipchains` filtering software (which is included on the accompanying CD-ROMs). We discuss firewalls in greater detail in Chapters 5 and 6.

✓ **FTP (File Transfer Protocol):** A protocol that lets you get files and software from FTP sites (all of which start with `ftp://` in the URL) that you can access with Netscape Navigator or a dedicated FTP client.

✓ **Internet gateways:** Software with which you can automatically connect your computer (and thus your private network) to the Internet, giving your private network a permanent, virtual connection for the price of a single phone line. Red Hat Linux includes the `diald` utility for just this purpose (see Chapter 5 for more info about `diald`).

✔ **Samba and NFS (Network File System):** Red Hat provides these two programs so that you can share files over a network. Because of its multi-tasking capability, virtual memory, and powerful file system, Red Hat Linux (with the help of Samba) works well as a file and print server for Windows systems, enabling PCs to communicate with the file system and printers attached to a Linux machine. Of course, Red Hat Linux and the NFS together can share files and printers with other Linux and Unix systems.

✔ **Telnet:** Supports users logging in and using machines remotely.

✔ **Turnkey systems:** No, that's not turkey. A *turnkey* system is put together once and then duplicated in hundreds or thousands of places. Turnkey systems are typically used for easy information kiosks, hotel reservation systems, doctor and lawyer office systems, and automotive diagnostic systems. Linux is perfect for a turnkey system because it provides the security, protection, and stability that these systems need, without requiring payments for each installed copy of the operating system.

✔ **Web servers:** Allow users to see Web pages. Many Internet service providers *(ISPs)* use Linux to deliver these services to their customers.

Chapter 2

Preparing Your Hard Drive for Red Hat Linux

- -

In This Chapter

▶ Finding out what you need to install Red Hat Linux

▶ Creating a boot disk if you can't boot from CD

▶ Repartitioning with `fips` so that Red Hat Linux can bunk with Windows

- -

*U*nless you have a brand-spanking-new hard drive with nothing on it, you must get your hard drive prepared before you can install Red Hat. This process is pretty straightforward when you have an entire hard drive to use for the installation, but harsh reality (or Windows) unfortunately often dictates that you may not have that luxury. But all is not lost! With the caveat that your hard drive needs to have enough free space to accommodate both operating systems, Red Hat Linux can happily coexist with other operating systems such as Windows — you just choose one operating system or the other when you start the computer.

This chapter shows you how to properly tenderize and marinate your hard drive so that Red Hat Linux can sit happily alongside Windows (or another operating system), and how to create a boot floppy disk that is necessary to get the installation process started on some older computers. Chapter 3 picks up where this chapter leaves off and shows you how to install Red Hat Linux.

Knowing What You Need to Do to Prepare Your Hard Drive for Red Hat Linux

Before you install Red Hat Linux on your hard drive, you need to do get your hard drive ready, especially if you intend to have Windows (or another operating system) installed on the same hard drive as Linux.

The following list describes the process you need to follow to prepare your hard drive for Red Hat Linux:

1. **Put on a red fedora hat (and have a mirror nearby so that you can see how cool you look!).**

2. **Make room on your computer for Red Hat Linux if you want to install it alongside Windows (or another operating system).**

   This step is totally unnecessary if you don't want Red Hat Linux to coexist with another operating system.

3. **Determine if your computer can boot from CD-ROM.**

   In the next section we show you how to test your computer to see if it can boot from CD-ROM.

   If you can boot from the CD-ROM and don't have another operating system you want to keep, you can safely skip this entire chapter and just move on to the actual installation in Chapter 3 (lucky you!). If you can boot from the CD-ROM and do have another operating system you want to keep, such as Windows, you don't need to haggle with the silly boot disk business in this section and can skip to the "Move Over Windows, Here Comes Something Meatier" section later in this chapter.

4. **Create a boot disk if your computer is not able to boot directly from CD-ROM.**

   We show you how to create a boot disk using either Windows (or MS-DOS) or Linux later in this chapter.

Finding Out If Your Computer Can Boot from CD-ROM

To start the Red Hat Linux installation process, you need some sort of boot disk (or disc), be it the *Red Hat Linux 7 For Dummies* CD1 that comes with this book (the easy way) or a boot floppy disk, which you have to create (the slightly less easy way).

If you have a computer that was manufactured around 1997 or later, then you can probably boot directly from the CD-ROM.

Testing whether or not your computer can boot from CD-ROM is really easy: place CD1 that comes with this book into your computer's CD-ROM drive and turn your computer on. If Red Hat Linux starts its preinstallation process, you're golden. If nothing happens, your computer is either not set by default to boot from CD-ROM or your computer isn't capable of doing so.

If your computer doesn't boot, that doesn't necessarily mean that it's unable to boot from CD; the option may be there but isn't turned on. You can try and follow these general steps to find out if your computer is capable of booting from CD-ROM (just about every BIOS is different from the next, and so it's impossible for us to make these steps anything but general):

1. **Boot (that is, turn on) your computer.**

   During the initial start phase, you should see some simple text displayed. While this is going on, you should see an instruction telling you what key to press to gain access to the menu that allows you to modify your computer's. For example, typical instructions are Press <F1> to Enter Setup or Press <DEL> to Enter Setup.

   BIOS stands for Basic Input/Output Settings. The BIOS controls the most basic functions of your computer that do not require an operating system like Red Hat Linux or Windows to work. For example, the BIOS controls what devices your computer uses to boot from.

2. **Press the correct key to enter the BIOS.**

   A BIOS setup menu is displayed. Most of the time, you need to press a function key (F1, F2, and so on) to enter the various submenus and then identify the submenu that controls your computer's boot sequence.

3. **When you see the menu that includes your computer's boot sequence, press the approriate function key to enter the menu.**

   This may take a bit of sniffing around, as some of the menus may have some fairly techie-sounding names. Go ahead and feel free to enter menus, just be very careful not to change anything. If you do accidentally change something and you're not sure how to fix it, exit your BIOS making sure to choose *not* to save changes when the BIOS asks you whether you want to save upon exit!

   Once you're in the boot sequence menu, it should be obvious whether your computer can boot from CD-ROM or not — if you toggle through the list of options there should be a reference to a CD-ROM alongside references to your floppy drive and your actual hard drive.

4a. **If you find a CD-ROM listing, follow these steps:**

   1. Select the CD-ROM option (or equivalent) as the first device in your computer's boot sequence.

   2. Press the Esc key to exit from the menu.

   3. Make sure to save the changes you made when your BIOS asks if you want to save.

   4. Reboot your computer from the CD-ROM.

4b. **If you *don't* see any way to make your computer boot from CD-ROM, exit your BIOS without saving changes and skip to one of the next two sections to create your boot disk from either Windows (or MS-DOS) or Linux.**

Creating a Red Hat Linux Boot Disk with Windows or MS-DOS

If you have an MS-DOS, Windows 9*x*/ME or a Windows NT/2000 system, then you can use your system to read the accompanying CD-ROM as well as create your boot disk. The CD includes a program called `rawrite.exe` that you can use to make the disks while you're running Windows.

If you need to use a PCMCIA card for a CD-ROM controller to install Linux (if you have a laptop computer with an Ethernet connection, for example), you have to create the PCMCIA version of the boot disk, which is also on CD1. In that case, substitute the `pcmcia.img` file for the `boot.img` file in the following instructions. If you need to install Red Hat Linux over a network — for example, if your PC or notebook does not have a CD-ROM drive but another computer on the network does — then you need to create a network boot disk. In this case, substitute the `bootnet.img` file for the `boot.img` file in the following instructions.

In the following instructions, I assume that your CD-ROM is drive D: and your floppy drive is A:. If your drive letter designations are different, substitute the appropriate letters for *D* and *A* in the following instructions.

To create a boot disk, follow these steps:

1. **On a Windows computer, open a command prompt by clicking the Start button and choosing Programs⇨MS-DOS Prompt (or Programs⇨Command Prompt on a Windows NT/2000 machine).**

   If you are running MS-DOS, then you are already at a command prompt, which should look similar to `C:\>`.

2. **Insert an MS-DOS formatted, high-density (1.44MB) 3½-inch floppy into the floppy drive.**

3. **Insert CD1 that came with this book into your CD-ROM drive.**

4. **Type** d: **at the command prompt and press Enter.**

5. **Type** cd \dosutils **at the command prompt and press Enter.**

6. **Type** rawrite **at the command prompt and press Enter.**

   `rawrite` opens and asks you to enter the disk image source filename.

7. **Type** d:\images\boot.img **at the command prompt and press Enter.**

   `rawrite` asks you to enter the location of the target disk drive where you want to create the boot disk.

8. **Type** a: **at the command prompt and press Enter.**

   `rawrite` tells you to insert a formatted disk into your A: drive and press Enter.

9. **Verify that you have a formatted disk in your A: drive and press Enter.**

   `rawrite` copies the boot image to the floppy disk, which can now *boot* (start up) your computer and begin the Red Hat Linux installation process.

   Wait until the floppy disk drive light is out before removing the disk.

10. **Remove the boot disk and label it something ridiculously obvious like "Boot Disk" so that you know what it is later.**

Making a Boot Disk with Linux

If you don't have access to MS-DOS or Windows but do have access to another Linux system, this section is for you. To make a boot disk in Linux, you must log in as a user with permission to write to the 3½-inch floppy drive, which Linux refers to as /dev/fd0.

To create the boot disk and supplemental disk, follow these steps:

1. **Insert a blank, formatted floppy into your floppy drive and insert CD1 that came with this book into your CD-ROM drive.**

   Next you have to mount the CD (*mount* meaning to make the CD visible to the rest of the file system).

2. **Type mount /mnt/cdrom at the command prompt and press Enter.**

3. **Change to the images directory by typing cd /mnt/cdrom/images at the command prompt and pressing Enter.**

4. **Type dd if=boot.img of=/dev/fd0 at the command prompt and press Enter.**

   Linux copies the boot image to your floppy disk.

5. **You may dismount the CD-ROM (remove it from the rest of the file system) by typing cd / and pressing Enter and then typing umount /mnt/cdrom and pressing Enter.**

   Wait until the floppy disk drive light is out before removing the disk.

6. **Remove the boot disk from your disk drive and label it something obvious like "Boot Disk" so that you know what it is later.**

Move Over Windows, Here Comes Something Meatier

Before you install Red Hat Linux on your hard drive, you need to make room for it. Some people find space by getting rid of Windows and installing Red Hat Linux by itself, while others don't want to make such drastic changes and prefer to have Red Hat Linux and their other operating system coexist peacefully. The former configuration is referred to as a *standalone system* and the latter as a *dual-boot system.*

Chapter 3 shows you how to install and use a standalone Red Hat Linux system, and all discussions and examples in the following chapters assume you have a standalone system. However, many people find dual-boot systems to be desirable, and so we describe how to create one here using partitions.

A *partition* is a section of space on a drive used to organize files and directories. For example, the famous C: drive in MS-DOS and Windows is installed on its own partition on your hard drive. Most people wouldn't know this necessarily, because most systems come with only one large partition that hogs up the entire hard drive. You can reconfigure an existing Windows partition so that you can install Red Hat Linux on the same disk using one of two methods: shrinking the DOS partition by using *destructive repartitioning* and thereby wiping out all the data on the hard drive; or by using *nondestructive repartitioning,* which moves and confines existing data on the hard drive safely into its own partition, leaving the rest of your hard drive for Linux.

Microsoft's NTFS file system (Windows NT/2000 typically uses NTFS but can also use FAT32) cannot be altered with the tools provided by Red Hat Linux. Therefore, you can't create a dual-boot computer on an NTFS-formatted disk that does not already have an extra partition that you can use. If your NTFS-based computer has more than one partition, then you can use one of the partitions to install Red Hat Linux. You have to be willing, of course, to lose whatever is installed on that partition to do so.

We strongly suggest backing up any important files on your hard drive before performing any major work on repartitioning it. You don't want to lose any data or programs that you worked hard to install. Refer to your system's owners' manual to find out how to back up your system and how to restore the data if necessary.

Nondestructive Repartitioning with fips: Can't We All Just Get Along?

If you can't add another hard drive to your system, and your only choices are destructive and nondestructive repartitioning, then the latter is definitely the better choice if you want to keep existing data or another operating system on the same computer as Red Hat Linux. You still should back up your system, just in case you have to restore it afterward.

The fips utility works by dividing the drive into two partitions. The first partition includes your other operating system, such as Windows or MS-DOS.

The second partition, which begins at the end of the space used by DOS or Windows and encompassing the rest of the drive space, is the non-DOS partition where you install Red Hat Linux.

If you want to use the `fips` utility to repartition your hard drive, keep in mind that your DOS partition can hold only 2GB or less. If the amount of used space on your DOS partition is greater than 2GB, you won't be able to nondestructively repartition unless you either delete some files or move them to another drive.

If you decide to keep space on your hard drive for DOS or another operating system, try to keep that operating system in the first partition. Trust us — managing DOS and Linux together is going to be much easier this way.

The next two sections contain steps for defragmenting your hard drive and using `fips` to carve the drive into partitions.

Defragmenting your hard drive

Defragmenting a hard drive consolidates all the data on your hard drive within one partition, leaving the empty space behind for Linux. This is necessary because Windows is a slob as operating systems go, throwing data all over the hard drive rather than in any sort of logical order.

Follow the steps in one of the following two sections to defragment your hard drive while running Windows or MS-DOS.

Defragmenting in Windows 9x/ME or Windows NT/2000

The following steps show you how to defrag your hard drive in Windows 9x/ME or Windows NT/2000:

1. **Close all programs and windows on your system, leaving just the desktop and icon bar.**

2. **Double-click the My Computer icon on the desktop.**

3. **Select your C: drive by clicking it and choosing File⇨Properties⇨Tools.**

4. **Click Defragment Now.**

   The defragmentation program looks at the drive to determine whether it needs defragmentation.

   You may get a message telling you that you don't need to defragment because your hard drive is not very fragmented, but don't believe it. Under normal circumstances this may be true. But in this case, defragmenting your hard drive is necessary because you're going to move the end of the partition file system and make the partition smaller, erasing any data outside of that barrier.

5. Click Start.

The defragmentation window appears and the defrag process begins.

Defragmenting can take a long time, depending on the size of your hard drive.

By clicking the Show Details button, you can scroll up and down the large window to watch the defrag process in action, as shown in Figure 2-1. The colored blocks represent programs and data, and the white space represents free space on your hard drive that fips can allocate to the Linux file system. The movement of the blocks around the screen shows that the data is being moved forward on the drive. Expect to see white space appear toward the bottom of the window, which represents the end of your drive. At the end of the defragmentation process, no colored blocks should appear at the bottom of the window, and all the blocks should be compressed toward the top of the window.

After what may seem like a long time, defragmentation finishes. All useful blocks of information are now at the beginning of the drive, making it ready for the fips program in the "Resizing with fips" section later in this chapter.

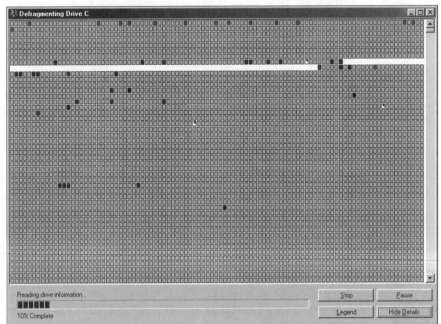

Figure 2-1:
The defrag program in progress.

Defragmenting in MS-DOS or Windows 3.x

Follow these steps to defragment your hard drive in Windows 3.*x* or MS-DOS:

1. **Close all programs and windows on your system.**

2. **If you're running Windows, exit from Windows into MS-DOS by choosing File⇨Exit Windows.**

3. **Type** cd \dos **at the command prompt and press Enter.**

4. **Type** defrag **at the command prompt and press Enter.**

   The defrag program asks you which drive to defragment.

5. **Use the letter keys on your keyboard to select the drive you want to defragment.**

   The defragmentation program looks at the drive to determine whether it needs defragmentation.

   You may get a message telling you that you don't need to defragment because your hard drive is not very fragmented, but don't believe it. Under normal circumstances this may be true. But in this case, defragmenting your hard drive is necessary because you're going to move the end of the partition file system and make the partition smaller, erasing any data outside of that barrier.

6. **Defragment the drive even if the program says the drive doesn't need defragmenting.**

   After what may seem like a long time, defragmentation finishes. All useful blocks of information are now at the beginning of the drive, making it ready for the fips program in the next section.

Resizing with fips

The MS-DOS fips utility is used to nondestructively resize your MS-DOS and/or Windows partitions. Newer versions of Windows 9*x* (including Windows ME) use a 32-bit file allocation table (called FAT32) and drive management that provide for single-drive configurations larger than 2GB. Older versions of Windows 95 used a 16-bit FAT (called FAT16, oddly enough); to use the space above 2GB, the drive had to be partitioned into logical drives of 2GB or less. Newer computers often have drives larger than the old 2GB limit. If the drive is repartitioned, the large drive management system is disabled, and DOS and Windows partitions are once again limited to 2GB.

To use fips, you must first exit your Windows interface and get to the MS-DOS prompt. To do so with Windows 9*x*, follow these steps (in Windows ME or Windows NT/2000, you need to reboot with an MS-DOS boot disk that includes the fips utility):

1. **Click the Start button.**

2. **Click the Shut Down button.**

3. **Select the Restart the Computer in MS-DOS Mode option.**

   If your computer is not capable of booting into MS-DOS mode (such as with Windows ME), then you have one other option: If you can obtain an MS-DOS boot floppy (one that has CD-ROM drivers configured on it), then you can boot from it; the CD-ROM drivers are necessary because you have to access the fips program on CD1.

4. **Copy the** fips.exe **program from CD1 to your boot disk.**

   For MS-DOS and earlier versions of Windows 95 you need to use the FAT16 version of fips.exe, which is stored in the \dosutils\fips15c\ directory. For later versions of Windows 9*x*/ME, the FAT32 version of fips.exe is found in \dosutils\fips20\ directory. You can find documentation on both versions in the fips.doc file, which can be found in the \dosutils\fips15c\ (for the FAT16 version) and \dosutils\fips20\ (for the FAT32 version) directories on CD1.

5. **Boot your computer from the floppy.**

   The computer restarts in MS-DOS mode.

6. **Type** cd a: **at the DOS prompt and press Enter.**

7. **Type** fips **at the prompt and press Enter.**

   Some messages appear and flash by, but you can ignore them all except the last one, which asks you to press any key.

8. **When you see the** Press any key **message, do so.**

   You see all the existing partitions on the hard drive.

9. **When you see the** Press any key **message, do so again.**

   You're getting pretty good at this! A description of the drive and a series of messages flash by. Then fips finds the free space in the first partition.

10. **When asked whether you want to make a backup copy of sectors, type** y **for yes.**

    The screen asks whether a floppy disk is in your A: drive.

11. **Place a formatted floppy disk into your A: drive and then press** y.

    A message similar to Writing file a:\rootboot.000 appears, followed by other messages and then the message Use cursor key to choose the cylinder, enter to continue.

    Three columns appear on the screen: Old Partition, Cylinder, and New Partition. The Old Partition number is the number of megabytes in the main partition of your hard drive. The New Partition number is the number of megabytes in the new partition you're making for the Linux operating system.

12. Use the left- and right-arrow keys to change the numbers in the Old Partition and New Partition fields to give you the space you need for both the Windows operating system and Linux (see Figure 2-2).

A minimum Linux system, without the X Window System graphical environment, requires about 40MB of hard drive space. A minimal graphical environment requires about 150MB of hard drive space. The full distribution, along with all the programs and compilers on the hard drive, requires about 680MB of hard drive space. Then you have the amount of data space you need for your own files. The amount of data space that you leave for the Linux and Microsoft operating systems is up to you, but the more space you leave the more storage space you have.

13. When you have the correct amount of hard drive space in each field, press the Enter key.

fips displays the partition table again, showing you the new partition that has been created for the Linux operating system. This new partition will probably be partition 2; your C drive is probably partition 1.

You also see a message at the bottom of the screen asking whether you want to continue or reedit.

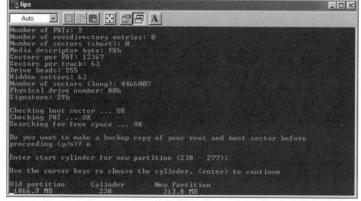

Figure 2-2:
The fips
program
carving up a
hard drive.

14. If you are satisfied with the size of your partitions, type c to continue (if you are *not* satisfied type r, which takes you back to Step 7).

Many more messages about your hard drive flash by. A message then appears, stating that the system is ready to write the new partition scheme to disk and asking whether you want to proceed.

15. Type y to make fips write the new partition information to the hard drive.

If you type **n**, fips exits without changing anything on your hard drive, leaving your hard drive exactly the way it was after you defragmented it.

16. **To test that nondestructive partitioning worked properly, reboot your system by pressing Ctrl+Alt+Delete.**

17. **Allow Windows to start and then run ScanDisk by clicking the Start button and choosing Programs⇨Accessories⇨System Tools⇨ScanDisk.**

    ScanDisk indicates whether you have all the files and folders you started with and whether anything was lost. Even if everything is found to be okay, consider keeping any backup files around for a while to be on the safe side.

Now you're ready to install the Linux operating system, which we show you how to do in Chapter 3.

Chapter 3

Ready, Set, Install!

．．．

In This Chapter

▶ Starting the Red Hat Linux installation

▶ Letting Red Hat Linux partition your hard drive for you

▶ Installing software

▶ Configuring your new installation

．．．

*I*nstalling Red Hat Linux isn't rocket science — it's more like nuclear science. No, no, just kidding! Don't run! Just relax, sit down, grab your favorite drink, and contemplate the excitement about to unfold: the installation and configuration of Red Hat Linux! After you're done, you'll have a powerful computer capable of performing most, if not all, of your daily chores — all for the cost of this book! That's pretty amazing when you think about it: For a few bucks, you get the same amount of operating power that cost a million dollars just a few years ago!

This chapter walks you through the Workstation installation of Red Hat Linux, which automates otherwise horrifically complicated decisions that no sane person would want to haggle with, such as partitioning your hard drive and selecting software. The Workstation installation includes the GNOME graphical user interface (GUI) and all of the tools that an average computer user needs to survive. If you want software that the Workstation install doesn't provide, you can always add packages later.

You can run the Red Hat Linux installation system from a graphical interface or from a text-based interface. The graphical method is the default, and that's what we discuss in this chapter. In addition to the ease of using a mouse to point-and-click, the graphical method has the advantage of grouping similar configuration choices together. For example, the keyboard and mouse selection is presented within one window, not two, as in the text-based installation. If you really, really want to use the text-based install, or you have to do so (in some cases, the Red Hat Linux installation system can not use your graphics adapter, for example), we show you how in Appendix B.

If you choose any installation other than the Workstation install — which we think the vast majority of users will be perfectly happy with — the instructions in this chapter will differ significantly from the steps you actually have to follow to perform the installation.

Installation Stage 1: Starting the Install

To begin installing Red Hat Linux, you need to boot or reboot (*boot* means to start, *reboot* means to restart) your computer with CD1 that comes with this book in your CD-ROM drive (if you can boot from the CD-ROM) or a boot disk in your main floppy drive (if you can't boot from CD-ROM). (In Chapter 2 we show you how to test whether or not you can boot from the CD-ROM and how to make a boot disk if you can't.)

Red Hat provides a complete and detailed installation guide on CD3 that comes with this book. If you have access to another computer — Linux or Windows — you can mount the Red Hat CD-ROM on that computer and look at the manual with Netscape or another browser. If you have another Linux computer, mount CD3 that comes with this book (the documentation CD-ROM) and open the `index.html` file in the `/mnt/cdrom/rh-docs/` directory on CD3; on a Windows computer, you want to look at the `index.htm` file in the `\rh-docs\` directory instead.

If you ever want to stop the installation process, simply eject the boot disk (if you're using the boot floppy), remove the CD from the drive, and reboot your machine. This does not affect your computer — other than losing the installation configuration information that you've entered if you enter before you've written the changes to disk at the end of the installation (see the last section in this chapter for more info). The point of no return comes when the installation process partitions your hard drive and starts writing software to it. If you stop at that point, you need to reinstall an operating system before using the computer again.

1. **Insert CD1 that came with this book (or a boot disk if you are using one) and boot or reboot your computer.**

   After your computer thinks for a while, the first installation screen appears displaying the `boot:` prompt, as shown in Figure 3-1.

2. **Press Enter.**

   A series of messages scrolls by, indicating whether your hardware is being detected by the Linux kernel. Most of the time — particularly with newer systems — Linux detects all the basic hardware and then a welcome message appears.

   If you want to use the text-based install, or you have to do so (in some cases, the Red Hat Linux installation system cannot use your graphics adapter, for example), we show you how in Appendix B.

```
                    Welcome to Red Hat Linux 7.0!

o  To install or upgrade a system running Red Hat Linux 3.0.3
   or later in graphical mode, press the <ENTER> key.

o  To install or upgrade a system running Red Hat Linux 3.0.3
   or later in text mode, type: text <ENTER>.

o  To enable expert mode, type: expert <ENTER>.  Press <F3> for
   more information about expert mode.

o  To enable rescue mode, type: linux rescue <ENTER>.  Press <F5>
   for more information about rescue mode.

o  If you have a driver disk, type: linux dd <ENTER>.

o  Use the function keys listed below for more information.




[F1-Main] [F2-General] [F3-Expert] [F4-Kernel] [F5-Rescue]
boot: _
```

Figure 3-1:
The first Red
Hat Linux
installation
system
screen.

If the hardware is not detected, you may have to reboot and add some options at the boot: prompt. For example, if the system doesn't detect your CD-ROM drive, you may have to type the following:

```
boot: linux hdc=cdrom
```

If you continue to have problems, you can get more installation information from Red Hat's online installation manual (if you can get access to a working computer, that is!) in HTML format located on CD3 in the /mnt/cdrom/doc/rhmanual/manual directory. You can mount the CD-ROM on another Linux or Windows system and view the document with Netscape.

The Language Selection window appears, as shown in Figure 3-2.

---Online Help---

Language Selection

Which language would you like to use during the installation and as the system default once Red Hat Linux is installed?

Choose from the list at right.

---Language Selection---

What language should be used during the installation process?

Czech
Danish
English
French
German
Hungarian
Icelandic
Italian
Norwegian
Romanian
Russian
Serbian
Slovak
Slovenian
Spanish
Swedish
Turkish
Ukrainian

? Hide Help   ◁ Back   ▷ Next

Figure 3-2:
Selecting
your
language.

3. Select a language and click Next.

You have a choice to use several languages, so choose the language that you speak, or, if you're feeling adventurous, one that you don't (not recommended).

The Keyboard Configuration window appears, as shown in Figure 3-3.

4. Select the keyboard model and layout that you want to use and then click Next.

The Mouse Configuration window appears, as shown in Figure 3-4.

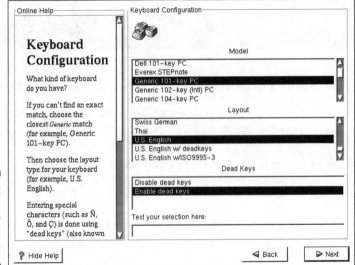

Figure 3-3:
Configuring your keyboard layout.

5. Select your mouse (squeak!) and click Next.

Red Hat provides a slew of mice to choose from. If you have a PS/2 mouse, all you have to do is select the manufacturer and number of buttons. If you have the older style of mouse that connects via a serial port, you have to select the manufacturer, number of buttons, and the serial port that it is connected to; you only have four serial ports to select from, and in many cases, it will be either `ttyS0` or `ttyS1`.

If you have a two-button mouse (either serial or PS/2), you can choose to have it emulate three buttons by clicking the Emulate 3 Buttons option. You emulate the third (middle) button by pressing both outside mouse buttons at once.

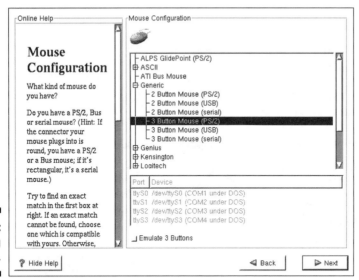

Figure 3-4: Configuring your mouse.

The Welcome to Red Hat Linux introduction window appears (see Figure 3-5) after you complete the initial configuration steps.

6. Click Next.

The Install Options window appears, as shown in Figure 3-6.

See the numbered list in the next section to continue with the installation.

Figure 3-5: Welcome to Red Hat Linux!

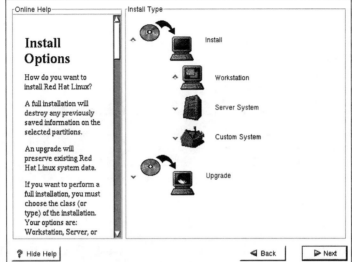

Figure 3-6:
Choosing
your
installation
type.

Installation Stage 2: Selecting and Slicing the Pie

Red Hat Linux gives you several installation types to choose from. The standard *Workstation* and *Server System* installations preselect your partitions and software for you based on whether you expect to use your computer as a personal workstation or a general server. We don't discuss the Server System installation here.

The Server System installation wipes your entire hard drive automatically, including partitions containing other operating systems such as Windows!

If you are running Windows NT (or Windows 2000) and choose to install the Workstation installation, then your NT boot record is overwritten and you will be unable to boot Windows NT (but your NT partition will not be erased, just rendered unbootable). An NT *boot record* is what enables a Windows NT system to start automatically when you start your computer. You can install Red Hat Linux 7 without overwriting the NT boot partition if you choose the Custom installation method and manually configure the Linux Loader (LILO). It is beyond the scope of this book to describe that process. For more information on the Custom installation, see the Red Hat Linux installation guide on CD3 however. If you have access to a Windows machine, then insert CD3 and use a browser to open the following path: `D:\RH-DOCS\rh1-ig-en-7.0\index.html` (assuming your CD-ROM is designated as D:). On a Linux computer the URL is `file:/mnt/cdrom/RH-DOCS/rhl-ig-en-7.0/index.html`. You can also view the installation guide at Red Hat's Web site by visiting the following URL:

```
www.redhat.com/support/manuals/RHL-7-Manual/install-guide/
```

You can also roll your own Red Hat Linux system by selecting the *Custom System* installation, which we also don't discuss here. Finally, if you already have Red Hat Linux installed, you can choose the *Upgrade* option and the newer software installs over the older software without changing your current partitions or user software (for this chapter, though, we assume that you're installing fresh).

Picking up from Step 6 in the preceding section, follow these steps to continue the installation:

1. Select the Workstation option and click the Next button.

The Automatic Partitioning window appears, as shown in Figure 3-7.

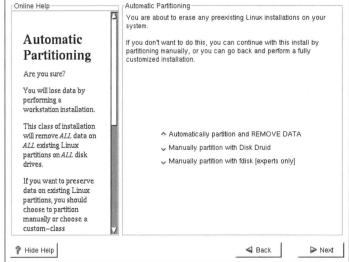

Figure 3-7: Choosing to let Red Hat Linux partition automatically.

2. Select the Automatically Partition and REMOVE DATA option and then click Next.

Red Hat divides the portion of your hard drive that isn't carrying another operating system into three partitions, or just partitions the whole hard drive if there are no existing partitions. The partitions the installation creates are *root* (/), *boot* (/boot) and *swap,* which is used internally by Linux and isn't accessable to you like the other partitions. You can click either of the manual options if you're an experienced Unix or Linux user and understand the concept of using multiple partitions, but we recommend that, unless you feel really lucky or are very experienced, you let Red Hat do the work here.

When your hard drive is partitioned, the portion of it not containing Windows or another operating system is wiped completely clean. This means that you can't recover existing information on this portion of the hard drive after it's partitioned, so be sure of what you're doing before you proceed!

The Network Configuration window eventually appears, as shown in Figure 3-8. We tell you how to configure your network in the next section.

If you don't have a network or just don't want to haggle with it right now, click Next and skip the next section.

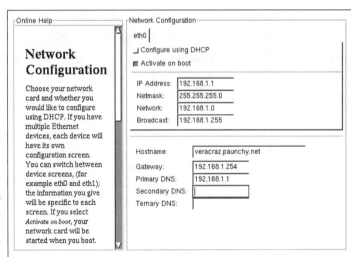

Figure 3-8: Setting up your network.

Installation Stage 3: Configuring Your Network

Now it's time to configure your network, if you have one. If your computer has an Ethernet adapter and is connected to a network, then enter your information as described in the following list. Even if you don't have a network to connect to, you can still optionally enter your computer's hostname in Step 3. If you don't have a network and don't want to set your hostname, then simply click the Next button.

As you fill in the text boxes, you may find that Red Hat Linux guesses what information is needed and fills in some sections automatically. If it has guessed incorrectly, simply change the information.

Picking up from the end of the last section, follow these steps to configure your system for a network:

1. **In the Network Configuration window (refer to Figure 3-8), click the Activate on Boot radio button or, if you're connecting to a network that uses the *Dynamic Host Configuration Protocol* (DHCP), select the Configure using DHCP option, click Next, and skip to Step 3.**

   Selecting this option ensures that your network starts when you boot your computer.

   If you selected the Configure using DHCP option, you can skip Step 2 because with DHCP your computer obtains its IP address, netmask, default gateway, and nameserver information from the DHCP server on your network.

2. **Type your IP Address, Netmask, Gateway (IP), and Primary DNS into the appropriate text boxes.**

   The following list gives a brief description of the four parameters, which your Internet service provider should give you (if you're not using DHCP).

   - **IP address.** This is the numeric network address of your Linux computer and is the address your computer is known as on your local network and — in many cases — the Internet. If you haven't registered your private network's (also known as local networks or LANs) address space with the InterNic (the organization that is in charge of distributing IP addresses), then you can use the public address space that goes from 192.168.1.1 to 192.168.254.254.

   - **Netmask.** Private networks based on the Internet Protocol (IP) are divided into subnetworks. The netmask determines how the network is divided. For addresses such as the one in the preceding bullet (192.168.1.1, and so on), the most common netmask is 255.255.255.0.

   - **Gateway.** This is the numeric IP address of the computer that connects your private network to the Internet (or another private network). Red Hat Linux guesses the address of 192.168.1.254, for example, if you choose an address of 192.168.1.{1-254} for the IP address. You can accept this address, but leaving it blank is a better option, unless that address is your actual gateway. Chapter 5 describes how to configure your Linux computer to connect to the Internet via a telephone connection. If you do that, then setting a default route now can interfere with your connection.

- **Primary DNS.** The Internet Protocol uses a system called Domain Name Service (DNS) to convert names such as www.redhat.com into numeric IPs. A computer that acts as a DNS is called a nameserver. Red Hat Linux again makes a guess based on the IP address and netmask that you use. We suggest leaving this box blank, however, unless you are on a private network with a nameserver or will be connected to the Internet (your ISP will supply a DNS). When you designate a nonexistent nameserver, then many networking programs work very slowly as they wait in vain for the absent server.

3. Type your computer's hostname, including the network name (domain) in the Hostname text box.

Suppose that you want to name your computer veracruz and your network name is paunchy.net, you type in **veracruz.paunchy.net**.

If you do not give your computer a name and domain name during the network configuration process, then it is referred to as *localhost. localdomain*. Otherwise, the welcome screen refers to whatever name you gave it: For example, in the preceding example you would see Welcome to veracruz.paunchy.net.

4. If you are connecting to the Internet directly through a modem, then leave the Gateway address blank, or, if you are on a LAN that has a gateway to the Internet, enter its address in the Gateway text box (you should obtain this address from your system administrator).

5. Type the primary DNS address in the Primary DNS text box.

DNS means Domain Name Server and is used by geeks and cool folk everywhere to change human names into Internet addresses. If you are connected to an ISP, they provide you with the DNS address. Otherwise, consult your friendly local system administrator for that information.

6. If you have access to secondary and tertiary nameservers (IPs), type in the appropriate text boxes.

Secondary and *tertiary* nameservers provide backup service to the primary nameserver. These are the IP addresses of the second and third DNS servers that your computer will use.

7. When you complete the form, click the Next button to continue.

The Time Zone Selection window appears, as shown in Figure 3-9.

The next section shows you how to configure your Red Hat Linux system.

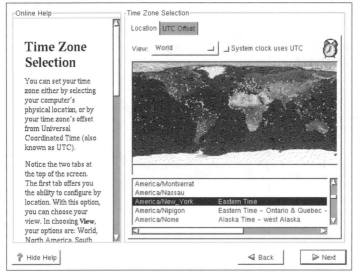

Figure 3-9:
Selecting
your time
zone.

Installation Stage 4: Configuring Your System

This section covers basic configuration for Red Hat Linux, at which time you set your time zone as well as the root user password. You can also add regular users and set their passwords. The following steps describe how to perform these basic tasks.

1. **In the Time Zone Selection window (refer to Figure 3-9), click the dot representing a city closest to where you live to select your time zone.**

   You can use the map to point-and-click your way to your time zone bliss. When you click one of the thousand points of light, the represented city and its time zone appear in the subwindow below the map. You can also click the slider bar at the bottom of the screen to locate the name of your city/time zone. After you find it, click the text to select your time zone.

2. **Click Next.**

   The Account Configuration window appears, as shown in Figure 3-10.

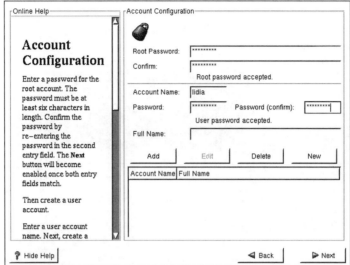

Figure 3-10:
Entering
your root
password.

3. Type your root password into both the Root Password and Confirm text boxes.

The password is for the root user, also known as the *superuser*, who has access to the entire system and can do almost anything — good and bad.

It's best to log in as the root user only to do system maintenance or administrative tasks. The root user is the only user with access to critical system files. To avoid making unwanted changes or deletions to these important files, add another user for yourself as described in Step 4 and use the root account only when you need to.

You have to enter the password two times to make sure that you typed it correctly. The password appears on-screen as asterisks when you type it in. Holy breach of security, Batman! You wouldn't want someone to be able to look over your shoulder and get your password, now would you?

4. (Optional) You can create user accounts in the bottom half of the screen by entering an account name, entering the password for the account into both the Password and Password (confirm) text boxes, and then clicking Add.

Your new user account name is displayed in the Account Name box. You can go on to add, delete, and edit new or old users until the cows come home. Enter any or all of the people who you want to be able to log in to your Red Hat Linux computer.

You don't have to add every user possible at this point. You can add (as well as modify or remove existing accounts) at any time after you've successfully installed Red Hat Linux by running the LinuxConf application (which we describe in Chapter 4).

5. **Click Next.**

The Selecting Package Groups window appears, as shown in Figure 3-11.

The final step of this section requires you to select the graphical window manager. If you intend to use graphics, you can choose either the GNOME or KDE system. GNOME is the default for Red Hat Linux and that's what we use throughout the rest of the book. KDE, however, is an excellent choice and many people prefer it.

6. **Select GNOME and click Next.**

The X Configuration window appears, as shown in Figure 13-12.

The next section shows you how to configure X Windows.

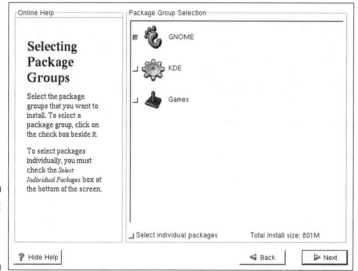

Figure 3-11:
Selecting
package
groups.

Checking out password ettiquette

Your password must be at least six characters long, but it's better to use at least eight. The more characters that you use, the harder the password is to break. If you're concerned about security at all, we recommend that you use a combination of uppercase and lowercase letters, symbols, and numbers to make your password as difficult to compromise as possible. In addition, don't choose anything that would be found in a dictionary or names or items that are easy to associate with you. In other words, your name, your name spelled backwards, your birthday, your dog's name, any word in any language, and so on are all poor choices. Beer, for example, is a poor selection for Jon's password, even though it has both uppercase and lowercase letters, because people easily associate him with that word.

A good way to come up with a good password is to select a phrase and destroy it. For example, take "I am not a number" and make it into something like "imN0tun#". Even though the end result does not spell out the phrase in any real way, it gives you all the cues to remember the essentially random characters ("I am" = "im", "not" = "N0t", "a" = "un" and "#" = "number").

Also, be sure to write your password down where it won't get lost and can't be easily found or stolen. For example, save your work passwords at home or else store them in a locked desk or safe. And don't write your password on a Post-it Note attached to your computer monitor, please!

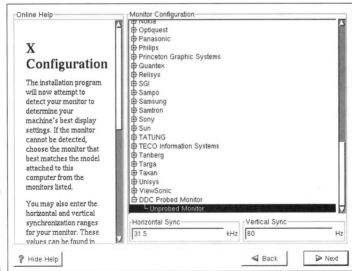

Figure 3-12:
Choosing
your
monitor.

Installation Stage 5: X Marks the Spot

Phew. You're almost at the finish line. Really!

One of the last things that you need to do is install X Server so that you can use the X Window System and a graphical user interface (or GUI) such as GNOME to interact with Linux. To configure an X Server you need to specify the video card and monitor for your system (if Red Hat didn't detect them automatically), including how much video memory the video card has, what speed it runs at, and a series of other options.

Picking up from the end of the last section, follow these steps to install the X Server:

1. **Select a monitor from the X Configuration window.**

   If your monitor is not included in the list, then you can select from within the Custom or Generic Monitor choices.

   Older monitors can't handle resolution rates and scan frequencies higher than what they were designed for. A monitor designed for a 640 x 480 resolution (and a low scan frequency) can't display a 2,048 x 1,024 resolution (and a high scan frequency), for example. If you try to make the monitor display a higher frequency than it's capable of displaying, it may burst into flames. (We didn't believe this either until we saw a monitor smoking.) Modern monitors, called *multiscanning monitors,* can automatically match themselves to a series of scan frequencies and resolutions. Some of these monitors are even smart enough to turn themselves off if the frequencies become too high instead of bursting into flames. Finding the documentation and matching your vertical and horizontal frequencies properly is the best way to go (particularly with older monitors). Lacking this information, try a lower resolution (VGA or SVGA) first, just to get X Window System running.

2. **The installation process will generally detect your video driver and configure the parameters for you. You can also specify the amount of memory on your video card.**

   Note that this memory is different than the amount of main memory. Most modern cards have 1, 2, 4, or 8MB of video memory. Use your arrow keys to move down the list.

   If you are an expert, you can also select the `Customize X option` and configure it manually.

If you don't know how much video memory your card has, try 1MB (the 1 Meg option). Although this setting limits the resolution of your screen, you will probably be able to get X Window System going. Later, you can experiment with the Xconfigurator program (described in Chapter 19) to figure out the best values for how much video memory you have, if the probe did not work properly.

3. **Click the Test this configuration button.**

4. **If you configured X correctly, this message appears:** Can you see this message?. **You have 10 seconds to either click the Yes button with your mouse or press the Enter key.**

5. **If you want to start X automatically at boot time, choose Yes. Otherwise, choose No.**

This book assumes that you answer yes to this option so that your Red Hat Linux computer starts X Windows and the GNOME window manager (if that's your default manager) every time you boot. If you choose no, whenever Linux boots you're faced with the unexciting command prompt where, after logging in, you can enter the startx command at the prompt to start X and your GUI.

If you choose No, then your system will start up in character-cell or text mode. You can always manually start X with the aptly named startx command or modify the /etc/inittab to automatically start X. The line id:3:initdefault should be changed to id:5:initdefault in the inittab file to do that.

After you make your choice, an informational screen appears, telling you you where the configuration file can be found, and also points you to the X README.Config file for more information.

6. **Click the Next button.**

If you have a problem with your X configuration, then you are regretfully informed about the situation. You have the option of quitting or going back and starting over. If you're game, go back and try, try again.

The About to Install window appears. At last you've reached the do-or-die stage — the point at which it's either go on and finalize the install (by writing to your hard drive) or to give it up with a whimper. See the next section for details.

Installation Stage 6: The Point of No Return!

Until this point no permanent changes have been made to your computer. The partitions you selected earlier have not been made permanent. No Red Hat Linux packages have been written to your disk. You can either stop completely or go back one or more steps by clicking the Back button.

If you want to stop the installation process completely, reboot your computer now and you will have to start all over again. You can reboot by pressing the reset button or by pressing the Ctrl+Alt+Del keys simultaneously. If you leave the Red Hat Linux installation CD-ROM in the drive, the computer restarts the installation process automatically when it reboots. If you remove the CD-ROM, then the previously installed operating system (if any) boots instead.

1. **After you suck in your breath and decide to take the plunge, click Next.**

   Your disk partitions are created and formatted and then the Red Hat Linux distribution is written to it. Yikes! The Installing Packages window tells you which package is currently being installed, as well as how many have been installed, how many remain to be installed, and the estimated time remaining.

   The installer then asks if you want to create a boot disk. This is a good option, just in case something happens to the boot partition on your disk. Microsoft products, for example, have a bad habit of overwriting the Master Boot Record (MBR) — and therefore your Linux booting system — when they are installed or even updated. Hard drive boot failures can also happen for any number of reasons — aliens and gremlins are well-known for wreaking havoc. The boot disk is a great tool for foiling these dastardly mischief makers.

   This boot disk is different from the one that you use to start the Red Hat Linux installation. This boot disk can start your Red Hat Linux computer in case the Linux boot information stored on your hard drive ever becomes corrupted.

2. **(Optional) Insert a blank disk into your main floppy drive, select the Create Boot Floppy option, and click Next to create a boot disk.**

   Before the system reboots, remove the CD and any floppy disks in your drives. Otherwise you'll be faced with going through the entire installation process again. If that happens, there's no need to groan — you can always re-reboot and remove the pesky critters.

   Your system reboots, and that's it! You're done installing Red Hat Linux! Chapter 4 shows you how to get started using your new system.

Chapter 4

Getting to Know Red Hat Linux

. . . .

In This Chapter

▶ Checking out the Linux file system

▶ Deciding on your interface: graphics versus text

▶ Comprehending logins and the root user

▶ Adding a regular user

▶ Stopping Linux

. . . .

*B*efore using Red Hat Linux, you need to check out a few of the basics. This chapter covers enough of the Linux fundamentals to get you started, including topics such as starting and stopping Linux; making user accounts for your friends and family, and understanding the difference between graphical and nongraphical applications.

Linux is a multiuser system, so you — and every other user — need an individual name and password to protect your information and keep your tasks separate from other people's tasks. You also find out how to create user accounts in this chapter.

Introducing the Linux File System Tree

Linux, like Unix, refers to everything as a file, giving each device, file, and directory a *file address* by which it can be identified. Linux refers to disks and disk partitions by using a system of letters and numbers; for example, /dev/hda could be the name of the first IDE hard drive, and /dev/sdb could be the name of the second SCSI hard drive.

The Linux file system can be viewed like a tree turned upside down, as shown in Figure 4-1, which shows three *subdirectories* (a directory within a directory) of root. The top of the upside-down tree is represented by a / (slash) and is called the *root directory,* or just root. A series of limbs, branches, and leaves extend below the root: limbs are mount points, the branches that extend from the limbs are directories, and the leaves on those branches are your files. Each *mount point* is a disk partition or remote file system (such as your CD-ROM drive) that is *mounted,* or made visible to, a directory of the limb above it. When a disk partition or remote file system is mounted on the directory branch, it turns that branch into another limb, allowing even more branches to be positioned and attached below the mount point.

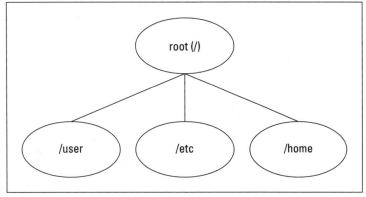

Figure 4-1:
The Linux
file system
is like an
upside-
down tree.

Linux needs at least a root partition in your directory structure (the upside-down tree) and a swap space partition. The root partition is used to store all of your personal and system files and directories, and *swap space,* the Hamburger Helper of the computer world, is used by Linux to extend your memory beyond the limit of your random access memory (RAM). If you have 64MB of RAM and 64MB of swap, for example, you can run programs that use up 128MB of memory.

The Workstation installation method used in Chapter 3 automatically sets up your root and swap partitions, as well as an additional boot partition that is used for storing the Red Hat Linux kernel and other files used for booting your computer.

The only time in this book that you need to access the boot partition is in Chapter 10 where the Linux kernel is modified so that you can burn CD-ROMs.

Giving Linux the Boot

To *boot* a computer means simply to start it (and to *reboot* means to restart it). Follow these steps to boot your Red Hat Linux system for the first time:

1. **Make sure that your computer is turned off.**

2. **Turn on the power to the monitor if it's separate from the main system.**

3. Turn on the computer's main power switch.

After a short time, the Red Hat boot menu appears on your screen, as shown in Figure 4-2. If you only have Red Hat Linux installed on your computer, then you are given only one choice of operating systems to boot: Linux.

The default operating system is the one at the top of the list. If you have installed Red Hat Linux along with another operating system, you can change the one that boots by default. See the "Changing LILO's default operating system" sidebar nearby for details.

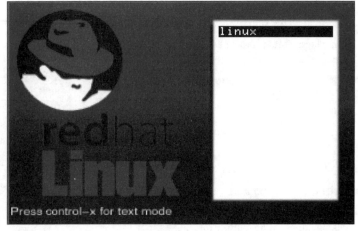

Figure 4-2:
The Red Hat
Linux boot
window.

You can exit from the Red Hat Linux graphical boot menu by pressing Ctrl+X. This places you at the — old style — LILO boot prompt. LILO's sole purpose in life (LILO stands for Linux loader, by the way) is to boot your Linux system and keep track of any other bootable systems on your machine. When the LILO boot: prompt appears, you can press the Tab key to see all the names for booting various operating systems or versions of operating systems.

4. Use the up or down arrow to highlight the word Linux (if it's not high-lighted already) and press Enter.

If you are running more than one operating system — for example, Red Hat Linux and Windows — you can select any of the listed operating systems to boot, but we assume here that you choose Linux.

After you press Enter, Red Hat Linux boots your system. During this process, a lot of information is displayed on your screen. The information is gleaned by Red Hat Linux as it probes your computer in order to determine what hardware — disk drives, printers, and so on — it has.

If you don't press anything, the default operating system (Linux sets itself as default when you install it) starts automatically after a five-second delay.

Changing LILO's default operating system

If you dual boot between Red Hat Linux and another operating system, you have to choose which operating system to boot right after your computer boots or LILO chooses the default operating system, which it sets up as Linux. But you can change which operating system boots by following these steps:

1. **Boot Linux and log in as the root user.**

2. **Click the Main Menu button and choose Programs➪System➪LinuxConf.**

   The Main Menu button looks like a footprint and is located on the toolbar in the lower-left corner of your desktop.

3. **Click the boot mode button at the bottom of the window.**

   The Boot configuration window opens.

4. **Click the default boot configuration button.**

   The default boot configuration dialog box opens, displaying a radio button for each operating system installed on your computer.

5. **Click the radio button of the operating system that you want to make the default operating system.**

6. **Click the Accept button.**

   The default boot configuration dialog box closes and control is returned to the Boot configuration window.

7. **Click the Quit button once in the Boot mode window and click it again in the Linuxconf window.**

   After a few seconds you are prompted to activate the change that you just made.

8. **Click the Activate the changes button.**

   You now have a new default operating system!

Logging In

When you use Linux, you must log in as a particular user with a distinct login name. Why? Linux is a multiuser system, and as such, it uses different accounts to keep people from looking at other people's secret files, erasing necessary files from the system, and otherwise doing bad things. The unique identity also helps to keep the actions of one person from affecting the actions of another, because many people may be using the same computer system at the same time. A benefit of this strategy is that Linux systems are essentially invulnerable to viruses, simply because each user's files and directories can not be used to corrupt the system as a whole as it can with Windows systems.

As Red Hat Linux boots, you see all sorts of messages scrolling by on the screen. After the scrolling stops, the login screen shown in Figure 4-3 appears.

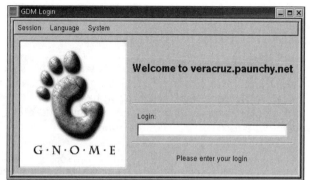

Figure 4-3:
The GNOME
login
screen.

If you chose during installation not to have X start automatically when you boot your system, then you see the simple login: prompt.

If you make a mistake while typing the password or your login, the system asks you to retype it.

We strongly recommend that you do most of your experimentation with Linux as a nonprivileged user and log in as the root user only when necessary. By operating as root, you run the risk of corrupting your system, having to reinstall again, or losing data, because you can delete or change anything you want. When you are logged in as a regular user, you can accidentally erase your own files and data but you can't erase someone else's files or system files.

The Command-Line Interface (CLI) versus the Graphical User Interface (GUI)

Red Hat Linux installs the X Window System by default. You can perform most of the administrative tasks with the GUI-based tools (GUI stands for *graphical user interface*) that Red Hat provides. Most of the how-to instructions in this book use the X-based applications and utilities. We do that because they are generally easier to use and this is not a systems administration-oriented book.

Occasionally, a utility or program doesn't run graphically, and other times using nongraphical methods and systems is just more interesting or convenient. Believe it or not, some geekier Linux users actually prefer to use a text-based, command-line interface, or what most call a *shell*. In cases where the shell interface is desirable or even necessary, it's important to know how to do some basic administrative tasks with the shell.

Text-based systems are generally run from a *shell,* which acts as a text-based interface between the Linux operating system and you. The bash shell, which Red Hat Linux uses by default, displays a prompt like [bubbleboy@veracruz bubbleboy]$. You enter commands at the shell prompt, and that's where the term *command-line interface* (or CLI) comes from.

You can start a shell from within the GNOME interface by starting a terminal session (also known as a terminal emulator). The GNOME system comes pre-configured with an icon on the GNOME Panel (the Panel is the bar at the bottom of your screen) that looks like a computer monitor. Clicking this icon starts a terminal session that you can use within GNOME, as shown in Figure 4-4. You can crack open more shell info in Chapter 14.

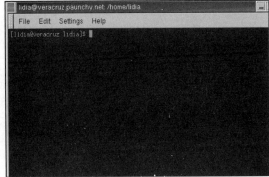

Figure 4-4:
A GNOME
terminal
session.

Creating an Account with LinuxConf

If you have cause to add new users (say if you have a home network), or you forgot to create a nonroot user during installation, this section shows you how. Red Hat offers you the LinuxConf administration tool to make your life easier.

To use LinuxConf to create a new account for general use, follow these steps:

The following instructions assume that you're using the GNOME window system, which is the Red Hat default. LinuxConf works the same, however, if you're using the KDE window system (KDE also comes with Red Hat Linux, although you have to voluntarily elect to install it).

1. **Log in as root.**

   LinuxConf can also work without X in a text-based menu mode. No differences exist between the graphical and text-based modes other than the look and feel.

2. **Click the GNOME Main Menu button and choose Programs⇔System⇔ LinuxConf.**

   The Main Menu button looks like a footprint and is located on the toolbar in the lower-left corner of your desktop and works in a similar fashion to the Windows Start button.

   The LinuxConf help window appears, as shown in Figure 4-5.

   The first time that you start it, it shows the Welcome to LinuxConf window. This is simply an informational screen. Press Enter to continue.

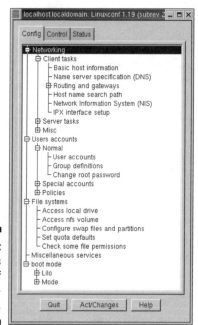

Figure 4-5: Red Hat's LinuxConf administration tool.

3. **Select the User Accounts option by clicking the plus sign (+), clicking Normal menu items, and then clicking the Users Accounts submenu.**

   The User account program starts, as shown in Figure 4-6. You use this program to add, delete, and modify user accounts on the system.

4. **Click the Add button.**

   The User account creation form appears, as shown in Figure 4-7.

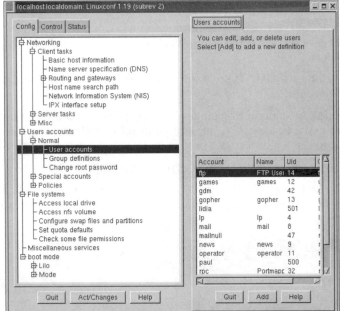

Figure 4-6:
The User
account
program.

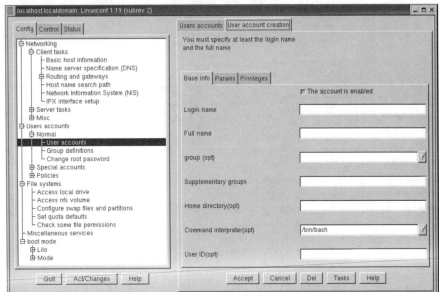

Figure 4-7:
The User
account
creation
form.

5. **Fill in information about yourself in the text boxes of the User account creation form. The following list describes the purpose of each field.**

   Most of this information is self-explanatory. Here are a few hints:

   • Everything but the username is optional.

   • Your login name is also the name that you will use to send and receive e-mail, so choose the name carefully. Make your login name short and use all lowercase letters. Names that seem cute or appropriate now may not be later. And avoid choosing a name that is too long, because you may have to type it several times a day. You may also have to give your e-mail address over the telephone, so a login name such as *phool* will result in missent messages, leaving you feeling very phoolish.

   • You can enter your full name if you want. That information is saved in the /etc/passwd file which anyone with an account on your system can read. This information is generally useful to system administrators because it allows them to connect a person with each account. It's probably superfluous if you're configuring your personal system.

   • Among your many choices for a default shell, /bin/bash is a good choice (bash is a popular shell that is the default for Red Hat Linux). For more on shells, check out Chapter 14.

6. **Click Accept.**

   The account is created, and the Changing Password window appears.

7. **Enter a password.**

   Red Hat Linux uses the Pluggable Authentication Module (PAM) that prevents you from entering trivial or otherwise dangerous passwords, but don't use that as assurance that your new password is a good one. A good password can't be found in any dictionary, because password crackers have programs that automatically try all dictionary words to crack your password. Also, information such as birthdays and anniversaries — or anything someone could associate with you — aren't good choices. Good passwords are short phrases of alpha-numeric characters that can't be found in any dictionary, with nonalphabetic characters, that make sense to you and you alone. For example, if you like the phrase "give me a break" you might convert that into gvm3abrk. Just don't forget it, or write it on a Post-It note and put it on your computer monitor!

   The new password should be different from the one you use for root.

   As you type the password, little asterisks, rather than the actual password, appear on-screen in case someone is looking over your shoulder as you type (Linux is showing its paranoid side here).

8. **Type the password again and press Enter.**

   The program makes you retype the password to ensure that the password you typed is the one you thought you typed. If you don't retype the password exactly as you did the first time (which is easy to do because it doesn't appear on the screen), you have to repeat the process starting with Step 7.

9. **Click the Quit button.**

   If everything is all right, the Linuxconf window has an entry for your new account.

10. **Click the Quit button to exit.**

Creating an Account without X

If X isn't working, or if you want to work from a terminal emulator, you can still add the nonprivileged user account that we advise you to add earlier in the chapter. To do so, follow these steps:

1. **Type** useradd *name* **at the command prompt, where** *name* **is the login name for the new login account.**

2. **Type** passwd *name* **at the command prompt and press Enter.**

   This changes the password of the new account, which had a default password assigned to it by the useradd command in Step 1. What good is a password if you use the default one?

    See the Warning icons in the last section for hints on creating a good password.

   As you type the password, little asterisks, rather than the actual password, appear on-screen in case someone is looking over your shoulder.

3. **Type in your password again.**

   Linux asks you to retype your new password to ensure that the password you typed is the one you thought you typed. If you don't retype the password exactly as you did the first time (which is easy to do because it doesn't appear on the screen), you have to repeat the process.

4. **Type in a password for the new login.**

   Linux updates the password for the new login.

Ending Your First Session

Logging off of the system and restarting the login process is simplicity itself. To do so, click the GNOME Main Menu button (which looks like a big foot in the lower-left corner) and choose Log out. The Really log out? Window appears and you're asked to confirm that you want to log out. If you do — do you really? — then click the Yes button and you're outta there. Click No if you don't want to log out.

You can also choose to reboot or halt your computer from this window by clicking either the Halt or Reboot buttons and then clicking Yes to confirm your decision. Depending on which you choose, your system proceeds to stop completely or else reboot. You can also press the Ctrl+Alt+Backspace keys to shut down your current session. This method is less graceful but still effective, especially in case some renegade process freezes your X session.

Part II
Got Net?

In this part . . .

Once you've created your own Red Hat Linux workstation, it's time to hit the great outdoors. Chapter 5 shows you how to find an Internet Service Provider (ISP). Next, you find out how to make the necessary connection to your ISP and start surfin' da Net. From there, we show you how to protect yourself from the worst aspects of the Net by building a simple, but effective, firewall.

Many people have access to existing computer networks at work, school, and home. Small, local networks are often referred to as Local Area Networks, or LANs for short. Chapter 6 shows how to connect your computer to a LAN. If your LAN has an Internet connection, this chapter also describes how to configure your workstation to use it. We then show you how to modify the firewall introduced in Chapter 5 to use on a LAN.

Now you're ready to journey into the great uncharted territory of the World Wide Web. Chapter 7 shows how to surf the Net with Netscape. Netscape is included on the *Red Hat 7 Linux For Dummies* CD-ROM so that you can get up and running quickly to browse like crazy.

Okay, now that you're out in the wilds of computerdom, how will you communicate? Smoke signals? Yodeling? E-mail? That's the ticket, and you find out how to send and receive e-mail in Chapter 7 as well.

Chapter 5

Connecting to the Internet with a Dialup Modem

● ●

In This Chapter

▶ Finding an Internet service provider (ISP)

▶ Configuring your modem

▶ Manually connecting to your ISP

▶ Automatically connecting to your Internet service provider

▶ Configuring your Internet connection with LinuxConf

▶ Starting and stopping the Internet service software

▶ Creating a simple but effective firewall

● ●

Surfing the Internet is a lot of fun and a surprisingly useful activity. Come on, admit it: You know you want to tie up your phone line for hours in order to annoy your family or roommates, browse sites with ridiculous addresses such as www.theonion.com, and chat chummily with people you'd never dream of speaking to in person. The catch is that before you join the fray of the new online universe, you've gotta have access to the Internet.

This chapter describes how to use a modem to connect to an Internet service provider (or ISP), and create your bridge to the Internet. You also find out how to create a firewall to protect your system from anyone on the Internet who wants to do you harm. After you're hooked up to the Internet, you too can go to a party and drop the casual phrase, "I found this while surfing the Net this afternoon . . . on my Red Hat Linux system." If you've never been the life of the party in the past, this will certainly make you immediately more popular.

This chapter assumes you're connecting to the Internet using a standard dialup modem. Faster connections, referred to as *broadband connections,* are not covered in this book because there are so many kinds and they're all so radically different to set up. To hook up through DSL or cable or some other new-fangled method, ask your service provider for necessary software and instructions for Red Hat Linux (and pray they have them).

If you have access to a network that has a broadband connection, Chapter 6 describes how to connect to it and gain access to the fast connection. You can then surf until the cows come home in light speeds compared to a dialup modem.

Desperately Seeking an ISP

To get connected using a dialup modem, you have to successfully hook up a modem to your computer and then find a good Internet service provider (ISP) to dial in to. The process of connecting your modem to your computer is outside the scope of this book, due largely to the almost infinite possible modem/computer configurations. See the materials that came with your modem for instructions on hooking it up.

The best way to find a good ISP is by word of mouth. Ask your friends and acquaintances who live nearby (if they live far away, their opinions won't mean much) which ISPs they use and whether they're satisfied with them. Getting personal recommendations is a good way to find out both the good and bad points of an ISP that you can't find through normal channels like a Yellow Pages advertisement.

If you don't have any friends and your acquaintances won't speak to you, then try finding a local Linux User Group (LUG) to ask. You can look up LUGs at Red Hat's community Web page at www.redhat.com/apps/community or you can ask a friend with Web access to do so if you can't.

If you can't find a reference, look in your local Yellow Pages under Internet or Internet Service Providers. List the names and telephone numbers of any ISPs that you find. These companies are probably local companies, which are often superior to larger operations because the management and support structure is more accessible to you. Just start calling each one and asking them if they support Linux.

A local ISP may not be the best choice for you if you do a lot of traveling, in which case mobile access is the most important service you need. The following national/worldwide ISPs are a sample of what's currently available for Linux.

ISP	Toll-free Phone Number (U.S. Only)
AT&T WorldNet:	800-967-5363
CompuServe:	800-336-6823
eFortress:	888-930-1030
Mindspring:	888-677-7474

ISP	Toll-free Phone Number (U.S. Only)
SprintNet:	800-473-7983
CompuglobalHypermeganet:	555-867-5309

Okay, so ignore that last listing, which is just a bad Simpson's pun.

After jotting down some candidates, call to make sure that they support Linux and offer a dialup PPP service. PPP (which stands for *point-to-point protocol*) is what Linux uses to connect to the Internet. A PPP connection enables your computer to become part of the Internet, which itself is just a lot (and we mean a *lot*) of interconnected computers and network devices — thus the term *Internet* (as in "internetworking").

Also find out how and what kind of service they provide. ISPs that can host Web pages for you are a plus, as are ISPs that can filter junk e-mail, or *spam*. And any good ISP can handle 56 Kbps modems. Even if you use a slower modem, their system is able to handle your system. If you upgrade to 56 Kbps, then they're ready for you.

Most local ISPs are small to medium- sized organizations that cannot afford to staff their lines 24 hours a day, 7 days a week. Many small ISPs, however, are owned and run by technical people who monitor their systems for what seems like 24 hours a day. They often are logged in while at home and periodically monitor their e-mail — a good indicator of this is if they have a generic e-mail address such as `help@swcp.com`. If you get lucky, or really do your homework, then you'll connect with one of these ISPs and get excellent service.

Now is a good time to verify that your own telephone service is billed at a flat rate and not metered. If you have metered service, you'll run up huge phone bills while spending hours chatting about lone gunmen and interdimensional space travelers.

After you choose your Internet service provider and arrange payment, the ISP provides you with certain pieces of information, including the following:

- ✔ Telephone access numbers
- ✔ A username (usually the one you want)
- ✔ A password (usually the one you supply)
- ✔ An e-mail address, which is typically your username added to the ISP's domain name
- ✔ A primary Domain Name Server (DNS) number, which is a large number separated by periods into four groups of digits
- ✔ A secondary Domain Name Server (DNS) number, which is another large number separated by periods into four groups of digits

> ✔ An SMTP (mail) server name
>
> ✔ An NNTP (news) server name
>
> ✔ A POP3 or IMAP4 server name, which is used to download e-mail from the ISP's server to your machine

Deciding on a Modem

To use Linux with the Internet, you must have at least one of the following devices:

> ✔ A modem and a telephone line
>
> ✔ A DSL or ADSL connection
>
> ✔ An ISDN connection
>
> ✔ A cable modem connection
>
> ✔ A sattelite-based ISP connection
>
> ✔ Access to a LAN *(local area network)* that has an Internet connection
>
> ✔ Mental telepathy

Modems are the most common method for making personal or small business Internet connections, and thus this chapter covers modems. The other methods provide higher speeds but cost more and require more work to set up; except for the ISDN connection, they also provide connections that are continuously turned on. But due to the virtually infinite number of configurations with these faster connections, we don't cover them in this book.

Modems are either internal or external. An *internal modem* plugs into a PCI or ISA slot on your computer's motherboard and receives its power from the computer. An *external modem* comes in its own case, requires its own power supply, and connects to the computer via a serial (RS232) connection. Both types of modems use your phone jack to connect to the Internet.

Internal modems are generally less expensive than external ones, but external modems have several advantages. You can easily turn them on and off, you can connect them to a computer without opening the computer case, and if your telephone line is struck by lightening, your computer won't be damaged by the charge passing through the modem. On the other hand, internal modems are cheaper and require fewer external cables. Also, internal modems need only a telephone line cable, whereas external modems require a telephone line, a serial connection, and power supply cables.

A third type of serial line modem is a *PCMCIA card* (sometimes called a PC card). These cards are used most often with laptop computers. Most laptops come with internal modems.

Avoid WinModems like the plague, as these modems are designed for Windows computers only. They're cheaper than regular modems because they're lazy (or smart depending on how you look at it) and depend on the Windows operating system to do much of their work for them. Linux drivers are only now beginning to appear for such modems.

Configuring Your Internet Connection

After you attach your modem, you need to configure it so Red Hat Linux can use it to connect to your ISP. The Red Hat Dialup Configuration Tool does a good job at detecting and then configuring your modem and a dialup account to connect your computer to your ISP and thus to the Internet.

1. **Click the Main Menu button and choose Programs⇨Internet⇨ Dialup Configuration Tool.**

   The GNOME Main Menu Button is the icon that looks like a big foot in the bottom-left corner of your screen.

   If you are not logged in as root, you are prompted for the root password in the Input dialog box. Two windows open up simultaneously the first time that you start the Dialup Configuration tool. The Internet Connections window, shown in Figure 5-1, displays the modems and PPP accounts that the tool knows about. The window has a blank screen if no Internet connections have been configured yet. The Create a new Internet Connection window, shown in Figure 5-2, is used to find the modems and create the PPP accounts.

2. **In the Create a new Internet Connection window, click Next.**

   The Select Modem window appears, as shown in Figure 5-3.

Figure 5-1: The blank Internet Connections window.

Figure 5-2:
The Create
a new
Internet
Connection
window.

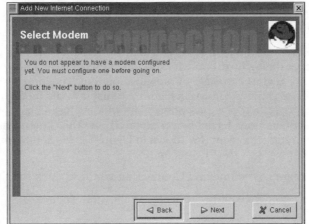

Figure 5-3:
The Select
Modem
window.

3. Click Next again.

The Searching for modems dialog box appears, as shown in Figure 5-4. The Dialup Configuration Tool scans your computer for modems. When it finds one, the window shown in Figure 5-5 appears (although the information displayed may differ).

If Linux doesn't find a modem, or you click the Cancel button, it displays the Enter a modem window shown in Figure 5-6 and guesses that a modem is attached to your first serial port — /dev/ttyS0. You can modify the modem settings, if you wish, in this window. (Please see the next two sections — "Using Windows to Locate your Modem" and "Using Red Hat Linux to Locate your modem" — for instructions on how to get information about your modem.)

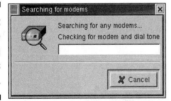

Figure 5-4:
The
Searching
for modems
dialog box.

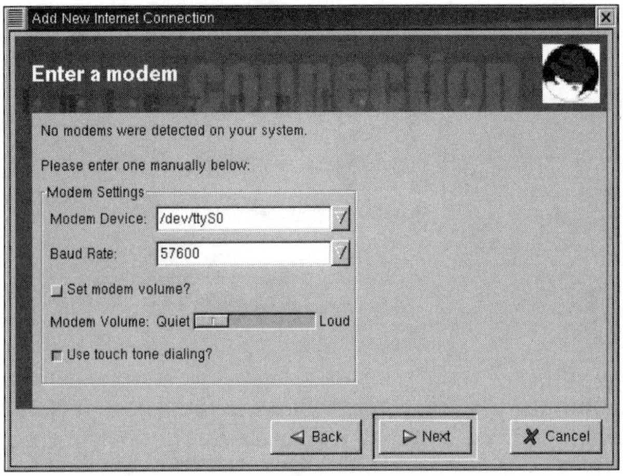

Searching for modems

Searching for any modems...
Checking for modem and dial tone

✗ Cancel

Add New Internet Connection

Enter a modem

No modems were detected on your system.

Please enter one manually below:

Modem Settings
Modem Device: /dev/ttyS0

Baud Rate: 57600

☐ Set modem volume?

Modem Volume: Quiet ▭ Loud

☐ Use touch tone dialing?

◁ Back   ▷ Next   ✗ Cancel

Figure 5-5:
The Modem
found
window.

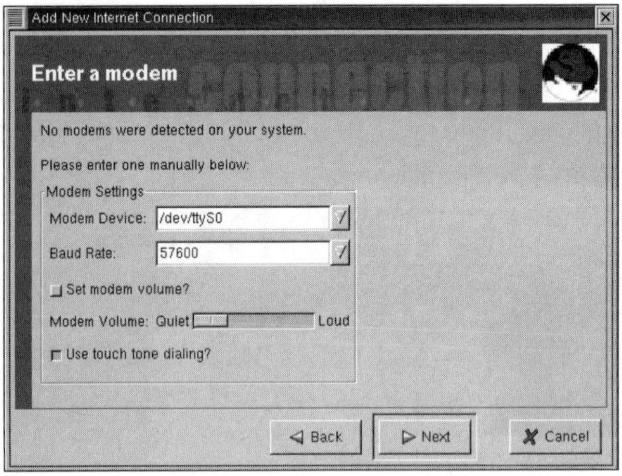

Add New Internet Connection

Enter a modem

No modems were detected on your system.

Please enter one manually below:

Modem Settings
Modem Device: /dev/ttyS0

Baud Rate: 57600

☐ Set modem volume?

Modem Volume: Quiet ▭ Loud

☐ Use touch tone dialing?

◁ Back   ▷ Next   ✗ Cancel

Figure 5-6:
The Enter a
modem
window.

4. Click Next yet again.

The Phone number and name window appears, as shown in Figure 5-7.

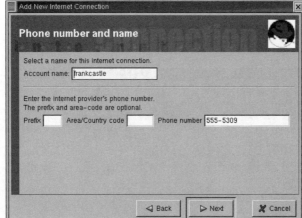

Figure 5-7:
The Phone
number and
name
window.

5. Enter a name for your new connection in the Account Name text box and your ISP's phone number in the Phone Number text box.

You can choose any name that you want for the account name (you can see that we call our account name `Myconnection` in Figure 5-7). You should also enter your ISP's prefix and area or country code if necessary in the appropriate text boxes.

6. Click Next when you're finished filling in the info.

The User name and password window appears, as shown in Figure 5-8.

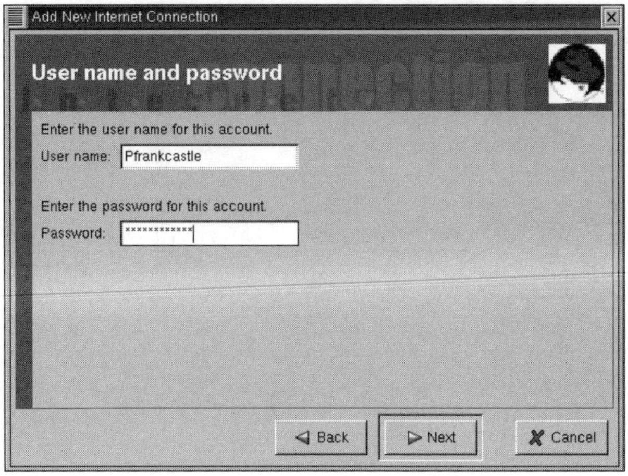

Figure 5-8:
The User
name and
password
window.

7. **Enter your PPP account name in the User Name text box and your password in the Password text box and then click Next.**

Your PPP account name and password are often different than your login account and password. You need to be authenticated by your ISP when you dial up and attempt to establish a PPP connection. You have to supply the information for your PPP account when you do this and it may be different than your user account. Talk to your ISP for more information about what information to supply here.

The Other Options window appears, as shown in Figure 5-9.

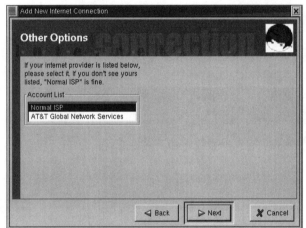

Figure 5-9:
The Other
Options
window.

8. **Select the Normal ISP option and then click Next if your ISP is not AT&T Global Network Services (if you use AT&T, click the selection for it and the Next button).**

Your account information is stored, and the Create the account window appears displaying your information, similar to Figure 5-10.

9. **Click Finish.**

The Internet Connections window, which is grayed out (as in Figure 5-1) if there are no accounts to show, comes to life and displays your new account, as shown in Figure 5-11. If you click the Modems tab, you see the information about your modem, as shown in Figure 5-12.

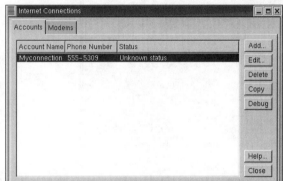

Figure 5-11:
The
Accounts
tab of the
Internet
Connections
window.

Figure 5-12:
The
Modems tab
of the
Internet
Connections
window.

Locating your modem with Linux

Linux uses device files to communicate with peripherals. Device files occupy the /dev directory and are equivalent to Windows drivers — you need them so that your hardware works.

Your modem can connect to one of four serial ports available on your PC. A *serial port* is the mechanism that your computer uses to communicate with a device, such as a modem. An external modem is generally connected to port /dev/ttyS0 or /dev/ttyS1 (although it's possible to configure it as /dev/ttyS2 or /dev/ttyS3). If you have an internal modem, then it can be any one of the tty devices.

During the boot process, Red Hat Linux provides a utility called kudzu that automatically tries to locate new devices when you boot your system. kudzu is good at detecting equipment like modems (both internal and external). When kudzu detects a new device, it prompts you to configure the device, and you should let it do so. kudzu's one hard-workin' little guy. Make note of what device it is attached to.

If kudzu is unable to find your modem, then it's not unreasonable to find it by process of elimination. This method is crude but effective. The following two numbered lists describe how to find your modem. The first method is for external modems, sending a string of characters to it and looking for the light-emitting diodes (LEDs) to light up. The second method is for internal modems, which don't have LEDs, and use the hideous screeching sound of your modem to track it down.

1. **If you have an external modem, then you can find it by running the following command from a command prompt:**

   ```
   echo "anything" > /dev/ttyS0
   ```

   Honestly, it doesn't matter what you put between the quote marks in the preceding commands, it just has to be some text — *any* text.

   If your modem is connected to the target serial port, you should see the LEDs light up in a short burst.

2. **If your modem isn't found, try sending the string to** /dev/ttyS1, /dev/ttyS2 **and finally** /dev/ttyS3 **by altering the number at the end of the command in Step 1 to match the port you're targeting.**

Life is a bit harder if you have an internal modem because you don't have a visual response. You can, however, listen to the modem's speaker to find out what's going on. To do so, follow these steps:

1. **If you have an internal modem, enter the following command at a command prompt:**

```
echo "atdt5555309" > /dev/ttyS0
```

If you hear the modem pick up and dial, you've won the game of hide-and-go-seek and know what device it is connected to. You can then skip to Step 4.

2. **If you don't hear anything, then make sure that you have the speaker turned on by entering the following command and then retry Step 1:**

```
echo "atv" > /dev/ttyS0
```

If you hear the modem pick up and dial, you've found what device it is connected to and can skip to Step 4.

3. **If you still can't hear anything, then try using the other serial ports by substituting** ttys1, ttys2, **and finally** ttys3 **in the command in Step 2 and trying it again until you find one that works.**

4. **After your modem is found, send the following command to the modem to kill the connection:**

```
echo "atz" > /dev/ttyS0
```

Getting desperate with dip

If your modem still isn't found after trying one of the two methods in the last section, you can use the dip dialup program. You can use dip interactively; that is, dip allows you to enter a command and immediately see the result — a great advantage when experimenting or troubleshooting modems.

To use dip to find your modem, follow these steps:

1. **Type dip -t at the command prompt and press Enter.**

   The dip> prompt appears (surprise!).

2. **Enter the following commands at the** dip> **prompt and press Enter after each:**

```
DIP>port ttyS0
```

```
DIP>dial 555-5309
```

If the modem picks up and dials, you've won! You can go on to Step 3. If the modem doesn't pick up, then dip returns you to the command prompt, and you should pick up with Step 4.

3. **If your modem is found, press the Enter key to immediately kill the connection.**

If the modem picks up and dials, you're done! You can skip Step 4. If the modem doesn't pick up, then dip returns you to the command prompt, and you should pick up with Step 4.

4. **Quit dip and then restart the program so that you can try ports ttyS1, ttyS2, and ttyS3 (to do so, just modify the first command in Step 1 to match the serial port you're targeting).**

Locating your modem with Windows

If you're running a Windows 9*x*/ME or a Windows NT/2000 system, then you can see which port your modem is connected to by following these steps:

1. **E-mail Bill Gates and ask him for your configuration.**

   If he's in court all week, see Step 2.

2. **Choose Start↪Settings↪Control Panel.**

   The Control Panel window appears.

3. **Double-click the Modem icon.**

   The Modems Properties dialog box appears.

4. **Select the Diagnostics tab.**

   You should see your modem listed with a COM line number beside it. This is the Windows designation for your modem's serial communications line. Thus, if the number 1 appears, that means Windows knows it as COM1; if it's a 2, then it's on COM2, and so on. These number designations translate directly to the matching number of ttyS0, ttyS1, ttyS2, and ttyS3 in Red Hat Linux.

Setting up DNS

Finding your way around the Internet would be nearly impossible if not for the Domain Name Service (DNS) system. This system converts the dot.com type of Internet name format into a numeric Internet Protocol (IP) address. An example of an IP address is 198.59.115.2. All the information that flows across the Internet (Web browsing, e-mail, and so on) is carried by IP packets that have source and destination IP addresses. So when you go to browse www.redhat.com, for example, that name is converted into a numeric IP address by DNS.

Unless you want to do all your browsing and e-mail by remembering numeric IP addresses, you must set-up your own DNS. Your ISP provides you with one or two DNS server addresses such as 198.59.115.2. You need to tell Linux about the DNS servers before you can browse the Internet. To do so, follow these steps:

1. **Log in to Linux as root.**

2. **Start the LinuxConf system administrative tool by clicking the Main Menu button and choosing Programs⇨System⇨LinuxConf.**

   The LinuxConf window appears, as shown in Figure 5-13.

3. **Choose Networking⇨Client Tasks⇨Name Server Specification (DNS).**

   The Resolver Configuration window appears (see Figure 5-14).

   The look and feel of LinuxConf has changed considerably since Red Hat Linux 6.2. The new iteration now does a better job of grouping similar functions by dividing the menus with tabs. You now click a tab to open up a group of similar functions. In version 6.2, the entire selection of menus was displayed in one screen — so much information was displayed that it was difficult to use.

4. **Type the domain name of your ISP in the Default Domain text box and press Enter.**

5. **Type the name server address in the IP of Name Server 1 text box.**

6. **(Optional) If you have a secondary name server, type it into the IP of Name Server 2 (opt) text box.**

   Figure 5-14 shows a completed Resolver Configuration window.

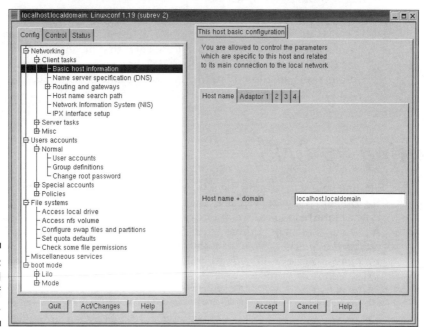

Figure 5-13:
The initial
LinuxConf
window.

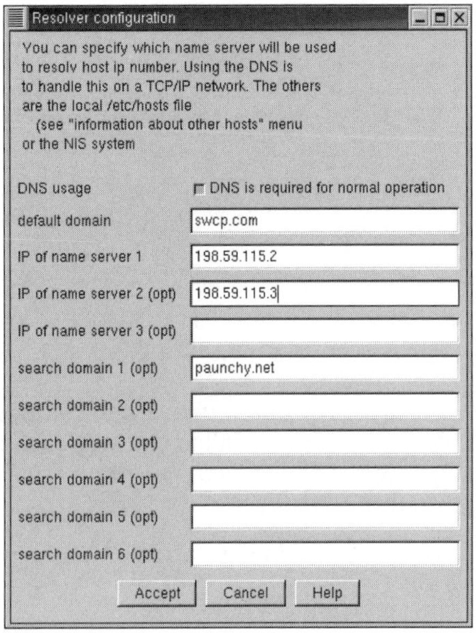

Figure 5-14:
The
Resolver
Configura-
tion
window.

7. **Click the Accept button.**

8. **Click the Quit button.**

9. **Click the Activate the Changes button.**

   LinuxConf exits and your settings are saved for future use.

Firing Up your Internet Connection

Red Hat Linux provides the Red Hat PPP dialer utility to help you establish a PPP connection, using the PPP configuration that you set up with the Dialup Configuration Tool (which we described earlier in the "Configuring Your Internet Connection" section) to make the connection.

To connect to the Internet with the Red Hat PPP dialer, follow these steps:

1. **Log in to Linux as any user.**

2. **Click the Main Menu button and choose Programs➪Internet➪RH PPP Dialer.**

   The Choose window appears displaying all of the network interfaces that you have, as shown in Figure 5-15.

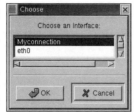

Figure 5-15:
Choosing
your
connection
from the
Choose
window.

3. Click the PPP interface and then click OK.

If you have an Ethernet (network) adapter, then it shows up as eth0. Your internal Linux network interface — called the loopback (or lo) — also shows up. You can ignore them because they don't have anything to do with connecting with your modem.

The Start window appears, as shown in Figure 15-16.

Figure 5-16:
Starting
your new
connection.

4. Click Yes and the PPP dialer dials your modem and logs in to your ISP's PPP account.

Once your connection is established, the PPP connection status window (shown in Figure 15-17) graphically displays the amount of your modem's capacity that you're using.

5. When you're finished using the Internet, you can close the connection by clicking the button (with a dot) in the PPP status window (see Figure 15-17).

The Change connection status? dialog box appears.

6. Click the Yes button to end your connection.

Figure 5-17:
Your PPP
connection
status
window.

Fire! Fire! Heh, Heh. Fire!: Securing Your System with a Firewall

After you connect to the Internet, you run the risk of the bad guys running amok with your computer; bad guys known by some as black hats (as opposed to red hats, which are of course the ultimate in cool). You may also have heard them called hackers, crackers, Trojan Horses, white hats, and so on. Whatever their name and whatever their intention, they all pose the threat of breaking into or otherwise harming your computer. This section describes how to build a firewall to help protect your Red Hat Linux computer from the bad elements found on the Internet.

The firewall described in this section will allow you to make RealAudio connections, but you must follow the directions given in the "Getting RealPlayer through your firewall section" in Chapter 11. There we describe how to configure RealPlayer to use the HTTP protocol in place of its native RTSP and PNA. RealPlayer works with this firewall since HTTP is allowed to pass through to the Internet. PS

You may think that there's safety in numbers. After all, literally millions of people, businesses, and organizations are connected at any one time. What do you — a simple person with a simple computer — have to be concerned about? The bad guys are usually interested in big money or big publicity, right?

Well, that line of thinking is all true, and chances are that you'll never suffer bad times. But that's a risk that you may or may not want to take. Linux offers a rather simple method for protecting yourself. The ipchains RPM that is packaged with Red Hat Linux can be used as a *firewall* — a tool for preventing unauthorized access to your computer.

Linux is a multiuser and multitasking operating system, meaning that more than one task can be run at once, and that, unlike with Windows, more than one person can be logged in at once. This offers an attractive launching point for black hats. If someone can gain access to your Linux computer while it's on the Internet, then that person can use your machine to launch attacks against other machines, and you become the proxy that helps the bad guys hide their identities.

Building a simple but effective firewall

The ipchains utility filters IP packets, which are the backbone of the Internet (IP stands for Internet Protocol, in fact). When you're connected to the Internet, all the information (graphics and text) that you send and receive is sent in the form of IP packets. All the information that enters and leaves your computer via the Internet is packaged in the form of IP packets. You can use `ipchains` to accept or deny IP packets based on their destination, source address, and ports.

Ports are another aspect of the Internet Protocol — one that you shouldn't care about. Suffice it to say that ports are used to control the internal workings of the Internet for such things as Web browsing.

Creating your firewall filtering rules

The `ipchains`-based firewall that we describe in this chapter allows you to access all of the primary Internet services except FTP. No one can access your machine or even see it. (Tools such as `nmap`, which we describe briefly in the sidebar at the end of this chapter, are readily available on the Internet and can be used to scan your computer and find out what type of operating system you have as well as what services it offers.)

FTP is used to transfer files from one place to another. You can modify the rules to allow FTP but that makes creating your firewall a little more complicated. You can find more extensive and complete rules in the directory on CD 3. Look for `ipfilter.rules` and `ipfilter.reset`.

The following steps describe how to protect yourself by building a firewall based around a PPP connection, but they can easily be modified to work with other types of connections:

1. **Log in to your system as root.**

2. **Create a script with the following** `ipchains` **rules in it:**

The lines preceded by the hash (#) symbol are comments so that you have some clue what the code following the comments are doing. You don't have to type them into the script.

```
# The next line activates the kernel module that allows
        RealAudio
# connection through your firewall
modprobe ip_masq_raudio

# Flush out all existing rules
ipchains -F
ipchains -X

# Set default filters to deny everything
ipchains -P input   DENY
ipchains -P output  DENY
ipchains -P forward DENY
```

```
# Allow all internal network traffic
ipchains -A input  -i lo -j ACCEPT
ipchains -A output -i lo -j ACCEPT

# Allow all private network traffic (If you have config-
      ured an Ethernet interface on a local network)
ipchains -A input  -i eth0 -j ACCEPT
ipchains -A output -i eth0 -j ACCEPT

# Allow all TCP packets out to the Internet
ipchains -A output -p TCP -j ACCEPT -i ppp0  -s 0.0.0.0/0
      1024:65535 -d 0.0.0.0/0

# Allow all TCP SYN packets back in (the return packets)
ipchains -A input -p TCP -j ACCEPT -i ppp0 ! -y -s
      0.0.0.0/0

# Allow DNS UDP packets out to the Internet
ipchains -A output -p UDP -j ACCEPT -i ppp0  -d 0.0.0.0/0
      domain

# Allow DNS UDP packets back in from the Internet
ipchains -A input -p UDP -j ACCEPT -i ppp0  -s 0.0.0.0/0
      domain
```

3. **Save the script as** `ipfilter.ppp` **to the** `/usr/local/etc` **directory.**

   Next you need to create the script that will be used to turn off the firewall.

4. **Use a text editor to create the following script and then save it as** `ipfilter.reset` **to the** `/usr/local/etc` **directory.**

```
ipchains -F
ipchains -X
ipchains -P input   ACCEPT
ipchains -P output  ACCEPT
ipchains -P forward ACCEPT
```

   Next you have to make the file executable.

5. **Click the Main Menu button and choose Programs⇨File Manager.**

   The File Manager window appears.

6. **Navigate to the** `/usr/local/etc` **directory and right-click the** `ipfilter.ppp` **file.**

7. **Click the Permission tab and then click all three permission buttons (so they look pushed in) that are immediately below the Exec column heading.**

8. **Click OK.**

   You can now run the `ipfilter.ppp` script in order to turn on your firewall.

9. **Repeat Steps 6 through 8, substituting `ipfilter.reset` for `ipfilter.ppp`.**

   You now have two scripts that turn on and off your firewall. The following section describes how to use the scripts.

Firing up your firewall

To activate your firewall, follow these steps:

1. **Log in as any user and connect to the Internet.**

2. **Start the GNOME file manager by clicking the Main Menu button and choosing Programs➪File Manager.**

   The File Manager window appears.

3. **Navigate to the `/usr/local/etc` directory and start the firewall by double-clicking the `ipfilter.ppp` script.**

4. **Try connecting to a Web site with Netscape Communicator.**

   Everything should work as usual.

   You can manually start the filter script by entering the following command at the command prompt in the terminal window:

   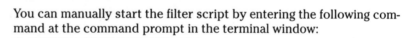
   ```
   ipfilter.ppp
   ```

Displaying your firewall rules

If you want to display the firewall rules, follow these steps:

1. **Open a terminal session by clicking the terminal icon on the GNOME Panel.**

   The Panel is that big menu bar at the bottom of your screen. The terminal icon looks like a monitor.

2. **If you're not already the root use, yype `su -` at the command prompt in the terminal window and press Enter to become root.**

3. **Enter the root password.**

4. **Type in the following command to display the firewall rules.**

```
ipchains -L
```

Make sure you use a capital "L" as the option.

5. **You should see a list displayed in the terminal window, as follows:**

```
Chain input (policy DENY):
target      prot opt      source       destination   ports
ACCEPT      all  ------    anywhere     anywhere      n/a
ACCEPT      all  ------    anywhere     anywhere      n/a
ACCEPT      tcp  !y----    anywhere     anywhere      any ->
            any
ACCEPT      udp  ------    anywhere     anywhere      domain ->
            any
Chain forward (policy DENY):
Chain output (policy DENY):
target      prot opt      source       destination   ports
ACCEPT      all  ------    anywhere     anywhere      n/a
ACCEPT      all  ------    anywhere     anywhere      n/a
ACCEPT      tcp  ------    anywhere     anywhere      any ->
            any
ACCEPT      udp  ------    anywhere     anywhere      any ->
            domain
```

The first *chain* (which is simply a set of rules used for a common purpose or function) is for incoming — or input — IP packets. You can see that the default policy is to deny all IP packets. The first two rules tell `ipchains` to allow all internal packets on the logical loopback (`lo`) and Ethernet (`eth0`) interfaces. The next rule allows the return packets from outgoing connections to come back in. The last rule allows the incoming UDP domain packets, which are used for domain name service (DNS).

The next chain — forward — denies all packets from being forwarded through your Linux computer. Forwarding is only necessary if you use your computer for routing or other advanced networking functions.

The last chain — output — defines what IP packets are allowed out of your computer. The first two rules are for your `lo` and `eth0` interfaces again and allow all internal traffic. The next rule allows any and all IP packets destined for the Internet to leave through the firewall. The last rule allows domain (DNS) packets to go out to the Internet.

You can make your `ipchains` rules tighter by allowing only certain types of packets out to the Internet. You can specify certain ports and addresses that are allowable, for example. This makes your firewall incrementally safer but also more restrictive.

Testing your firewall

Your new firewall is no silver bullet, but it does provide a great deal more protection than if you didn't have one. Treat it for what it is — a good, sturdy lock. It's the beginning of your Internet security, but not the end. But don't trust it without first making sure it works.

To test your firewall, follow these steps:

1. **Throw some gasoline on your computer and light a . . . no, no, just kidding. Don't do that, especially if you plan to sue.**

2. **Try to Telnet to your ISP or University account; any computer account that's external to your own computer will do.**

   (Telnet is a network program that allows you to connect to a remote computer and interactively enter commands.)

3. **If you don't know it already, find out what your temporary (dynamic) IP address is by entering the following command at the command prompt:**

   ```
   who | grep login
   ```

   where *login* is your, well, login your name. This command should show an IP address in numeric form, similar to the following:

   ```
   iamme (192.168.1.250) ...
   ```

   Please note that the preceding IP address has been changed to protect the innocent. The address is what is known as a public address and will (should) never exist on the Internet anyway.

4. **Try to Telnet back to your Linux computer by typing in the actual address that you received in Step 3 in place of *IP_address* in the following command:**

```
telnet IP_address
```

If your firewall is set up correctly, nothing should happen. If you turn off your firewall, however, then you should be able to log in to your Linux computer.

For more information on firewalls and security, search the Internet for security-related topics. The SANS (www.sans.org), USENIX (www.usenix.org), Red Hat (www.redhat.com), and CERT (www.cert.org) Web sites are all good places to start. The companion documentation CD-ROM (CD3) also has some good HOWTO documents on the subject.

Kicking your firewalls tires really hard

A good test of a firewall is to get your ISP to run a port scan against your firewall. A port scanner throws IP packets in various tortured forms at your computer and then reads the response to those packets — if any — and tries to determine what services your are running. Port scanners can even detect what operating system you are running.

nmap is an excellent free port scanner and is probably the tool that your ISP will use to scan you. It's beyond the scope of this book to describe how to use it. But if you want to investigate its use on your own, you can get it from www.insecure.org. The nmap package comes with good documentation that describes its use.

Chapter 6

Connecting Red Hat Linux to a Local Area Network (LAN)

In This Chapter

▶ Configuring your local network connection with LinuxConf

▶ Starting and stopping your local network connection

▶ Routing to the outside world

▶ Creating a simple but effective firewall

---

*T*his chapter shows you how to connect your Red Hat Linux computer to a local area network (LAN). This is different than connecting directly to the Internet via an ISP as described in Chapter 5. When you connect to the Internet, you use a modem to communicate with an ISP, which then connects you to the Internet. In this case, you connect directly to a LAN with an Ethernet adapter. Ethernet-based LANs are much faster than modem/ISP connections. If your LAN has an Internet gateway, then you can connect to the Internet, too.

If you configured your Ethernet card during the installation process described in Chapter 2, then great! You can skip this chapter or browse through it. Otherwise, use this chapter to configure your Ethernet adapter for the first time or reconfigure networking for your Red Hat Linux machine.

Although forming a private network isn't exactly rocket science, describing in detail how to connect two or more computers together to do so is still beyond the scope of this book. The job is not terribly difficult but would take too much space given all of the possible configurations. Many good books are available that show how to do that, and you can consult the Linux documentation found in the /usr/doc/HOWTO directory of your Red Hat Linux installation. See the Ethernet-HOWTO, Networking-Overview-HOWTO, NET-3-HOWTO, and NET-3-4-HOWTO on CD3 that came with this book for more information on networking.

Going Local

The invention of Linux has revolutionized the use of networks. Creating a LAN prior to Linux was complicated and expensive (in this book the term LAN and private network are used interchangeably). LANs were nearly the exclusive domain of big corporations, universities, and other such monstrous organizations.

But TCP/IP networking was built into Linux from the beginning. In the mid-1990s, if you could afford a couple of PCs, a few $150 10Mbps (megabits per second) Ethernet adapters — also known as network interface cards, or NICs — and a cheap piece of coaxial cable, a LAN was born! Prices have crashed since then, fortunately, falling to earth like David Bowie: Can you believe a 100Mbps NIC now costs as low as $15!

You only have to configure a handful of networking subsystems to get your Red Hat computer on a network. They are listed below:

✔ Load your Ethernet NIC kernel module

✔ Configure your NIC

✔ Configure your routing table

✔ (Optional) Configure your domain name service (DNS). If you do not want to create your own DNS server, then you need to configure a complete routing table (/etc/hosts) on every computer on your LAN.

Performing these three or four steps is pretty heavy lifting, but the load is eased in general by using the graphical LinuxConf system administration tool to configure your network. You can also use individual commands to perform the same configuration. Both methods are described in this chapter. Have fun!

Connecting to a LAN with LinuxConf

To connect your Red Hat computer to an existing local area network (LAN), you need an Ethernet adapter installed on your computer and a network hub, or switch, to connect it to. After you set up the hardware, you simply need to configure your network settings.

Note that if your LAN also has an Internet connection, then you can set up your computer to communicate with the Internet, too. A high-speed Internet connection is best, but it doesn't matter in terms of the network configuration.

Configuring your basic host information

To get your Red Hat Linux computer working on a LAN, you must first configure its Ethernet adapter. The Ethernet adapter is the device that electrically connects your computer to your LAN. In order to work with the other computers on your network, your Ethernet adapter must be given a network address and a few other pieces of information.

Follow these steps to configure your Red Hat Linux Ethernet adapter by using LinuxConf:

1. **Log in as root.**

2. **Start LinuxConf by clicking the GNOME Main Menu button and choosing Programs⇨System⇨LinuxConf.**

   The first time that you start up LinuxConf, the introductory screen Welcome to LinuxConf is displayed. Click the Quit button to exit from the screen and continue to the main LinuxConf screen.

3. **In the Config tab on the left, click Networking⇨Client Tasks⇨Basic Host Information.**

   The This host basic configuration window appears, as shown in Figure 6-1.

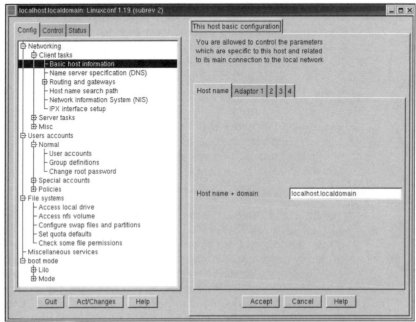

Figure 6-1: The This host basic configuration window.

4. **Type a host name in the Host Name + Domain text box and click the Accept button**

   If you are connecting to a network not controlled by yourself, then you have to first confirm the hostname that you want to use. Otherwise, use whatever dull one they give you.

5. **Click the Adaptor 1 tab.**

   The configuration fields for your Ethernet adapter appear.

6. **Click the Manual option.**

7. **Type the host name and domain name of your computer together in the Primary Name + Domain text box.**

   This combination includes the hostname that you entered in Step 4 plus the name of your network, for example `veracruz.paunchy.net`. If your computer is connected to a LAN that has a domain name, then you must use that name. If you have a single computer or one connected to your own network, then you can use any name that you want.

8. **(Optional) Type an alias (or nickname) for your computer.**

   Using an alias makes it simpler to refer to a computer. For example, instead of having to refer to my machine as `veracruz` you can use an alias like `vera` or `cruz`.

9. **Assign an IP address to your computer by typing it in the IP Address text box.**

   IP addresses are analogous to street addresses; they provide a number that uniquely identifies your machine from all others. Public IP addresses do not require any registration with the powers that be — the InterNIC organization that distributes IP addresses. Confusing? Not really. Public IP addresses are not routed on the Internet and can be used on LANs for your own use.

   If you're on a network with registered IP addresses, then get an IP address from your system administrator. Otherwise, go ahead and use a public IP address. (Use any class C address between 192.168.1.1 and 192.168.254.254. For example, 192.168.128.5 or 192.168.1.20.)

10. **Type the netmask for your IP address in the Netmask (opt) text box.**

    The Internet Protocol defines only three network address classes: A, B, and C. Only class C addresses are assigned by the InterNIC. We use only class C addresses here. If you're not using a class C address, then you're probably experienced in the ways of TCP/IP and know what netmask to use. (You can use non-standard netmasks to subdivide your network into sub-subnets of, for example, 64 machines. This is rarely necessary and creates networks that can be very confusing to use.) Otherwise, don't fool with Mother Nature, buddy: Use a class C address.

11. **Type the network device, which should be** eth0, **in the Net Device text box.**

Ethernet adapters are referred to as `ethx`, where `x` can be a number from 0 on up (Adapter 1 is `eth0`, Adapter 2 is `eth1`, and so on.)

The window with your Ethernet adapter information should look similar to Figure 6-2.

You should not have to enter information into the Kernel Module, IO Port (opt), or IRQ (opt) text boxes because Linux is good at detecting this information directly from the device.

Kernel modules are the Linux equivalent to Microsoft Windows device drivers. Red Hat Linux generally is able to detect what Ethernet adapter you have and automatically load the correct module. If Red Hat is unable to detect your Ethernet adapter, then it's unlikely that you can find the correct one from the supplied list. You can still go ahead and try; there's no harm in trying.

12. **Click the Accept button.**

You must now configure your name service, a process that we cover in the next section.

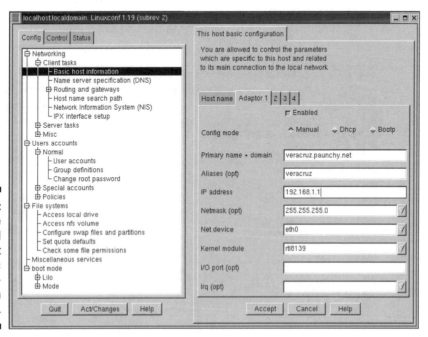

Figure 6-2: The completed This host basic configuration window.

Name that name server: Configuring DNS

You now need to configure your DNS information. This is the same process described in Chapter 5, but in this case that you're connecting to a LAN and you may have access to a local DNS server. If your LAN provides a DNS server, then you can use it as your primary name server (DNS). You can still specify your ISP server as your secondary DNS server.

1. **Log in as root.**

2. **Click the Main Menu button and choose Programs⇨System⇨LinuxConf.**

   The Linuxconf window appears.

3. **In the Config tab on the left, click Networking⇨Client Tasks⇨Name Server Specification (DNS).**

   The Resolver configuration window appears, as shown in Figure 6-3.

4. **Type the default domain name of your network into the appropriately named Default Domain text box.**

   A domain name is a two part name separated by a period. For example, paunchy.net is a domain name. This is the domain name discussed in Step 7 of the preceding section. It's the network name of the example LAN being constructed here. You should, of course, replace the paunchy.net domain name with the name of your LAN.

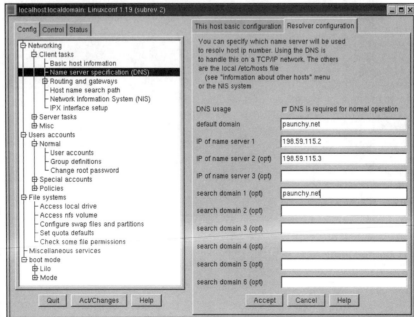

Figure 6-3:
The
Resolver
configura-
tion
window.

5. **Type the IP address of your DNS server in the IP of Name Server 1 text box.**

   IP addresses are made up of four sets of numbers separated by periods (192.168.1.250, for example). Your ISP provides you with an IP address when you subscribe.

6. **If you have one, type the IP address of your secondary name server in the IP of Name Server 2 (opt) box.**

   Most ISPs provide a backup DNS server address.

7. **(Optional) If you are connected to a network that has multiple domain names, then you may want to provide additional search domain names in the Search Domain 1 (opt) text box.**

   If you set up a domain name called `eng.paunchy.net` on your LAN, then you want to enter that name here. You can then use just the name of the machine you're looking for. For example, if you have a machine named `pumas.eng.paunchy.net`, then you can refer to it as simply `pumas` (rowr!). Without the secondary domain name, you have to use the entire name — `pumas.eng.paunchy.net` — instead of just `pumas`.

8. **Click the Accept button.**

9. **Click the Quit button.**

10. **After the screen changes, click the Activate the Changes button.**

    LinuxConf exits. Your settings are saved and ready for future use.

Getting away with your Internet gateway

The last step in connecting your computer to a LAN is to configure the Internet gateway. The *Internet gateway* is the computer, or dedicated device (router), that directs IP packets from your LAN to the Internet. To configure your Internet gateway, follow these steps:

1. **Log in as root.**

2. **Click the Main Menu button and choose Programs⇨System⇨LinuxConf.**

3. **In the LinuxConf window, under the Config tab, click the Networking button.**

   The Network Configurator window appears.

4. **In the Network Configurator window, on the Client Tasks tab, click the Routing and Gateways button.**

   The Routes to other networks window appears.

5. **Click the Set button.**

The Defaults window appears.

6. **Enter the IP address of your LAN gateway in the default gateway text box.**

If you want to be able to access the Internet through your LAN, you must specify the default gateway here. If you are connecting to an existing network at work or other professionally run organization, then contact your system administrator to get your default gateway address. If you are running your own network that is connected to the Internet via a router and high-speed device such as DSL, ISDN, or a cable modem, then you should enter the address of the router as your gateway.

For example, Paul has a DSL connection to the Internet. He also has a Red Hat Linux system connected to the DSL device that acts as his LAN's router (it has two Ethernet adapters — one connected to the DSL device and one to his LAN). The Red Hat Linux router is responsible for directing all of the LAN's Internet-bound traffice to Paul's DSL connection and is, therefore, his Internet gateway and has an address of 192.168.1.254. The gateway address that is assigned to all computers on his LAN is the same — 192.168.1.254.

7. **Click the Accept button.**

8. **Click the Quit button.**

9. **After the screen changes, click the Activate the Changes button.**

LinuxConf exits. Your settings are saved and ready for future use.

Manually starting your Network

Sometimes LinuxConf configures your network stuff but doesn't activate it. Why does this happen? Who knows — it may be because LinuxConf is still relatively young and will get better with time. In the meantime, you can start your networking systems another way.

You can use the /etc/rc.d/init.d/network script to start and stop your networking system. To start your network modules, NIC, and routes, log in as root and run the following command:

```
/etc/rc.d/init.d/network restart
```

All networking components are stopped and then started again. Alternatively, you can use /etc/rc.d/init.d/network start to simply start and configure your Ethernet adapter and routes. The /etc/rc.d/init.d/network stop command turns off all networking on your system.

If LinuxConf doesn't work as it should (and sometimes it just won't), you have to manually configure your LAN. We show you how to do so in Chapter 18.

Protecting Your Red Hat Linux Workstation with a Firewall

After you connect your Linux machine to your LAN, you must consider providing yourself with more protection. Building your own firewall is equivalent to storing your valuables in a safe that's behind the locked doors of your home. Locking your front door is more important, but the amount of time and money you spend on a safe depends on how much you have to protect.

While the firewall described in Chapter 5 is essential for your safety, the one used here is optional if your LAN is already protected by a firewall.

The firewall described in this section will allow you to make RealAudio connections, but you must follow the directions given in the "Getting RealPlayer through your firewall section" in Chapter 11. There we describe how to configure RealPlayer to use the HTTP protocol in place of its native RTSP and PNA. RealPlayer works with this firewall since HTTP is allowed to pass through to the Internet.

The simple IP filtering firewall introduced in Chapter 5 can readily be modified to work with a LAN (Ethernet) connection. By placing a firewall on your Red Hat Linux computer, you greatly increase your security. If you use your Red Hat Linux computer on a network with more than one person, you must at least consider the insider threat. Not that the people you work, or exist with, are untrustworthy, but you have to consider all possibilities. We hope we don't sound paranoid. (Even paranoids have enemies!)

Anyway, all the information that enters and leaves your computer via your Ethernet NIC is packaged in the form of IP packets. You can use ipchains to accept or deny the IP packets based on their destination and source address and ports.

Creating your firewall filtering rules

The ipchains-based firewall described here is similar to the one from Chapter 5, but this one has been modified to work on a Red Hat Linux workstation that is connected to a LAN. This firewall works on the same principle of denying most network traffic but judiciously allowing enough through to let you access your LAN and the Internet.

We provide a copy of the `ipfilter.reset` firewall script described here on the main (/) directory of CD3.

The following steps describe how to protect yourself by building a firewall. The rules are based around a PPP connection but can easily be modified to work with other connections.

1. **Log in as root.**

2. **Create a script called `ipfilter.eth0` in the `/usr/local/etc` directory.**

   This script starts your firewall. Type the following `ipchains` rules into it. (The lines preceeded by the hash (#) symbol are comments.)

   ```
   # Flush out all existing rules
   ipchains -F
   ipchains -X

   # Set default filters to deny everything
   ipchains -P input    DENY
   ipchains -P output   DENY
   ipchains -P forward DENY

   # Allow all internal network traffic
   ipchains -A input  -i lo -j ACCEPT
   ipchains -A output -i lo -j ACCEPT


   # Allow all TCP packets out to the Internet
   ipchains -A output -p TCP -j ACCEPT -i eth0  -s 0.0.0.0/0
            1024:65535 -d 0.0.0.0/0

   # Allow all TCP SYN packets back in (the return packets)
   ipchains -A input -p TCP -j ACCEPT -i eth0 ! -y -s
            0.0.0.0/0

   # Allow DNS UDP packets out to the Internet
   ipchains -A output -p UDP -j ACCEPT -i eth0  -d 0.0.0.0/0
            domain

   # Allow DNS UDP packets back in from the Internet
   ipchains -A input -p UDP -j ACCEPT -i eth0   -s 0.0.0.0/0
            domain
   ```

3. **If you want to run RealAudio (described in Chapter 11) connections, then add the following line to the script.**

   ```
   modprobe ip_masq_raudio
   ```

4. Create the following script (which turns off IP filters) in the /usr/local/etc **directory and name it** ipfilter.reset.

```
ipchains -F
ipchains -X
ipchains -P input   ACCEPT
ipchains -P output  ACCEPT
ipchains -P forward ACCEPT
```

5. Make scripts executable by running the following command (the script can only be run by root):

```
chmod 770 /usr/local/etc/ipfilter.*
```

Firing up your firewall

To activate your firewall, follow these steps:

1. Log in as root.

2. Start the firewall by typing the following:

```
/usr/local/etc/ipfilter.eth0
```

3. Try using your computer to access the Internet.

For example, try connecting to any Web site with Netscape Communicator. Everything should work as usual.

4. Next, look at the rules that you've set up by typing ipchains -L **at the command prompt and pressing Enter.**

5. You should see a list, as follows:

```
Chain input (policy DENY):
target     prot opt     source       destination   ports
ACCEPT     all  ------   anywhere     anywhere      n/a
ACCEPT     all  ------   anywhere     anywhere      n/a
ACCEPT     tcp  !y----   anywhere     anywhere      any ->
           any
ACCEPT     udp  ------   anywhere     anywhere      domain ->
           any
Chain forward (policy DENY):
Chain output (policy DENY):
target     prot opt     source       destination   ports
ACCEPT     all  ------   anywhere     anywhere      n/a
ACCEPT     all  ------   anywhere     anywhere      n/a
ACCEPT     tcp  ------   anywhere     anywhere      any ->
           any
ACCEPT     udp  ------   anywhere     anywhere      any ->
           domain
```

The first *chain* (which is simply a set of rules used for a common purpose or function) is for incoming — or input — IP packets. You can see that the default policy is to deny all IP packets. The first two rules tell ipchains to allow all internal packets on the logical loopback (lo) and Ethernet (eth0) interfaces. The next rule allows the return packets from outgoing connections to come back in. The last rule allows the incoming UDP domain packets, which are used for domain name service (DNS).

The next chain — forward — denies all packets from being forwarded through your Linux computer. Forwarding is only necessary if you use your computer for routing or other advanced networking functions.

The last chain — output — defines what IP packets are allowed out of your computer. The first two rules are for your lo and eth0 interfaces again and allow all internal traffic. The next rule allows any and all IP packets destined for the Internet to leave through the firewall. The last rule allows domain (DNS) packets to go out to the Internet.

Red Hat Linux 7 introduces a new method for launching basic network services called xinetd. For those familiar with the previous versions of Red Hat Linux and all other Linux distributions, you will not find the inetd daemon anymore; the new system replaces the inetd.conf file in the /etc directory with xinetd.conf. The xinetd.conf file gets its configuration information from individual system files. For example, if you install the Telnet server package (telnet-server-0.17-7.rpm), the xinetd.d Telnet configuration file is stored in the /etc directory. This package is not installed by default with the Workstation installation option. You can install the xinetd RPM package to use the new system.

Configuring ipchains to start automatically

Red Hat Linux now provides a mechanism for starting an ipchains-based firewall: the /etc/rc.d/init.d/ipchains startup script to be exact. The /etc/sysconfig/ipchains configuration file provides the script with the firewall rules. But the configuration file is difficult to create unless you already have a running firewall. After you have your firewall running, enter the following command:

```
ipchains-save > /etc/sysconfig/ipchains
```

The `ipchains-save` command reads and then displays your current set of rules. The > symbol redirects the output to the `/etc/sysconfig/ipchains` file, in this case, and henceforth your Red Hat Linux workstation starts your firewall automatically at bootup.

You can also start and stop the firewall manually. The `/etc/rc.d/init.d/ ipchains stop` command turns off the firewall; the `/etc/rc.d/ init.d/ipchains start` command turns it on, and the `/etc/rc.d/init.d/ ipchains restart` command first stops and then starts the firewall.

Chapter 7

Surfing the Web and Managing E-Mail with Netscape Communicator

· ·

In This Chapter

▶ Tailoring Netscape Communicator to your liking

▶ Checkin' out da Web

▶ Receiving and reading e-mail

▶ Sending your first e-mail message

· ·

*O*nce upon a time, there was a company called Netscape that created a browser to surf the Internet. The browser was called Netscape Navigator and it could to be downloaded from the Internet for free. Netscape put it in the hands of millions of people — including us, your authors — who could use it to access the exploding number of Web servers. Netscape Navigator made history and changed the world. Many think of Navigator as the tool that was most responsible for popularizing the Internet.

Over time, Netscape Navigator became Netscape Communicator, a larger program that can not only surf the Web but can also organize e-mail, let you participate in newsgroup discussions, download files, create Web pages, and even listen to music, all through a single graphical interface.

In this chapter, we show you how to set up Netscape Communicator for your Red Hat Linux system so that you can surf the Net and send and receive e-mail.

Netscape Communicator can do far more than we describe in this chapter, as our goal is to describe how to use its basic features. For more information about Netscape Communicator, check out the features available under the Help menu, such as the Reference Library or Help contents. You can also check out *Netscape Communicator 4.5 For Dummies* by Paul Hoffman (published by IDG Books Worldwide, Inc.).

Red Hat Linux 7 comes with Netscape Communicator 4.75, and that's the version of Netscape we discuss in this book. But by the time this book is published, Netscape will have released their snazzy new Netscape 6 browser that took the company over two years to complete. Check out Netscape 6 at the following URL:

```
http://home.netscape.com/browsers/6/index.html
```

Checking Out Communicator

CD1 of your *Red Hat Linux for Dummies* companion CD-ROMs includes a copy of Netscape Communicator Version 4.75, which is installed with Red Hat Linux by default. Netscape Communicator has several main features, including:

- ✔ **Navigator:** The Web browser that allows you to surf the Web.

- ✔ **Messenger:** The e-mail and newsgroup reader client, which includes an address book that you can use to store the e-mail addresses and other information of everyone with whom you communicate.

- ✔ **Composer:** The HTML editor that Netscape provides for creating or modifying the contents of Web pages.

- ✔ **Netscape Radio:** The Web-based radio client, which enables you to choose from one of 15 channels that play nonstop music. Configuring your computer to access radio stations requires that you have your sound system working and the RealPlayer plug-in.

Setting Up Netscape Communicator

The first thing that you want to do is to tailor Netscape Communicator to your preferences. You can do this *offline* (without connecting to the Internet). Follow these steps to customize Communicator to your liking and set up Communicator to be your e-mail client:

1. **Start Communicator by clicking the Netscape "N" icon on the GNOME Panel.**

   The Welcome to Red Hat Linux screen appears in Navigator, as shown in Figure 7-1.

Figure 7-1:
Navigator
displaying
info about
Red Hat
Linux 7.

2. **Choose Edit⇨Preferences.**

   The Preferences window appears, as shown in Figure 17-2.

   On the left side of the Preferences window is the Category window, which you can think of as a map of where you are in the Preferences window.

3. **Click the arrow next to the Navigator category to collapse it.**

   Here is where you determine what Web page appears when you start Communicator; as well as which Web page loads when you click the Home button on the Navigation toolbar.

4. **In the Home Page area of the Navigator window, fill in the Location field with the URL of the Web page you'd like to be your home page.**

5. **(Optional) If you want, select a History number.**

   Communicator remembers where you have been and lets you select (and go to) a previous location. How long Communicator remembers (and thus how big the list becomes) depends on how many days of history you choose. If you are short on disk space, then choose a lower number like 1 or 2 days. Otherwise, leave the default setting alone.

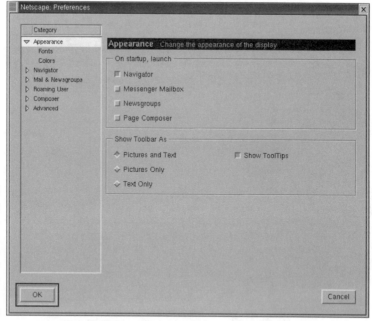

Figure 7-2:
The
Netscape
Communi-
cator
Preferences
window.

6. In the Category window, click Mail & Newsgroups and then click the Messages submenu.

The Messages window, shown in Figure 7-3, is where you can set defaults for outgoing messages. This window is also where you can select the option of automatically quoting e-mail that you reply to, which means that Communicator includes (or *quotes*) the original message in your reply. This feature is often useful when you want to comment on specific items that someone has written.

The Formatting subcategory offers options for how Communicator formats your outgoing message, such as whether you want to send plain text e-mail or HTML-formatted e-mail. The latter option is fine if you know that the recipient reads e-mail using an HTML-enabled e-mail client (such as Netscape Messenger) rather than a text e-mail reader. You can also choose to send yourself an automatic e-mail copy of every e-mail you send.

You may want to deselect the two options of always sending HTML messages and automatically quoting and including the original message in a reply. (Some folks prefer not to receive HTML in their e-mail messages, and don't want their text quoted back at them.) To deselect an option, just click to remove the check mark.

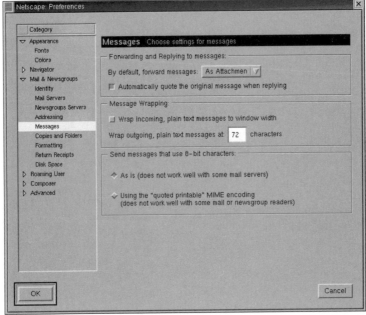

Figure 7-3:
The
Messages
window
offers
options for
sending
e-mail.

7. Click the Identity submenu under the Mail & Newsgroups category.

The Identity window appears, as shown in Figure 7-4. Here you can add your e-mail address, return address, and organization name, and specify a different reply-to address if you don't want people replying to the same e-mail address you send from.

8. Enter your e-mail address in the Email Address text box.

You can also enter your full name and organization name in the appropriate text boxes, but this is purely optional. If you want your return address to be different than your e-mail address, enter it in the Reply-to Address text box. You can also create a file that contains a signature that is appended to every message you send. If you create such a file, then enter its name in the Signature File text box.

9. Click Mail Servers under the Mail & Newsgroups category.

The Mail Servers window appears, as shown in Figure 7-5. Your ISP or local system administrator supplies you with access to machines called *servers* that send and receive your e-mail even when you are not connected to the Internet. When you do connect to the Internet, your computer tells the server to deliver the e-mail or send your messages.

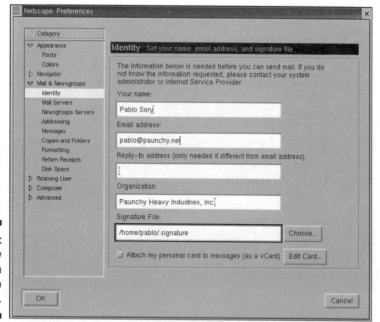

Figure 7-4:
The Identity window in all its drab glory.

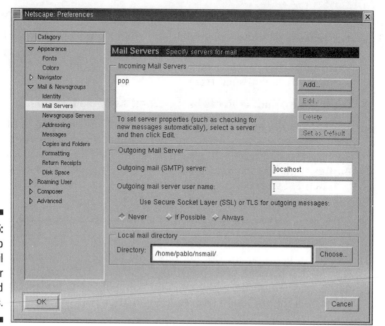

Figure 7-5:
Setting up the e-mail server names and addresses.

10. **Enter your incoming and outgoing mail servers by following these steps:**

    1. Click the Add button, type the name of the incoming server into the Server Name text box and your username into the User Name box, and then click OK.

    2. Type your outgoing server name into the Outgoing Mail (SMTP) Server text box.

       The name of this and the name of the incoming server are usually the same, but if you're using a special mail service called POP (Post Office Protocol), which allows you to download e-mail to your system from the server, your ISP gives you a name for their POP server. IMAP4 is an even newer protocol for doing similar procedures as POP, and if your ISP has an IMAP4 server, they should tell you that also.

       IMAP4 is more powerful and secure than POP. You should select IMAP4 if possible.

    3. Type your username for your mail server into the Outgoing Mail Server User Name text box and click OK.

11. **If you want to participate in a news server, under Mail & Newsgroups click Newsgroups Servers and then click the Add button.**

    The Newsgroups Servers window appears, as shown in Figure 7-6.

    Netscape Communicator enables you to read Usenet newsgroups, which are a series of discussion groups that have been active for many years. Usenet groups were one of the first uses of the Internet, and they have been disseminating information (and misinformation) for many years.

    A dialog box appears.

12. **To participate in a newsgroup, fill in the name of your news server (provided by your ISP) in the Server text box.**

    Message groups can be quite active, so you should fill in the last option in the window, which specifies how many messages you want to receive before being asked.

    Now you're all set to run Netscape Communicator and see the world. Click OK and go, go, go!

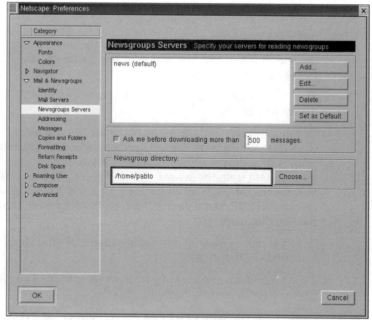

Figure 7-6:
Setting up
newsgroup
server
information.

Navigating the Net with Navigator

After you've configured your browser properly, you need to connect to the
Internet. If you connect with a modem, see Chapter 5 to configure your connection if you haven't already. After you're connected to the Net, type the
following URL in the Netsape Location text box:

```
http://www.mylinuxbooks.com
```

Netscape Communicator shows Paul's Web page, as shown in Figure 7-7. If
you put your mouse cursor over the *Red Hat Linux 7 for Dummies* link, this
book's Web page pops up as shown in Figure 7-8, including information about
the book such as scripts, corrections (errata), and other useful links.

Delete the URL in the Location text box and replace it with another one, such
as www.netscape.com or anything you want to try. Press the Enter key to
send the browser off to another Web page. You can always click the Back
button to return to where you were before, or click the Forward button to go
forward to a page from which you've just come.

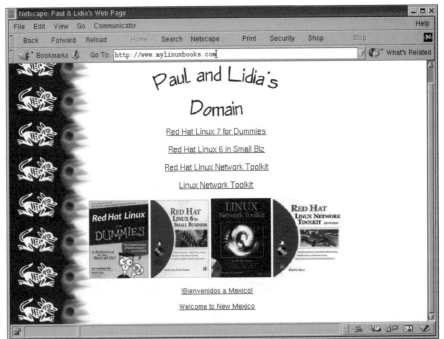

Figure 7-7:
Paul's www.
mylinux
books.
com site.

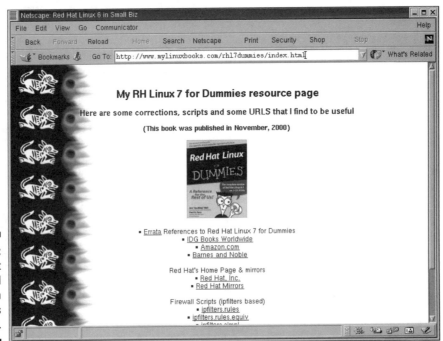

Figure 7-8:
You can get
additional
information
about this
book here.

Here are a few interesting URLs related to Linux that you can try:

www.redhat.com

www.linuxtoday.com

www.linux.com

www.li.org

www.ssc.com

Another way of opening a new Web page is to choose File⇨Open New Location. Netscape displays the Open Page dialog box, shown in Figure 7-9, where you can type the new URL and then choose whether you want to use open that URL in Navigator (to browse) or Composer (if you want to edit the Web page the URL points to).

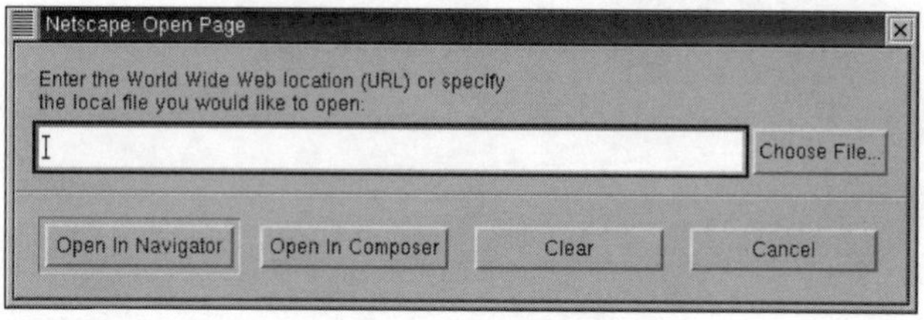

Figure 7-9:
The Open
Page dialog
box.

Netscape: Open Page

Enter the World Wide Web location (URL) or specify
the local file you would like to open:

Choose File...

Open In Navigator | Open In Composer | Clear | Cancel

You can also use this the Open Page dialog box to open a file of HTML code that's local to your system. If you decide to load a local file, click the Choose File button. The File Browser dialog box, shown in Figure 7-10, springs up so that you can search the file system to find the file you want.

Web pages can also contain graphics, as shown in Figure 7-11. Type http://electriclichen.com/linuxbierwanderung into the text box and see the cute penguin (the mascot of the Linux world) going off to drink a beer while working on Linux with his notebook.

You can even send sounds through the Web (although illustrating this capability is a little difficult). Sounds are transmitted over the Internet as files, and you can play them after they reach your browser, computer, and sound card.

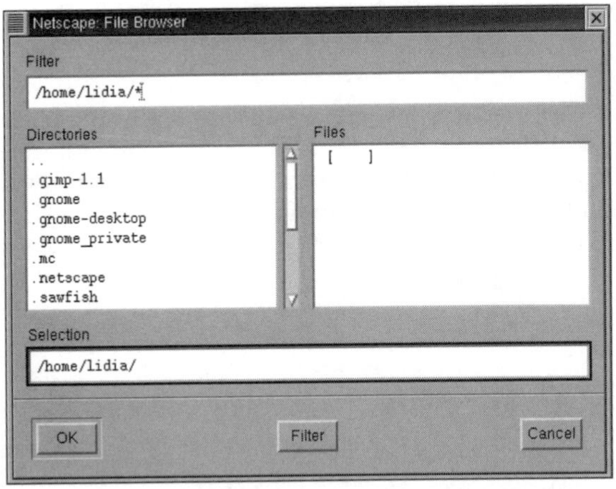

Figure 7-10:
Navigating
through
local files.

Figure 7-11:
A penguin
and his
beer — you
can send
images
through
the Web.

Working with E-Mail

Now that you can surf the Internet, you probably want to tell people about your adventures. Well, Netscape Communicator can send and receive e-mail, too. This section describes how to send and receive messages with Netscape Messenger, Communicator's e-mail program. We show you how to set Communicator up to be your e-mail client in the "Setting Up Communicator" section earlier in this chapter.

Getting your e-mail

To get your e-mail you first need to start Netscape Messenger by starting Communicator and choosing Communicator⇨Messenger. Netscape Messenger appears, as shown in Figure 7-12.

To get your mail, simply click the Get Msg icon. This icon tells Netscape Communicator to make contact with your mail server and see whether any e-mail messages are waiting for you. If you have no new e-mail, a message at the bottom of the screen tells you so. If you do have e-mail, the subject and sender appear in the center of the screen, and the e-mail message itself appears in at the bottom of the screen, as shown in Figure 7-13.

If you have multiple e-mail messages, you can see each one by clicking the Subject line in the middle window. You may reply to, forward, or delete a particular message by highlighting its Subject line and clicking the appropriate icon (Reply, Forward, or Delete). When you click the Reply icon, the address of the person you're replying to appears automatically in the To field of the reply. When you forward a message, a copy of the message is sent as an attachment to the address you specify.

Sending e-mail

To send an e-mail message, you need to know the recipient's e-mail address. Just as a URL consists of certain components, an e-mail address is made up of the person's e-mail name (often the same as his or her login name) and domain name. For example, to send an e-mail to the President of the United States, you address it to president@whitehouse.gov.

Your ISP should have given you an e-mail address, and you can ask your friends for their e-mail addresses. (It's ironic that in order to get your friends' e-mail addresses, you end up spending a lot of time on the telephone.)

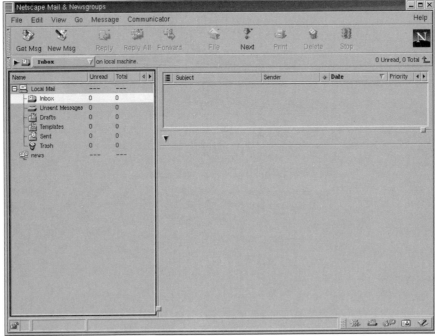

Figure 7-12:
The
Netscape
Inbox -
Netscape
folder
window.

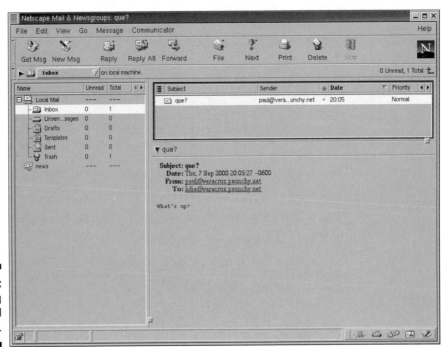

Figure 7-13:
Receiving
an e-mail
message.

With the Mail & Discussions window on the screen, click the New Msg icon. The Compose window, similar to Figure 7-14, appears.

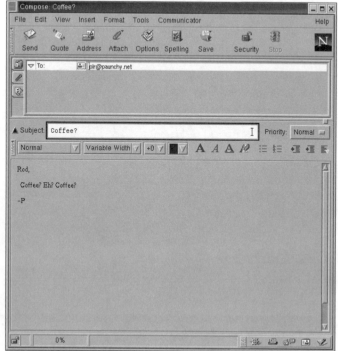

Figure 7-14: The Compose window for composing new messages.

Below the row of icons near the top of the window is the word *To* is a white space where — after you click in it — you can type the e-mail address of the person you' are trying to reach. Just for fun, try sending a letter to your own e-mail address. Then if you receive it properly, you'll know that you did everything correctly. Just follows these steps to do so:

1. **Click in the To field and type your own e-mail address.**

2. **Click in the Subject field, and type any subject, such as** test.

3. **Click in the body of the message and type a brief message.**

4. **Click the Send Now icon.**

   Even if you are sending a message to yourself, it won't appear instantaneously. It still has to travel through the telephone line, be analyzed by the server, and sent back to you, so be patient.

You can also attach a file, an image, or even a sound to your message and send it to friends. who also use Netscape Communicator (or another MIME-compliant mail reader). To attach a file to your letter, simply click the Attach icon at the top of the Compose window. The Attach File dialog box appears, shown in Figure 7-15, allowing you to search your hard drive for the file you want to send.

After you select the file, the browser asks whether or not you want to encode it using with Base64 or Uuencoding. Either one is okay for sending mail to your friends, but Base64 is probably the more popular in the Microsoft world.

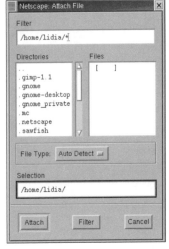

Figure 7-15:
The Attach
File dialog
box for
selecting a
file to attach
to a
message.

Part III

Linux, Huh! What Is It Good For? Absolutely Everything!

The 5th Wave   By Rich Tennant

"I'M GONNA HAVE A LITTLE TROUBLE WITH THIS 'FULL MOON' ICON ON OUR GRAPHICAL USERS INTERFACE."

In this part . . .

Y ou have finished your initial journey. Red Hat Linux is
up an' running, and you have mastered the basics of
the Internet and LANs. You've looked at the map enough
to know where you are. Now, the big question is: What do
you do with it?

Well, one thing that you can do with the computer is warm
your feet while you watch the screen saver kick in. You
can also confide to all of your friends that you have a
"Red Hat Linux box" at the next party you go to. Wow,
that'll make you popular as they clamor to know when
your stock options mature. Or, you can actually use your
new Red Hat Linux workstation to get things done.

Chapter 8 introduces you to the wonderful world of the
GNOME windows environment. GNOME is a friendly li'l
guy who likes to put a friendly face on Linux. With
GNOME, you can set up the "look and feel"' of Linux so
that you feel comfortable and at home. Chapter 9 takes
you a bit further and introduces many of the cool things
that you can do from GNOME.

Next, in Chapter 10, the serious fun starts. Can you say,
"par–*tay*?" Chapter 10 starts by describing how to set up
your sound card. From there, we show you how you can
listen to audio CDs and MP3. We also show you how to
record the sound from CDs. Finally, you become your own
recording studio by recording audio — and data if you're a
nerd — to CD.

Chapter 11 takes the audio thing one step further. It shows
how to use the commercial product RealPlayer to listen to
streams. No, not water streams, but audio and video
streams flowing from the Internet. You can listen to radio,
audio clips, and watch video, too. RealAudio provides a
free version of its player (that we use here), which you
can download from the Net. We also use two of the
CD/MP3 players — xmms and gtv — that come with Red
Hat Linux to play MP3 audio and video. With this knowledge, you never have to leave your couch again. Now,
that's living!

Chapter 8

Gnowing GNOME

*T*he Linux operating system comes with two interfaces in one, a command-line interface (like that found in MS-DOS) and the graphical X Window System, also known as just X, with GNOME sitting on top of X. X itself is said to sit on top of the command-line operating system, allowing total access to the operating system through a graphical interface. (Some operating systems, such as Windows ME, provide you with only a graphical interface.)

In this chapter, you find out a little bit about X, as well as the basics for working with GNOME. You also get to mess around with the GNOME Panel and desktop (the Panel is similar to the taskbar on a Windows computer). We also show you some cool but simple maneuvers to manage your windows (such as moving them, changing their size, bringing them to the front, and hiding them in the background), lock your screen, log out of GNOME, and stop X altogether.

GNOME is the default graphical user interface (GUI) for Red Hat Linux. You can also use the K Desktop Environment (or KDE) if you want, but for the purposes of this book we assume you stick with GNOME as your default.

Introducing the Amazing X Window System

The GNOME desktop environment provides Red Hat Linux's graphical interface by default (although you can use KDE if you want). GNOME and its Sawfish window manager run on top of the X Window System, also known simply as X, which is the software underneath GNOME that makes your Red Hat Linux computer able to display graphics. Unlike in the Microsoft world, Linux is not defined by its graphical interface. Microsoft Windows includes both the operating system — the software that makes for a usable computer — and its familiar graphical interface. The two are closely intertwined and essentially inseparable. Linux and X, however, are completely separate animals.

So what? Well, for one, separating the two makes for a more reliable and robust workstation. Without the burden of having to incorporate graphics into itself, the Linux operating system can remain a lean, mean fighting machine. The X Window System concentrates on providing graphics and does not interfere with the operating-system. Separating the two also makes for varied and interesting development efforts.

The version of X that comes with Red Hat Linux 7 is quite sophisticated and simple to use. This was not always the case. It took a lot of natural — dare we say Darwinian — selection to arrive at the current arrangement of X, and the end result works very well.

X has three main parts, including the following:

- A graphics server
- A set of graphics libraries
- A set of graphics clients that normally use the graphics libraries

The *graphics server* is a program that talks to the video card, keyboard, and mouse on your system. It receives commands from the set of graphics libraries incorporated into programs. Sometimes these programs are executed directly on the same system where the graphics device resides; other times, these programs talk across a network to a graphics device on another system. Using X, you can run your program in one part of the world and someone can see the output of it in another part of the world over the Internet.

The server program, often called the *X Server,* is not part of the operating system, as it is in some other operating systems. Instead, X Server is a *user-level* program — a special and complex one.

The following sections discuss each of the three major types of programs that use X:

- Window managers
- Terminal emulators
- General applications

Comprehending window managers

Window managers, like GNOME's Sawfish window manager, are programs that receive commands indirectly from the user through mouse clicks and keystrokes. The window manager passes those commands to a set of graphics libraries, which then communicate with the X server to manipulate windows on the graphics device (usually your monitor screen).

The window manager acts like a playground monitor; it's the central point of control for the major windows seen on the screen (and even some windows that can't be seen). It blows a whistle when a window gets unruly. The window manager can serve also as a desktop, where you can use it to launch applications. A window manager isn't necessary, but it would be difficult to use more than one or two applications at once without also using a window manager. (The applications themselves would need to be written to allow resizing, window positioning, and so on.)

Window managers may also maintain an *icon bar,* which keeps icons easy to find and manage, as well as performing other functions. But the most important thing to remember about window managers in X is that they are just user-level programs like any other — they are not part of the system. You have a choice of window managers, and each has different capabilities, although a discussion of window managers other than GNOME and their capabilities is outside the scope of this book.

The *Red Hat Linux For Dummies* CD-ROMs contain several window managers including the GNOME Sawfish window manager, KDE, and the previous Linux standard Fvwm. GNOME is the default for Red Hat Linux and so GNOME is the window manager used in this book. KDE is similar to GNOME in that it is a modern system but we leave it up to you to explore if you wish. You can also use good old Fvwm to start applications (and stop them of course), move windows, shrink windows, expand windows, and do everything but wash windows. Just think, you can use your system without ever typing a command!

Going old-school with the terminal emulators

The second main type of program under X is the *terminal emulator,* a program that emulates the old-style terminal console from within the GUI. You may be wondering why you would want to simulate a dumb, inexpensive terminal when you paid a lot of money for a neat graphics monitor. Shouldn't every program be graphical?

Well, in the early days of X, few graphical programs were available. Most programs were written to run on nongraphical interfaces and did not include the libraries that create graphical programs on an X Server. Therefore, to run both graphical and nongraphical programs, the dumb terminal had to be emulated through software.

When you start a terminal emulator, it usually executes a shell and gives you a command-line prompt. You type commands at this command prompt, and the results are output to the terminal emulator window.

Waxing vague with general applications

The third main type of program is the *general application,* and this can range from text editors such as xedit (which looks a lot like a terminal emulator but is much different) to applications such as xfig (which manipulates images) and xpaint (which enables you to draw objects) to games such as Doom. These programs would be impossible (or at least very hard) to run in a nongraphical interface.

Getting Earthy with GNOME

To check out the GNOME interface, log in to your Linux computer and you should see the GNOME window environment appear (unless you specified otherwise during installation), as shown in Figure 8-1. By default, the GNOME Hint screen starts when you log in.

If X does not automatically start when you boot your computer, then you need to start X manually by entering the conveniently named startx command at a command prompt. If X fails to start, consult Chapter 19.

Figure 8-1:
The GNOME login window and environment.

GNOME consists of the following three major elements:

✔ **The desktop:** Quite simply, the desktop is the space where you do your work. The desktop comes preconfigured with several icons that include links to your home directory, Red Hat's home page, the Dialup Configuration tool, your floppy disk, and the Trash bin. In Figure 8-1, you can see these icons along the left edge of the screen.

When you click the home directory or floppy disk icons, the GNOME File Manager (the Midnight Commander application) is started up and displays the contents of those directories. The *File Manager* is a graphical system for working with files and directories in your home directory as well as the entire file system.

✔ **Standard applications:** Programs such as the GNOME File Manager, the GNOME Help Browser, and so on.

The GNOME Help Browser provides a comprehensive and easy to follow tutorial, and will take you through all GNOME basics. The Help Browser also provides a good reference.

✔ **The Panel:** The menu bar that runs across the bottom edge of your GNOME screen.

Mucking about with basic window manipulation

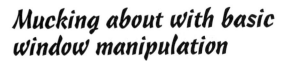

GNOME performs all of the basic graphical functions that you expect a GUI to do. You can move windows, resize them, minimize them, and so on. The following sections show you how to perform typical window manipulations in GNOME:

Getting focused

Before you can do anything to a window, you have to get its attention. When you have a window's attention, it's said to have *focus*. Depending on how you've set up GNOME, you can give a window focus with GNOME in several ways, including the following:

✔ Click the window's name in the Panel.

✔ Click the window's title bar, which is at the top of the window.

✔ Click a part of the window itself, which typically also makes the window the topmost one.

✔ If you're working in an office with a lot of people, then you can shout "Hey you, wake up!" While this tactic isn't likely to wake your window up, it sure is fun.

In this book we stick with the Red Hat/GNOME default of clicking a window to focus it.

Moving day

To move a window, click anywhere on the window's title bar and hold the left mouse button down. As long as you continue to hold the left mouse button down, the window moves anywhere that you move your mouse. Release the button and the window stays there.

Resizing windows to your heart's content

Sometimes a window is a little too big or a little too small, and you know life would be much easier if you could just nudge that window into shape. To do that, position the mouse cursor on either the lower-left or lower-right corner of a window until the cursor changes into a double-sided arrow. Left-click the mouse button and pull the window's outline to your desired size. Release the mouse button and the window takes the new size.

Another way to resize a window is to click the far, upper-left corner. A menu appears. Click the Window Size submenu and you get another menu that allows you to toggle either the height, width, or entire window between its normal (default) size and the entire desktop.

Making a molehill out of a mountain

Now that you've put a lot of windows on the screen, how can you get rid of a few or all of them? Well, you can *minimize* (or *iconify*) a window by clicking the bold, underscore button towards the upper-right corner, which removes the window from the desktop and places it in a storage area on the right side of the Panel. If you're feeling in a particularly devilish mood, you can be more drastic and *close* a window.

Here are a few ways to get rid of a window, starting with the least drastic and escalating to outright window death:

- ✔ Take advantage of any exit buttons or menu options that the window or application in the window give you. For example, many applications allow you to choose File⇨Exit or File⇨Quit to close the application.

- ✔ Click the X button in the upper-right corner of the window's title bar to close the window.

- ✔ Click the upper-left corner of the window or the title bar and then choose either of the Close or Destroy options in the menu that appears. Close attempts to contact the application and ask it nicely to stop itself, where Destroy doesn't care what the application thinks and stops it immediately.

✔ You also have the option of completely closing the application by right-clicking its icon in the Panel and choosing either Close or Kill App in the menu that appears. The difference between the two is that Kill app will close the program if it does not respond to the Close command. Kill app isn't as nice as Close and potentially could cause problems if you are running a program like a database that is actively manipulating data.

You can return a minimized window to the desktop by clicking the icon that corresponds to the window on the Panel.

Making a mountain out of a mole hill

To make a window fill up the entire screen, click the Maximize button in the upper-right corner of the window. If you check out those buttons to the right of the title bar of a typical window, the Maximize button is the one in the middle; it looks like a square and is similar in action to the Cascade button in Windows.

Playing with the Panel

The GNOME Panel is the menu bar along the bottom of the desktop. The Panel is similar to the taskbar in Windows, providing a location to place common menus and applets for easy starting or viewing. The Panel also gives you a view of the virtual desktop (described later in this chapter) and lets you keep track of minimized windows.

By default, Red Hat Linux places icons on the Panel for accessing the GNOME Help Browser, the Configuration tool, the GNOME terminal emulation program, and Netscape Communicator 4.75. You can start any of those programs by clicking their icon. There is also a simple clock placed at the far right of the Panel.

Another important element of the Panel is the Main Menu button at the far left, which is used to access all the standard GNOME applications and configuration tools. Click the Main Menu button, which looks like a small footprint located in the lower-left corner of the screen. The menu shown in Figure 8-2 appears. You can choose from any of the menus displayed when you click the Main Menu button. For example, if you hover your mouse over the Programs menu, you see the submenu displayed in Figure 8-3.

The Programs submenu is pretty much self-explanatory. For example, the System menu contains programs used to configure GNOME and other systems tied to GNOME and X. The Multimedia menu provides access to your CD player, while the Internet menu provides access to applications that help you connect to the Internet.

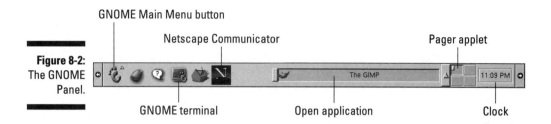

Figure 8-2:
The GNOME
Panel.

GNOME Main Menu button

Netscape Communicator

Pager applet

GNOME terminal

Open application

Clock

You can use the Panel submenu to modify the configuration and behavior of the Panel itself. For example, if you click the Main Menu button and choose Panel⇨Add to panel⇨Applets⇨Clocks⇨AfterStep Clock, you get the nifty clock applet added to the Panel. The AfterStep clock is more attractive than the simple one that is displayed by default. (You can remove the original clock by right-clicking its icon and selecting the Remove from panel option.)

One of the other interesting functions of the Panel menu is the Add New Launcher function. Click the Main Menu button and choose Panel⇨Add to panel⇨Launcher buttons. The Create launcher applet window appears, as shown in Figure 8-3. By entering the pathname of an application, you can add a new applet to the Panel that *launches,* or starts, that application.

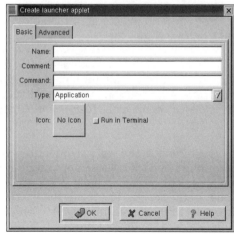

Figure 8-3:
The Create
launcher
applet.

Give it a try. For example, if you download the StarOffice desktop productivity suite (which includes a full-fledged word processor, spreadsheet, and so on — we describe StarOffice in Chapter 12), you can add an applet for it to your Panel so you don't have to haggle with menus to launch it. From the Create launcher applet window, add the name, any comments, and the command to launch the program. The instructions in Chapter 12 have you install StarOffice into your home directory — for example /home/login/office52/soffice —

so if you wanted to add a StarOffice applet to your Panel you would enter this pathname (switching *login* for your login name) into the Command text box. If you click the No Icon button, you are given a few pages of standard icons that you can use to distinguish your new applet from others on the Panel; in our case we chose the `gnome-tigert.png` as our icon mascot. Figure 8-4 shows the finished applet launcher window.

Figure 8-4:
The StarOffice launcher applet is born.

After you finish editing the Create Launcher Applet window, click OK. The icon is added to your Panel, as shown in Figure 8-5. You can create a launcher for any application on your Linux computer in the same way.

Figure 8-5:
The StarOffice launcher applet icon on the Panel.

You can create an icon on your desktop for any application found in the GNOME Main Menu menu. Just click the Main Menu Button, find the menu item for the application that you want an icon for, and then left-click the application and hold the mouse button down. While continuing to hold down the button, drag the mouse cursor to any open area on the GNOME desktop. Release the mouse button and an icon for that application is placed on the desktop. You can then start the application by double-clicking the icon.

Working on your virtual desktop

After using GNOME for awhile you can probably tell that it's possible to create lots and lots of windows on the screen. You may even lose windows behind other windows. Perhaps you wish that your monitor was larger just so you could open up more windows and do more things at one time, or maybe you just don't want to close down or minimize one application before going to another application.

Well, monitors are expensive, and a lot of systems can have only one graphics card, so you're probably stuck using a single monitor. But you don't have to be stuck with one *screen.* X, with the help of GNOME, can give you both virtual screens and virtual desktops.

A *virtual desktop* enables you to have more than one desktop screen to work on. It's like having four tables (desks) spread in front of you. You have the option of organizing your work — terminal screens, window applications like Netscape, and such — on different desktops. The default for Red Hat Linux GNOME is four virtual desktops. The virtual desktop display icon — the *pager applet* — on the far-right side of the GNOME Panel controls the virtual desktops.

By clicking any of the four Desk Guide buttons, you are placed in the corresponding desktop. Click the lower-right one, and you go to that screen. Give it a try!

You can easily switch between desktops by turning on Edge Flipping. When active, Edge Flipping allows you to switch to an adjacent desktop by moving the mouse cursor to the edge of the screen. After a short delay, you are placed in the new desktop. Edge Flopping — er, flipping — is turned off by default in Red Hat Linux's installation of GNOME. To turn it on, click the Main Menu button and choose Programs⊅Settings⊅GNOME Control Center. In the Control Center that appears, click Sawfish Window Manager and then click Workspaces. Click the Edge Flipping tab. From the window shown in Figure 8-6, click the Select the Next Desktop When the Pointer Hits Screen Edge option, and then click the Hitting Screen Edge Selects the Next option and change it from viewport to workspace. You can also change the time you have to wait for the flip by changing the Milliseconds to Delay Before Flipping number.

You may notice that the upper-left block in the pager applet (the virtual desktop display), shown back in Figure 8-2, seems to be colored or seems to contain some smaller blocks. That upper-left block represents the virtual desktop you are in right now. The smaller rectangle within the upper-left block is a window (in this case, it's The Gimp, which is the graphical image manipulation tool used to create the figure).

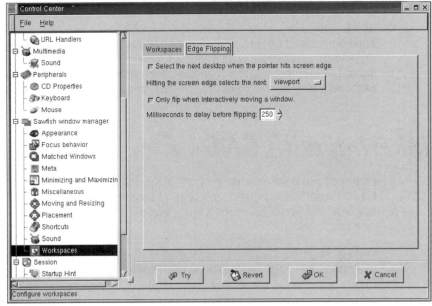

Getting out of GNOME or X

If you want to leave your computer on but don't want to leave your computer open to anyone just walking along, you can save the time of logging out of your GNOME desktop by using the screen lock. To do so, click the Main Menu button and choose Lock Screen. The screensaver is displayed. To return to productive life and your desktop, press any key or wiggle your mouse and enter your password in the X Screensaver window that appears.

Securing your computer while you step out

GNOME preconfigures an icon for locking your screen. This is actually one of the best security features that you can use. You must enter your password to get your screen back after using this icon.

To use this icon, click the little padlock icon that sits almost all the way to the left of the GNOME panel. Your screen locks up and you must enter your password to get back in. Locking your screen is a good idea when you're going to be away from it for even a minute or two.

Locking up the shop

When you've finished for the day and want to go home (or just upstairs), you need to log out. Click the Main Menu button and choose Log out. The Really log out? screen appears. Click Yes to log out. You also have the options to *halt* (shut down) or reboot your computer.

eXterminating X

When you can't get your applications to respond to you, you can simply stop X, which kills all the programs running under it. To do so, press the Ctrl+Alt+Backspace keys all at once. If you started X manually, you can then log out of the account. If X is started automatically at boot time (as this book assumes), then you will get the X login screen and you can log back in.

Tinkering with GNOME

Once you are familiar with the GNOME basics, you probably want to know how to modify it. To do so, you need to pay attention to two configuration systems: the GNOME Control Center system and the Sawfish Configuration system.

You can start the GNOME Control Center by clicking the Main Menu button and choosing Programs⇨Settings⇨GNOME Control Center. The Control Center appears, as shown in Figure 8-7. Here you can modify all the basic properties of GNOME. Choose Desktop⇨Background and you can set the color and other aspects of the desktop. Choose Desktop⇨Screensaver⇨Xjack and you switch from the default random screensaver to the "All work and no play makes Jack a dull boy" screensaver. Not a bad selection for those long winters spent at peaceful resorts with plenty of time to write Linux books!

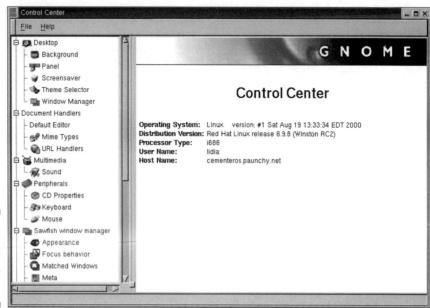

Figure 8-7: The GNOME Control Center window.

The Control Center also lets you configure things other than screensavers with maniacal rantings. We leave it to you to explore the wonderful world of setting your keyboard bell and such. This system gives you lots of flexibility.

You can reach the Sawfish window manager via the Control Center. Open the Control Center and the Sawfish window manager menu appears towards the bottom of the screen. Use your mouse cursor to move the slider bar down so that the entire menu visible, as in Figure 8-8.

Focus Behavior and Appearance are the important menus here. The Focus Behavior menus let you change the style of how windows appear as they are moved and resized. More importantly, the Focus Behavior menus enable you to change the way windows are controlled by the movement of your mouse. This is called *keyboard focus*.

By default, you have to click a window to bring it to the surface. You can change this so that merely moving the mouse cursor to a window focuses it. The sloppy focus behavior works as a compromise by bringing focus to a window when you move the mouse there, but not raising it to the top of the screen until you click the mouse button.

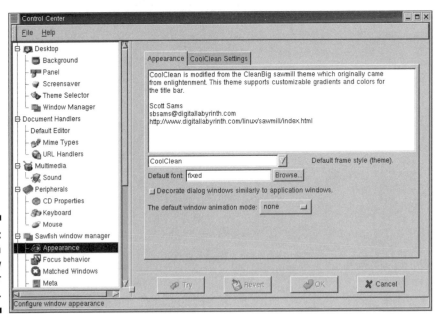

Figure 8-8:
The Sawfish window manager menu.

The Appearance menu gives you the ability to change the window frame styles; a *frame style* is the way a window border looks. For example, click the Default Frame Style (Theme) and you get a selection of window borders. They're fun to play with and give you the ability to customize your windows to your taste.

The Miscellaneous section provides control over settings such as how long it takes for tooltips to appear and for keyboard focus to take effect. The other options provide control over the remaining look and feel of your desktop; for example, you can control the number of virtual windows displayed, your audio system (if you have one), and other such things. There are too many other menu options and combinations to describe here, so be adventurous and give the Sawfish window manager a cruise!

Chapter 9

Gnowing More Graphical Stuff

*I*n this chapter, you find out how to use some of the useful programs that come with GNOME. Although space prohibits us from showing you all the programs, we give you a good sampling of what's available.

Becoming a GNOME File Manager

Being the boss doesn't make you a bad person. It's just a job. Right? Well that little GNOME guy is a good worker and doesn't get paid much. Just press a key here, click a button there, and you can boss him around like Dilbert. GNOME even comes with its own file manager that saves you work and makes room for those long lunches.

The GNOME File Manager follows in the tradition of all good file managers, graphically displaying the files and directories on your computer. You can copy, move, delete, and execute files by pointing and clicking. You can also create directories, view file details, and the like. Not a bad deal considering that it works for free.

Waking up the little guy

Red Hat Linux configures the GNOME File Manager to start automatically when you log in. The File Manager appears toward the end of the login process, as shown in Figure 9-1. Should you want to start it manually — after you've closed it, for example — then click the Main Menu button and choose Programs⇨File Manager.

The main menu follows the familiar File, Edit, and so on menu format and does all the things that you would expect those menus to do. The toolbar immediately below the main menu enables you to quickly move up one directory (Up) and redo previous moves (Back and Forward). It also lets you rescan a directory, go to your home directory, and change the way that icons are displayed. The Rescan function, for example, is useful if you create a new file via a terminal screen. The file doesn't show up in the File Manager until you move to another directory and return, or else rescan.

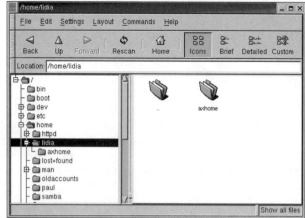

Figure 9-1:
The GNOME
File
Manager.

Putting him through his paces

Most people use file managers to do the basics: copying, moving, and deleting files and such. We introduce those things here and leave the rest (advanced functions) for you to explore on your own.

Moving files and directories

Moving a file or directory is as simple as clicking it and holding down the mouse button, and then dragging the mouse cursor over the directory that you want to move it to. Release the button and you have moved your file or directory.

You can move multiple files by clicking and holding the mouse button and then dragging the mouse cursor over the files that you want. The mouse cursor creates a rectangular outline and highlights all the files within that box. Next click anywhere within the highlighted box and drag the mouse cursor to the desired directory. Release the mouse button and the files move to the specified directory.

Copying files and directories

Copying a file or directory is a bit more complicated then moving one. Rather than simply clicking an icon and dragging it someplace, you have to right-click the file or directory icon and choose copy from the menu that appears. The menu lists all the options available from the File Manager. Choose Copy and another dialog box appears, as shown in Figure 9-2. Within that dialog box, you can manually enter the pathname of where you want to copy the file, or you can use the Browse function. If you choose Browse, yet another dialog box appears, and you can click and search for the target directory.

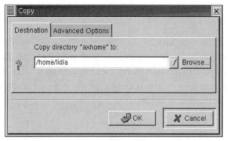

Figure 9-2:
The File
Manager
Copy
dialog box.

You can copy multiple files and directories in the same manner that you move them (see the previous section); you simply trace a box around the files that you want to copy by clicking and dragging the mouse cursor. Next, right-click any of the highlighted icon names (but not the white space around the icon and names themselves), and you get a menu with three options: Copy, Move, and Delete. Choose Copy and follow the directions described in the last three sentences of the preceding paragraph.

Deleting files and directories

Deleting files and directories is much the same process as copying them. You right-click the desired file or directory icon choose Delete from the menu that appears. You're then prompted to verify that you really want to delete that file or directory. Exercise your normal caution and self-preservations skills before clicking Yes.

Deleting directories is naturally a little more complicated. When you choose to delete an entire directory and it is not empty, you're prompted to delete it recursively, which means that any subdirectories will be deleted, too. Answer Yes and every file and directory within that directory is removed.

Finally, you can delete multiple files and directories. Again, you trace a box by clicking and dragging the mouse cursor. Right-click the icons or icon names (but not the white space around the icon and name). The simple menu, as described previously, appears. Select Delete and then answer Yes in the confirmation window.

You can change the confirmation behavior of moving, copying, or deleting functions. Choose Settings⇨Preferences and select the Confirmation tab in the Preferences window. You can then toggle various options that control such behavior.

Creating directories

To create a new directory, choose File⇨New⇨Directory. The Create a New Directory dialog box appears where you enter the name of the new directory. Linux creates the directory in the current working directory, which is the directory that the File Manager currently shows.

Viewing files and directories

By default, files and directories display in iconic — symbolic — form. The only information that an icon shows is the name and whether an item is a file or directory. You can see more information by clicking the Brief, Detailed, or Custom buttons that appear on the main toolbar. Figure 9-3 shows the window after the Detailed button is clicked.

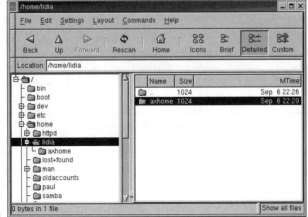

Figure 9-3:
Changing the File Manager's view.

The following list describes the differences between these views:

✓ **Icons view:** Displays the symbol (icon) and indicates whether an item is a file or directory. Regular file icons take several forms, but text and configuration files look like pieces of paper with a corner folded, and executable files look like pistons. Links, devices, and so on take other forms. Directories take the form of a partially open file folder. Icons are evenly placed across the entire File Manager screen.

✔ **Brief view:** Shows files and directories on individual lines. Directories are shown as smaller (closed) file folders. Regular files use various characters such as asterisks (*) and exclamation points (!) before the filename to represent executable files. Text and word-processing files, however, use no such characters and show only the filenames.

✔ **Detailed view:** Displays the size and time stamp of each file and directory, as well as their names.

✔ **Custom view:** Allows you to choose what file attributes to display. You can select the attributes by choosing Settings⇨Preferences and selecting the Custom View tab. From there, you can add and delete the attributes from a list of possible attributes.

You can reach these same views by clicking the Layout button and then clicking the radio buttons for Icon View, Brief View, Detailed View, or Custom View.

Finding files and directories

You can search for files and directories by using the File Manager's Find command. Choose Commands⇨Find File. In the Find File window, enter the directory in which you want to start your search (your current directory is the default) and the filename to look for.

You can also specify a string of characters to look for within the file or files.

Running programs and scripts

GNOME is such a hard worker that it happily launches commands for you. Choose Commands⇨Run Command and enter the name of the command you want to run in the Enter Command to Run dialog box. For example, if you enter the `xclock` command, the xclock appears on your desktop.

Managers are generally not that smart. But GNOME is and it tells the manager what to do when it encounters various file types. If you open a nonexecutable file, such as a PDF file, the file manager knows what program to use in order to view it.

GNOME recognizes various file types because it keeps a list — its own Rolodex of sorts. These file types are known as Multipurpose Internet Mail Extensions (MIME) types and they define what type of information a file stores. Consult Chapter 11 for more details on how GNOME keeps track of MIME types.

You can use the File Manager to create shortcut icons on your desktop that point to files or applications. Just left-click any file or application shown in the File and then, while holding the mouse button down, drag the mouse cursor to any blank part of the desktop and release the button. An icon is placed on desktop. You can then start the application by double clicking its icon. If the icon points to a data file (such as a text file, for example) and GNOME knows how to handle its MIME type, then GNOME launches the appropriate application to open the file. Otherwise, GNOME prompts you to tell it which application to use to open it.

Checking Out Some Handy Linux Programs

GNOME not only does the work described in the previous sections of this chapter, but it also works overtime. Many cool programs are bundled along with Red Hat Linux. A few of the particularly useful ones are described in the following sections.

Getting graphic with the Gimp

The Gimp is more than just a graphics-viewing program — it's also a great graphical manipulator. Click the GNOME Main Menu button and choose Programs⇨Graphics⇨The Gimp to start The Gimp.

The Gimp opens up several screens, including a Tip window. If you choose File⇨Open, you can open graphics files and view and even modify them. You can also copy any window, or your entire screen, by using The Gimp's Acquire function. Choose File⇨Acquire⇨Screen Shot. You can then save any images that you want. (This is how most of the figures in this book were obtained.)

Coordinating with ical

ical is a nice calendar that's available on Linux. You can use it not only to display your own calendar but also to combine other calendars, such as your boss's calendar or a calendar of holidays. You set up calendar items to recur daily, weekly, or monthly — all with different alarm settings. The ical program includes excellent online documentation under the Help key, so we don't go into a lot of detail about the program.

To take the calendar program out for a spin, follow these steps:

1. **Click the Main Menu Button and choose Programs⇨Applications ⇨Ical.**

   A window similar to Figure 9-4 appears.

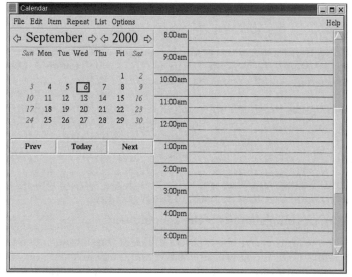

Figure 9-4:
The ical
calendar
program.

2. **Click the lower-left area of the calendar (under the Prev, Today, and Next buttons).**

   This step creates a new *notice entry,* as shown in Figure 9-5. Notice entries are messages to you and typically have no specific time frames. You can think of them as sticky notes that you put up on the wall. Because it has no time associated with it, you can't set an alarm to remind you of a notice entry.

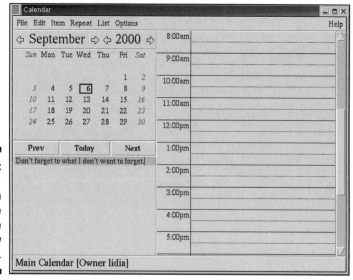

Figure 9-5:
The ical
program
with one
notice
window
selected.

3. **Type some text as a reminder.**

4. **Customize the notice, if you want.**

5. **Using the Repeat menu at the top of the screen, select whether the notice should be repeated, when it should be repeated, how many times it should be repeated, and so on.**

Now that you've created a notice on the calendar, you're ready to find out how to make an appointment. An appointment has all the attributes of a notice (it can be repeated, edited, and so on), but it also has alarms that remind you of the event. Follow these steps to schedule an appointment:

1. **Find the day and time frame for your appointment and then click the horizontal box that appears to the right of it.**

2. **Type the information for the appointment.**

If you want to move the box to a different time frame, move the cursor to the middle of the appointment box and then click and hold the middle mouse button (or hold both buttons down if you're using a two-button mouse). Positioning squares appear, as shown in Figure 9-6. Drag the appointment box to another time frame and then release the button.

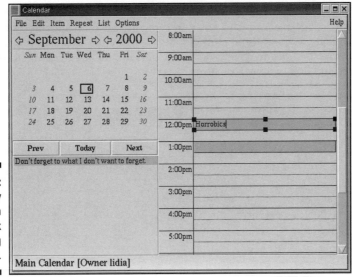

Figure 9-6:
The entry box with black positioning squares.

If you want to make the appointment longer, move the cursor to the black sizing box in the middle of the lower line of the appointment box, click and hold the mouse button, and drag the positioning squares to make the box bigger or smaller.

3. **Click the Repeat menu at the top of the screen and choose a repeat scheme that meets your requirements.**

4. **To close the calendar program, choose File⇨Exit.**

Processing with your Linux calculator

When you're predicting the location of the next meteorite to hit Earth or trying to balance your checkbook, look no further than Red Hat Linux, which provides you with a handy scientific calculator that can emulate a TI-30 or an HP-10C.

To use the calculator in TI-30 mode, follow these steps:

1. **Click the Main Menu button and choose Programs⇨Utilities⇨Simple Calculator.**

   A calculator appears, as shown in Figure 9-7.

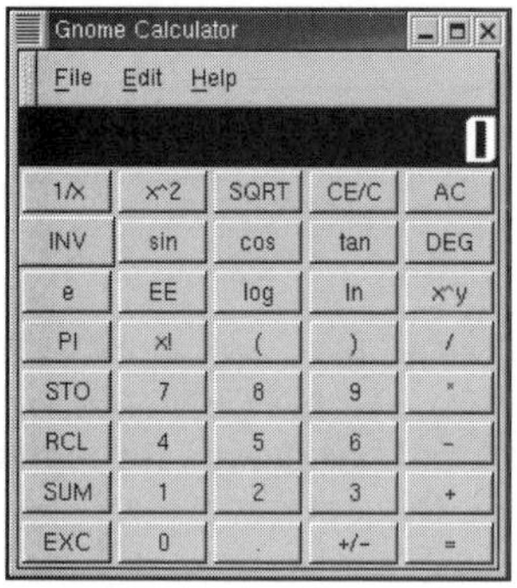

Figure 9-7:
The simple
calculator.

2. **Click the buttons and calculate away.**

   You can balance your checkbook, for example, but try not to get depressed when you do.

3. **When you're tired of all those numbers, choose File⇨Exit.**

Reading, writing, and gedit

GNOME gives writers one excellent tool: gedit, a simple text editor similar to Microsoft's WordPad or Notepad, if you've seen those. Use gedit for creating and modifying simple text files. You can access gedit by logging in as any user, clicking the Main Menu Button, and choosing Programs➪Applications➪gedit. Figure 9-8 shows the gedit window with a simple sentence written in it.

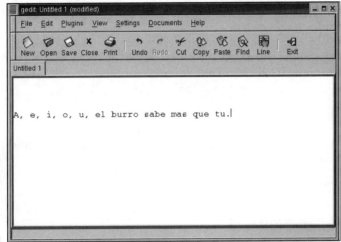

Figure 9-8: Behold the venerable gedit.

Reading PDF files

You can view portable document format (PDF) files with xpdf. PDF files are used to provide a lot of documentation on the Web. PDF files also provide the nice feature of being able to page forward and backwards through a document rather than having to view the whole thing at once.

Start xpdf by logging in as any user, clicking the GNOME Main Menu button, and choosing Programs➪Applications➪xpdf.

What you see isn't very interesting — just a blank page with some buttons pushed off to the bottom of the window. To open a file, you need to right-click your mouse button anywhere on the blank page and select Open. The xpdf: Open window pops up.

Download or copy a PDF file of your choice and open it up. An example of a PDF document from the US Immigration Service appears in Figure 9-9.

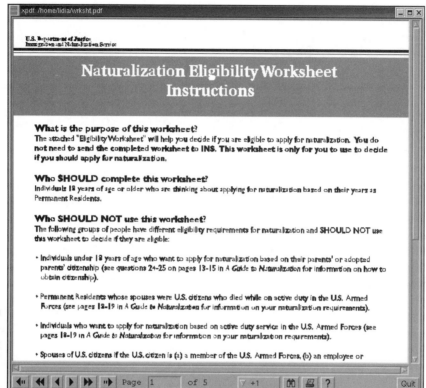

Figure 9-9:
A document
in the xpdf
viewer.

You can use the forward and backward buttons to page through the document. You can also use the Print button to print all or parts of a document. The binocular button is used to search for text. Have fun!

New applications are constantly being added to the GNOME universe. Go to www.gnome.org/applist to see what's available.

Chapter 10

Configuring Your Red Hat Linux Sound System

• •

In This Chapter

▶ Setting up your sound card

▶ Playing your CDs and MP3s

▶ Ripping your CDs

▶ Burning your own CDs

• •

*I*magine that you're sitting alone, working at your computer. Feeling lonely? Want a little company? Well, we can't provide friends, but we can show you how your system can provide some tunes.

In this chapter we show you how to have some fun with your Red Hat Linux computer. Red Hat Linux provides all the tools that you need to make your workstation into a sound system, including all the necessary applications to play CDs and MP3s, several CD and MP3 players, and tools for connecting your PC to a sound card and speakers

Setting Up Your Sound System

To keep this chapter from being a book in its own right, before we show you how to set up your sound system we first must assume that your computer has a working sound card installed and that your sound card is supported by Linux. (Assuming a lot, aren't we?)

You can configure and test your sound card at the same time by following these steps:

1. **Log in to Linux as root.**

2. **Insert CD1 that came with this book into the CD-ROM drive.**

GNOME automatically mounts the CD-ROM for you. If the CD-ROM fails to mount for any reason, please refer to Chapter 15 for instructions on mounting drives.

3. Start a terminal session by clicking on the GNOME terminal icon on the GNOME panel.

The GNOME panel is the menu bar along the bottom of your screen. The GNOME terminal icon looks like a computer monitor and is described in Chapter 14.

The following packages are used by Red Hat Linux to power the sound system: sox, awesfx, playmidi, and sndconfig. They are installed by default during the Workstation installation process we describe in Chapter 3.

4. Type the following command at the command prompt and press Enter:

```
sndconfig
```

The Sound Configuration Introduction screen appears, as shown in Figure 10-1.

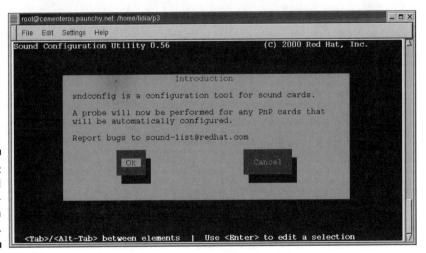

Figure 10-1:
The Sound
Configur-
ation
screen.

5. Read the information and press Enter.

If your sound card is Plug and Play (PnP), then sndconfig detects it and you can just press Enter and skip to Step 12. Once detected, the PCI Probe results window is displayed. Figure 10-2 shows the information that was detected about our sound card, your information will almost certainly be different. If it's not detected, continue on to Step 6.

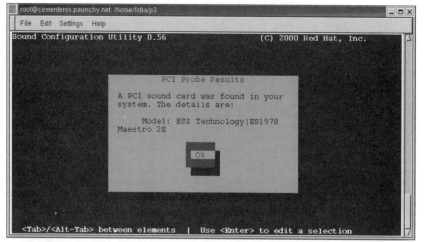

Figure 10-2:
The PCI
Probe
Results
dialog box.

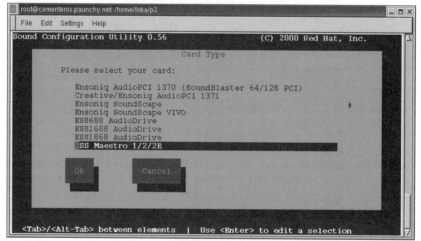

Figure 10-3:
The Card
Type dialog
box.

6. **If you know what your sound card is, use the up- and down-arrow keys to highlight your sound card and skip to Step 10 (if you don't know, continue to Step 7).**

7. **If you don't know what kind of sound card you have, you look at the files in the /proc directory by typing the ls /proc command at the command prompt and pressing Enter.**

The proc file system doesn't correspond to an actual (physical) hard drive. proc is a virtual file system that exists only within the mind of the Linux kernel. It is designed to provide information about Linux processes and hardware. proc provides a window into the running Linux kernel (operating system). You can find out a lot of information about your equipment from it.

8. **Type** cat /proc/sound **at the command prompt and press Enter, and once you determine the name of your sound, return to Step 6, or proceed to Step 9 if you can't discover your sound card name.**

The /proc/sound file contains information about your sound card. Our system shows the following sound card information, for example:

```
OSS/Free:3.8s2++-971130
Load type: Driver loaded as a module
Kernel: Linux veracruz.mp.sandia.gov 2.2.16-21 #1 Wed Aug
        9 11:45:35 EDT 2000 i686
Config options: 0
Installed drivers:
Card config:
Audio devices:
Synth devices:
Midi devices:
Timers:
0: System clock
1: Crystal audio controller (CS4236)
Mixers:
```

Note that towards the end it shows our CS4236 sound card. Yeah!

9. **If your** proc **file system doesn't contain information about your sound card, look at your computer's boot message log by entering the following command at the command prompt:**

```
more /var/log/dmesg
```

You can look at your computer's boot message log one page at a time by pressing the Spacebar (press Q when you want to quit). Look for any information that may be sound card related. For example, our CS4236-based sound card shows up as follows:

```
cs4232: set synthio and synthirq to use the wavefront
        facilities.
```

Look for words that suggest audio such as synthesizer, wave, and so on. Once you determine your sound card name, return to Step 6.

If all else fails, power down your computer and look at the sound card with your analog eyes. If that doesn't work, go out and buy a $20 sound card.

10. **Select the Ok button and press Enter.**

When we say to "Select the Ok button" we mean to press the Tab key until the Ok button is highlighted.

Appendix C describes some of the methods used to determine this information.

11. **Select the Ok button and press Enter.**

The Sound Card Test screen appears, as shown in Figure 10-4.

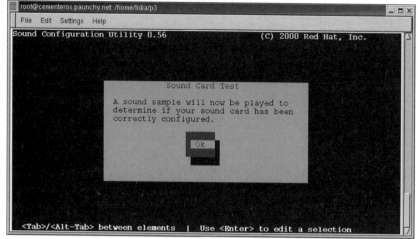

Figure 10-4:
Your sound
system is
about to be
tested.

12. **Press the Enter key to play the sound clip.**

    The sound clip is not just any sound clip: it's the voice of the big guy himself — Linux Torvalds, the inventor of Linux addressing the burning question of how you should pronounce the word Linux. (By the way, it's pronounced *Lin*–ux — with a short "i," like in the word "tin.")

    After you hear The Man, you're asked if you heard the message.

13. **If you heard the message, select Yes and press the Enter key.**

    The sndconfig program finishes, and you are returned to the GNOME terminal screen. Now that you have music in your life, you can enjoy blasting your neighbors' sensibilities late at night as you groove to your Red Hat Linux sound box. Have fun, but don't call us when the cops arrive.

    If you didn't hear the message, then you're sad and should select the No button and press the Enter key. This returns you to the Card Type screen (refer to Figure 10-3). Repeat Step 6.

    If you didn't hear the sound test sample, make sure that you have compatible speakers or earphones plugged into your sound card output. Plugging into the wrong output is actually quite easy. If you're not sure, turn down your speakers to a low setting and try plugging into the different audio outputs.

    If you're plugged in correctly, one of the following reasons may explain why you didn't hear the sound:

    - You chose the wrong sound card.

    - You entered the wrong parameters for the right sound card.

    - Someone else's stereo is way too loud.

Playing CDs and MP3s

Everyone wants a little music in their life. That's why you bought a $1,000 computer instead of a $300 stereo system, right? No? Well even so, you can use your Red Hat Linux machine as a music system if you want. This section describes how to set up your computer to play music CDs and MP3s.

Several CD players are available to Linux users: gtcd, xplaycd, and xmms are the ones that ship with Red Hat Linux. We use the xmms application here because it has a slick interface — the most important thing you could want — and plays both CDs and MP3s. Well, actually we see the MP3 thing as the reason to use it, but it does have a very nice look to it.

Log in as any user, click the GNOME Main Menu button, and choose Programs⇨Multimedia⇨XMMS. The xmms application appears, as shown in Figure 10-5.

Figure 10-5:
The xmms
main
screen.

The xmms program is installed by default as part of the Workstation installation. The xmms application is (surprise!) part of the xmms RPM package.

If you've used a CD player — that is, if you weren't raised by a family of wolves — most of the symbols in the xmms interface should be familiar (Paul's dog Oso often fiddles with xmms so he can listen to his friends bark out "Jingle Bells" — really!). Anyway, xmms does have a few unfamiliar buttons and options, which we describe in the following list:

✔ If you click the PL button a play list window pops up to the right. You can see what tracks are playing in this window. You can also select which tracks to play.

✔ Click the button immediately to the left of PL and the graphics equalizer shown in Figure 10-6 appears. What's the difference between a $300 equalizer you purchase in a store and xmms? About $300.

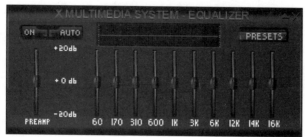

Figure 10-6:
The xmms
graphics
equalizer
window.

✔ The volume control slide is in the middle of the screen.

✔ The balance control slide is to the right of the volume control.

✔ You can open music files to play by right-clicking anywhere on the xmms window. A general menu window pops up, and you click File. From there, you can browse the files that you want to open.

✔ Other options exist for how to change the look and feel of xmms and other miscellaneous features. Right-click the window and select options or any of the other features.

Playing MP3 files

Not much changes when you want to play an MP3 file. You simply obtain the MP3 files from the Internet — for example, from `http://www.mp3.com`. You can then use the multimedia players, such as xmms (described in the last section) to play MP3 files. (MP3 files have the .mp3 suffix.)

You can also play streaming MP3s from the Internet. Chapter 11 describes that process.

Xmixer: Sounds for the rest of us

You can control your sound card volume and other features directly with the help of XMixer. XMixer is started by clicking on the GNOME Main Menu Button⇨Programs⇨Multimedia⇨Xmixer.

Figure 10-7 shows the XMixer window with all its buttons and slider bars. These controls may or may not match the capabilities of your sound card; the XMixer application is written for sound cards in general, as opposed to being written for a specific sound card.

For XMixer to work, you must have a sound card, a cable must attach the CD-ROM drive to the sound card, and the headphones must be plugged into the sound card (not the CD-ROM).

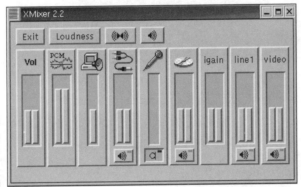

Figure 10-7:
The XMixer
window.

Most of the XMixer controls are labeled in Figure 10-7. Here's a little additional information:

✓ The Loudness control boosts the bass slightly for when you want low volume output (such as when your parents are home, the baby is asleep, or you have new batteries in your hearing aid).

✓ The Stereo Separation control is labeled with the red and black speaker connector wires, and is for cards that try to convince you that they have stereo separation capabilities.

✓ Each slider is made up of two columns, one for the left channel and one for the right channel. Place the cursor directly over one of the columns and drag the slider to move the column up or down. Move the cursor between the two columns to move both columns at the same time.

Some find it easier to use the middle mouse button to grab the top of the column. To do so, move the cursor to the top of a column, click and hold down the middle mouse button, and then move the mouse to pull the column up and down. If your mouse has only two buttons but you requested three-button emulation when installing your system, hold down both buttons at the same time to simulate the middle mouse button.

If you didn't ask for three-button emulation but want it now, follow these steps:

1. **Log in as root.**

2. **Type the following command at the command prompt and press Enter:**

```
/usr/sbin/mouseconfig
```

3. **Press the Tab key until the cursor is over Emulate Three Buttons and then press the Spacebar.**

   The Emulate Three Buttons radio button is located just above the Ok, Cancel and Help buttons.

4. **Select the Ok button and then press Enter.**

   You have installed three-button emulation for your mouse.

5. **Press Ctrl+Alt+Backspace to restart X Server and enable the emulation.**

Ripping CDs

Are you paranoid? If not, do you want to be? Well, cdparanoia can help fulfill all your fears. Just kidding. Really, cdparanoia is used for ripping the audio information — music files — from CDs to your hard drive or to other CDs.

The following steps show you how to use cdparanoia to copy music off of a CD and into a Linux file:

1. **Insert your favorite CD, log in as any user, and type the following command:**

   ```
   cdparanoia -Q
   ```

   You should see output similar to the following for a three-song CD:

   ```
   cdparanoia III release 9.7 (December 13, 1999)
   (C) 1999 Monty <monty@xiph.org> and Xiphophorus
   Report bugs to paranoia@xiph.org
   http://www.xiph.org/paranoia/

   Table of contents (audio tracks only):
   track        length              begin        copy pre ch
   ===========================================================
     1.    22157 [04:55.32]      0 [00:00.00]   no   no
            2
     2.    21100 [04:41.25]  22157 [04:55.32]   no   no
            2
     3.    20673 [04:35.48]  43257 [09:36.57]   no   no
            2
   TOTAL   65020 [13:32.05]  (audio only)
   ```

   The preceding output displays information about your CD. The first column shows the length, in sectors, of each track and how many minutes and seconds long they are. The second column shows where each track begins. The last column shows the number of channels on each track — two channels equals stereo; does anyone have a quadraphonic CD? The last row shows the totals.

2. **Next, try ripping a CD by entering the following command (which copies the first 60 seconds of a file):**

```
cdparanoia "1[:0]-1[:60]"
```

The command rips the CD and stores the music in the `cdda.wav` file.

To show some more ways to use the cdparanoia, the following commands rip the first track, tracks one through three and tracks four and five respectively:

```
cdparanoia "1"
cdparanoia "1-3"
cdparanoia "4-5"
```

You can choose the name of the file where `cdparanoia` saves the music by specifying the filename as the last option. For example, if you want the filename to be `tomwaits_o155.wav`, then type in the following command (the file is stored to your current working directory):

```
cdparanoia "1[:0]-1[:60]" tomwaits_o155.wav
```

To copy the entire CD use the 1– option. The "1" tells `cdparanoia` to start copying at Track One, and the "–" option tells it to continue to the end.

```
cdparanoia "1-" tomwaits_o155.wav
```

After you create the music file, you can listen to it with any of the CD players described earlier in this chapter.

Burning CDs

Back in the 80s ,when vinyl melted away under the invasion of CDs, it cost millions to build a CD factory where the CDs where created. Today, for roughly the $100 that it costs to purchase a CD burner (to *burn* means to record to CD), you can build your own personal factory. Amazing.

If you don't have a CD burner (or writer), this section won't do you a bit of good.

A recordable CD is referred to as a CD-R; a rewritable CD is called a CD-RW (the difference is that CD-Rs can only be recorded on once). CD burners look like regular read-only drives and are connected with either an IDE or SCSI interface.

If you have a SCSI-based CD-R, then you can skip the next section. But if you have an IDE-based interface, then you must recompile your Linux kernel to mimic a SCSI interface. The Linux CD recording application — `cdrecord` — is monolingual and can only speak SCSI.

SCSI doesn't mean that it's a dirty (scuzzy) interface: this acronym stands for *Small Computer System Interface.* Most inexpensive to moderate priced computers use an IDE interface to control both the CD-ROM drive and hard drive. SCSI interfaces also control hard drives and CD-ROM drives. You find SCSI interfaces on high-end computers because they provide higher performance and are more expensive.

Modifying Red Hat Linux to use cdrecord

Blast! If you have an IDE-based CD-R, you have to do some work to get your CD-R factory working. The heart of Red Hat Linux — the Linux kernel — must be recompiled so that `cdrecord` can speak correctly to your CD-R drive in SCSI-speak.

All Linux software starts out life in a raw form referred to as *source code.* Source code is written in languages — C, C++, Java, and so on — like English. But source code must be converted into a form that can be executed, or run, by the Linux kernel itself. The conversion process is referred to as *compiling.* The Linux kernel is no different than any other software and must be compiled in order to run.

A monkey wrench is thrown into the your Red Hat Linux workstation if you use SCSI emulation. Normally, your IDE/ATAPI CD-ROM drive, read-only or writable, is recognized by the Linux kernel as one of four devices: `/dev/hda1`, `/dev/hda2`, `/dev/hdb1`,or `/dev/hdb2`. But if you use a kernel with SCSI emulation, then it doesn't show up as any of those devices. Instead, it shows up as `/dev/sca0`, `/dev/scb0`, `/dev/scc0`, or `/dev/scd0`. To mount your SCSI emulated CD-ROM drive as you would a normal one, you have to change your habits a bit. The best way is to relink your `/dev/cdrom` softlink by entering the following command at a command prompt:

```
ln -s /dev/scd0 /dev/cdrom
```

assumeing that your SCSI emulated CD-ROM drive device file is `/dev/scd0`. If it's not, change the value of the parameter to either `/dev/sca0`, `/dev/scb0`, `/dev/scc0`, or `/dev/scd0` as appropriate.

A *softlink* is an essential pointer. By creating a softlink to the standard `/dev/cdrom` file, your Red Hat Linux computer knows exactly where to go find your CD writer.

Compiling a Linux kernel is real techie stuff, but it's not too hardcore, so don't be afraid. To recompile your Linux kernel so that you can burn CDs, follow these steps:

1. **Log in as root and insert CD1 that came with this book into your CD-ROM drive.**

2. **Open a terminal window.**

3. **To install the kernel source software, enter the following command at the command prompt:**

   ```
   rpm -ivh /mnt/cdrom/RedHat/RPMS/kernel-source*.rpm
   ```

   Red Hat Package Manager (RPM) files are used to install all the software that makes up Red Hat Linux. Managing RPM files is described in Chapter 16. Please note that you can use the graphical GnoRPM application, instead of the RPM command, to install the above package.

4. **Change to the kernel source directory by typing the following command:**

   ```
   cd /usr/src/linux
   ```

5. **Set up the kernel configuration by typing:**

   ```
   make menuconfig
   ```

   The Main Menu screen appears, as shown in Figure 10-8.

6. **Use the up- and down-arrow keys to select Block Devices and press Enter.**

   The Block Devices screen appears, as shown in Figure 10-9.

7. **Use the up-and down-arrow keys to select Include IDE/ATAPI CDROM support and then press the spacebar twice.**

   The <M> indicator changes to < >, which means that IDE/ATAPI CD-ROM support is turned off.

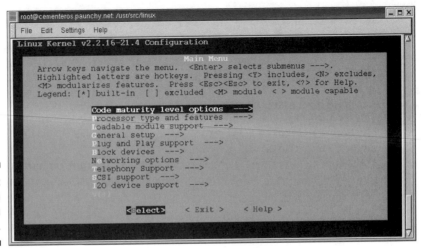

Figure 10-8: The Main Menu screen.

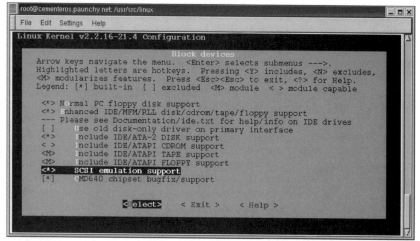

Figure 10-9:
The Block
Devices
screen.

8. **Select SCSI Emulation Support and press the spacebar once.**

   The <M> changes to <*>, which means that the SCSI emulation driver is compiled directly into the kernel. Normally, it's loaded on-demand as a kernel module, which is what the <M> specifies.

9. **Exit the Block Devices screen by pressing the Tab key twice and then pressing Enter.**

   You return to the Main Menu screen.

10. **Select Exit**

    You are prompted to save the new configuration.

11. **Select Yes and press Enter.**

    You return to the bash shell prompt.

12. **Type make dep at the command prompt and press Enter.**

13. **Type make bzImage at the command prompt and press Enter.**

    The recompiled kernel is named bzImage.

14. **Enter the following command at the command prompt:**

    ```
    mv /usr/src/linux/arch/i386/.../bzImage /boot
    ```

    The newly minted Linux kernel moves into the /boot directory.

15. **Update the Linux Loader (LILO) configuration that is found in** /etc/lilo.conf **to use the new kernel.**

    You can use any text editor to add the lines to the file /etc/lilo.conf file as shown below. Leave the existing LILO configuration alone and append a new entry labeled scsi-linux that is used to emulate the SCSI CD-ROM drive.

```
image=/boot/bzImage
        label=scsi-linux
        read-only
        root=/dev/hda1
```

The new /etc/lilo.conf, with the new entry added at the bottom, should look something like this:

```
boot=/dev/hda
map=/boot/map
install=/boot/boot.b
prompt
timeout=50
message=/boot/message
linear
default=linux

image=/boot/vmlinuz-2.2.16-22
        label=linux
        read-only
        root=/dev/hda1

image=/boot/bzImage
        label=scsi
        read-only
        root=/dev/hda1
```

The default line shows that your original Linux kernel is to be started during the boot process. The default kernel is the one that was installed as part of the Workstation installation class described in Chapter 3. This is the kernel that is loaded during the boot process unless you specify otherwise, which is what you're now doing by following these steps.

16. Type lilo **at the command prompt and press Enter.**

lilo reads the new /etc/lilo.conf file. The next time that you boot your computer, the Red Hat Linux kernel with SCSI emulation can be selected and used.

17. Reboot your computer.

18. When the LILO prompt appears, select the SCSI option.

Once your computer has been booted, you just need to install the cdrecord command.

19. Insert CD1 that came with this book into your CD-ROM drive.

20. Open a terminal emulator and type in the following command to install the cdrecord **package:**

```
rpm -ivh /mnt/cdrom/RedHat/RPMS/cdrecord*
```

The cdrecord package is installed. You can now use cdrecord to record your own CD-ROMs. The next section describes the process of making CDs.

Burn, baby, burn

The following instructions describe how to create, or *burn,* a CD-ROM. The instructions are the same whether you have an IDE/ATAPI or SCSI CD-ROM drive.

1. **Log in as root and insert a CD-R or CD-RW disc into your CD writer.**

   What can you burn? Well, the world's your oyster, and you can make a CD of anything you want — music or software. A good place to start is backing up your /home directory.

2. **First, choose an image to burn to CD.**

   Just for testing, you can make an ISO image by entering the following command at a command prompt:

   ```
   mkisofs -R -o filename filename
   ```

   where the first *filename* is the name of the output file and the second *filename* is the path to the file or directory that you want to burn to CD.

   For example, if you want to backup the */home/mydir* directory you would enter the following command:

   ```
   mkisofs -R -o mydir-31aug00.raw /home/mydir
   ```

3. **Next, determine what virtual SCSI device your system labels your IDE/ATAPI or SCSI CD-ROM drive as by entering the following command:**

   ```
   cdrecord --scanbus
   ```

   The output shows information similar to the following code:

   ```
   Cdrecord 1.8 (i686-pc-linux-gnu) Copyright (C) 1995-2000
           J!!rg Schilling
   Using libscg version 'schily-0.1'
   scsibus0:
       0,0,0    0) 'IDE-CD  ' 'R/RW 4x4x24      ' '1.04'
           Removable CD-ROM
       0,1,0    1) *
       0,2,0    2) *
       0,3,0    3) *
   ```

   This is the output you see if you have an IDE/ATAPI CD-ROM drive. SCSI-based systems, however, may show up with other values depending on their configuration. SCSI drives are recognized by their controller, target, and slice numbers. *Slice numbers* correspond to the three numbers in the above output. For example, if you have a SCSI-based CD-ROM drive that's connected as the third target on the first controller, then it shows up as: 0,3,0 above. (Slices are not used in this configuration and are always 0.) Whatever the numbers are, you simply need to use them in the dev= parameter described in the next step.

You can now write the file you chose (or created) in Step 2 to a CD.

4. **Take the** scsibus **values from Step 4 and use them with the** cdrecord **command by entering the following command:**

```
cdrecord -v speed=n dev=scsibus_values -isosize filename
```

Where *n* is the speed of your CD-ROM drive, *scsibus_values* are the virtual SCSI values obtained from step 3, *-isosize* specifies that you are recording raw data, and *filename* is the name of the file that is created.

For example, if you have a 4X speed ATAPI/IDE CD-ROM drive and want to create a CD from the *mydir-31aug00.raw* file, you should run the following command.

```
cdrecord -v speed=4 dev=0,0,0 -isosize mydir-31aug00.raw
```

The scsibus values from Step 4 — for example 0,0,0 — are used with the dev= parameter. The 0,0,0 value is combined with dev= to create the dev=0,0,0 parameter.

Please note that you need to set your speed according to what your CD-ROM drive can handle. You need to obtain the speed value from the documentation that came with your recordable CD-ROM drive in order to enter it as part of the speed parameter in the cdrecord command. Look for a value like *4X* or *8X*. Don't worry if you don't know them. If you set the speed too high, then your CD is just recorded at the lower level.

That's it! You computer writes the information to CD. Congratulations! You've created a new CD.

The process changes just a little bit if you want to burn music. First, you don't need to create an ISO image. Second, the following cdrecord command is used in place of the one shown in Step 3 of the preceding numbered list:

```
cdrecord -v speed=n dev=scsibus_values -audio filename
```

Where *n* is the speed of your CD-ROM drive, *scsibus_values* are the virtual SCSI values obtained from Step 3, *-audio* specifies that you are creating an audio disc and *filename* is the name of the file that is created.

For example, if you have a 4X speed ATAPI/IDE CD-ROM drive and want to create a music CD from the *tom_waits.raw* file, you should run the following command:

```
cdrecord -v speed=2 dev=0,0,0 -audio tom_waits.wav
```

Chapter 11

Screaming About Streaming Media and RealPlayer 7

*O*ne of the coolest Internet innovations is streaming audio and video. Streaming technology provides a continuous flow of sound and picture from a variety of sources in real time. Video streaming (movie, television, and so on) is still somewhat limited, especially on slower connections, but the force of streaming media is certain to explode in the near future as broadband connections become more common.

This chapter describes how to use your Red Hat Linux machine as both a radio and TV using the popular RealPlayer streaming audio/video client. After configuring your Internet connection, firewall, and Netscape browser in earlier chapters of this book, you're done with most of the heavy lifting. All you need to do is download RealPlayer 7 and configure it.

You can also play video and audio clips with the gtv player (although you can't play Real file formats in `gtv`, you need RealPlayer for that). gtv is a simple program that plays MPEG-formatted video files. gtv is installed by default on your Red Hat Linux machine. Click the GNOME Main Menu button and choose Programs⇨Multimedia⇨gtv.

Setting Up and Configuring Your Red Hat Vox Box

You can think of your Red Hat Linux computer as a simple appliance. Even though it does all of the usual, diverse computer-esque things, it can also work like any old, garden-variety radio. Downloading Real Audio's free

RealPlayer 7 software enables you to listen to radio stations — and any other streaming audio — from around the world, and to watch video (which we discuss towards the end of the chapter).

Downloading and installing RealPlayer 7

To get and make use of RealPlayer, you need four things: a working Internet connection, Netscape Navigator, a working sound system (all three of which are described in Chapters 6, 7, and 10, respectively), and the RealPlayer 7 software. To get RealPlayer, follow these steps:

1. **Log in as root, connect to the Internet, and start Netscape Communicator.**

   You can start Netscape by clicking the Netscape icon in the GNOME panel at the bottom of the screen.

2. **Enter the following URL in the Netscape Navigator Location text box and press the Enter key:**

   ```
   www.real.com
   ```

   Netscape displays the Real's home page.

3. **In the blue menu bar at the top of the page, click the <u>Download: RealPlayer</u> link.**

   The Real Audio download page appears.

4. **Click the <u>RealPlayer 8 Basic</u> link on the left side of the page.**

   You are prompted to enter your e-mail address, country, operating system, and so on, but don't bother entering anything but information about your operating system.

   That 8 in the step above isn't a typo: As of this writing, RealPlayer 8 doesn't work with Linux, but you still have to click this link to get to RealPlayer 7, which does work with Linux.

5. **Don't enter any information in the text boxes, just click the Select OS drop-down list and select UNIX.**

   The Select OS drop-down list doesn't include a Linux option. But by selecting UNIX, you go to the menu that does have a Linux option (Linux and Unix are fully compatible). The Community Supported RealPlayer Download Page appears, as shown in Figure 11-1.

6. **Fill in the fields with the requested information and select Linux 2.x (libc6 -386) as your operating system.**

   The non-RPM version is easier to install with the File Manager than the RPM. You can use the RPM version if you are familiar with the format and prefer it.

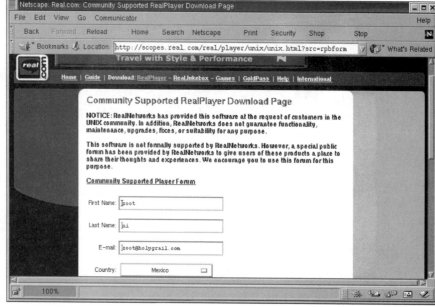

Figure 11-1:
The
Community
Supported
RealPlayer
Download
Page.

If you do not want to recieve extra e-mails (and who does?), click the Notify Me of Important News check box to remove the check mark so that you don't get e-mail from Real.

7. Click the Download Community Supported Player button.

The page shown in Figure 11-2 appears.

8. Click the location to download from the available options, preferably from a location geographically close to you.

If the locations nearest you are busy, try one that is in a time zone where it's night or early morning (thus, likely less busy).

The Save As window appears, prompting you to download the file.

9 Click OK.

The Save As dialog box appears.

10. Choose a location to download the file to and then click the Save button.

The file is saved to the directory you chose, or to the default directory if you didn't choose anything. We suggest saving it to the /usr/local/src directory, as shown in Figure 11-3, which is a good general purpose location for storing source files.

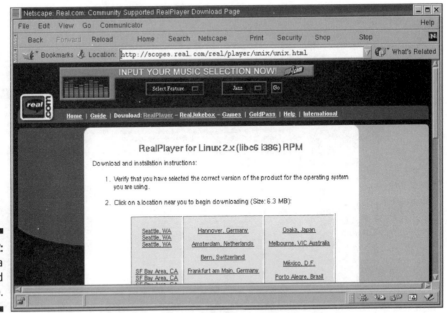

Figure 11-2:
Selecting a
download
site.

11. **Start the GNOME File Manager by clicking the Main Menu button and choosing Programs⇨File Manager and then open the directory to which you downloaded the RealPlayer 7 installation program.**

Figure 11-4 shows the File Manager being used to install RealPlayer.

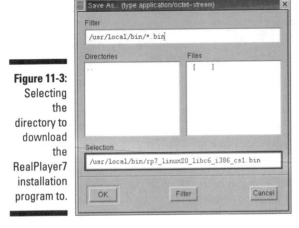

Figure 11-3:
Selecting
the
directory to
download
the
RealPlayer7
installation
program to.

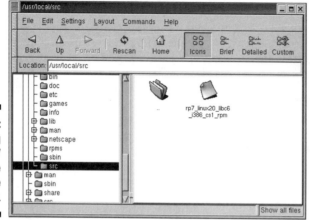

Figure 11-4:
Installing
RealPlayer 7
file from the
File
Manager.

12. **Choose File⇨Move and type a new filename with a .rpm extension into the Move dialog box that appears.**

    For example, Figure 11-5 shows the file being renamed to rp7_cs1.rpm, which is as good a name as any.

    The file needs to be renamed so that it matches the list of formats that the File Manager is programed to recognize. By renaming it with a .rpm suffix, the File Manager knows to launch the rpm command when you double-click the file.

Figure 11-5:
Renaming
the
RealPlayer
installation
file.

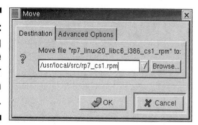

13. **Double-click the renamed file.**

    File Manager runs the rpm program and RealPlayer 7 is installed. After installation, RealPlayer launches itself and prompts you for your e-mail account, country, and zip code.

14. **Enter your information and click Next.**

    You are then prompted for your Internet connection type and speed.

15. Select your connection speed and click Finished.

RealPlayer plays its intro bump — a short piece of music, which you quickly learn by heart — and then sits there waiting to play you a tune (see Figure 11-6).

Figure 11-6:
The RealPlayer 7 Welcome window.

Launching RealPlayer from the Panel

After you've installed RealPlayer, you need to be able to start it. GNOME provides just such a capability from its applet launcher. You can create an applet launcher (an icon to click on) for RealPlayer on GNOME's Panel.

Being snubbed by QuickTime

Okay, in regards to Apple and Quicktime, we have bad new and good news. Want the bad news first? Of course you do. The bad news is that Apple does not support Linux with their QuickTime player or plug-in, nor does Microsoft with their Windows Media Player — at least not yet. Unfortunately, this means that if you want to see streaming movies in these two formats, you won't be able to view them through Linux. Many companies, however, make their video clips in multiple formats, and Real's plug-in currently has the greatest support in the streaming industry (Real claimed about 85 percent of the streaming market in recent studies). So take heart; for every one QuickTime clip that you can't view through Linux, there are probably nine that you can view through RealPlayer, and anyway it wouldn't be open source if Linux weren't snubbed by Apple and Microsoft!

Real themselves could also stand to support Linux better: RealJukebox by Real Audio is real good at converting CDs to MP3s and provides numerous ways to organize your MP3s. RealJukebox has all sorts of cool stuff that you can do, like change skins and themes, fade one track to another to create continuous music, add cover lyrics, cover art, and artist info to each track, and watch really nifty visualization effects. But you guessed it, RealJukebox has no Linux version yet. Come on, guys, get with the program!

The Panel is the gray bar that rests along the bottom of your screen.

Follow these steps to create a launcher applet for RealPlayer:

1. **Click the GNOME Main Menu button and choose Panel⇨Add to Panel⇨Launcher menus.**

2. **Enter a name for the RealPlayer launcher icon (try something obvious, such as RealPlayer 7).**

   You can optionally enter a comment in the Comment text box. The text that you enter is displayed in a tooltip that appeares over the icon when you hover the mouse cursor over it.

3. **Type realplay into the Command text box and press the Tab key.**

   RealPlayer supplies some images that can be used as the applet icon on the GNOME Panel, which you can now pick from.

4. **Click the Icon button at the bottom of the Launcher window to pick an icon for the launcher.**

   A window opens up that shows the default GNOME icons.

5. **Type /usr/local/RealPlayer7/Help/realplay/pics/RealLogo.gif in the text box and click the OK button.**

   The RealPlayer icon is displayed in the Launcher window, ready and waiting to launch RealPlayer.

6. **Click the OK button in the launcher window.**

   The new icon is inserted into the GNOME Panel, as shown in figure 11-7.

Figure 11-7:
The RealPlayer 7 launcher is added to the GNOME panel.

7. **Click the new RealPlayer launcher that you just created in the GNOME panel.**

   The RealPlayer window appears (see Figure 11-6).

Finding radio stations

"What can I play with this thing?" you may be asking, or more importantly, "How do I find stuff to play? Mom, I wanna play!" Well, you can find streaming radio content in several ways and places, including the following:

- Search with Netscape Search (click Communicator's Search button) to find individual stations and radio station databases and see if they have a RealPlayer supported streaming format.

- Stumble across RealPlayer files all around the Internet (look for the blue Real logo — they're everywhere when you start looking).

- Netscape Radio. Netscape Communicator, now a product owned by AOL, gives you access AOL's Spinner.com radio content (choose Communicator➪Radio). Netscape Radio requires you to have the RealPlayer plugin installed (the plugin installs when you install RealPlayer).

- Browse Real's content lists by following these steps:

    1. **Choose Content➪Live Stations in the RealPlayer window.**

       RealPlayer starts Netscape Navigator and the Real Audio Web page appears. The live station content list gives you access to Real Audio's content, as well as enabling you to search for other radio stations.

    2. **Click the <u>Find a Station</u> link to search for radio stations based on various criteria, such as location or call letters.**

       As of this writing, the RealPlayer database contains over 2500 stations.

    3. **Find your station, go to that Web site, and start the tunes.**

       You can access information about RealPlayer at `www.real.com/help`. The site supplies a frequently asked questions (FAQ) guide, a beginner's guide, and other useful information.

Real Audio, Inc. designs its own streaming audio/video formats (protocols). Microsoft, as you may guess, rolls its own, and some radio stations support only Microsoft's Windows Media Player, although many support both formats. You can differentiate Real Audio from Microsoft by the suffix that it appends to its files — RealAudio ends with `ram`, `ra` and `rm`, while Microsoft appends `asx` to its stuff. If you click the Windows Media button, you are asked whether you want to save the link as the file `kbac.asx`. That's because Netscape Navigator knows how to handle Real Audio broadcasts but not Microsoft ones — it has no MIME helper (application) that it can run.

Using RealPlayer

Internet radio stations often play an introduction message and/or advertisement, called a *bump*, when you connect and before playing the live feed. This happens because the radio station's URL points to multiple streams.

If you right-click the station's URL and choose the Save Link As option, then the individual URLs are saved to a file. The files generally end with an html — as in this case —, or a real audio metafile .ram suffix. Once you have saved the file, you can use the file to open the station

You can manually open the streaming radio feed. In RealPlayer, choose File➪ Open Location. The Open Location window appears, as shown in Figure 11-8.

Figure 11-8: Opening a radio station's audio feed.

When you type a station URL into the window's text box (for example, `pnm://rnr005sea.activate.net:7070/KBAC/live16.ra`) and click OK, RealPlayer appears and plays the radio station. You can now listen to the Morning Grind, The Lunch Lady, and Friday Funk. Wow, what more could you want out of life!

Skipping advertisements

When you save a station's URL as a file, a link to an advertisement is usually saved too. For example, when you save the KBAC radio URL, the `kbac.ram` file contains the following lines:

```
http://magweb2.magnitudenetwork.
    net/bumperAds/ad.ra

pnm://rnr005sea.activate.net:70
    70/KBAC/live16.ra
```

The first line is a URL that points to an advertisement bump that plays when you start listening to KBAC. The second line points to KBAC's audio feed. Clicking the URL causes the advertisement to play first, and then the audio feed. You can skip listening to the advertisement by editing the file and removing the first line.

Note that if you open the `kbac.ram` file (or any other station's file) directly from RealPlayer by choosing File➪Open File and entering the filename, the advertisement bump plays, and then the live broadcast starts.

RealPlayer, of course, uses the standard controls to play, stop, pause, mute, and pump up the volume. You can also display information about the stream, if available. You can display statistics about your Internet connection by choosing View➪Statistics; the player's audio stream speed is shown below the Clip Info subwindow.

MP3 on the Net

MP3 is a very popular medium for storing music and other audio information. You can create incredible music libraries on your hard drive and then store big chunks of it on a CD-R disc. You can even stream MP3 just like Real Audio, although streaming MP3 isn't as popular in the streaming world as Real Audio. That's not for lack of trying, though; many sites exist where you can listen to streaming MP3 music or radio-like feeds.

A good place to start is the well-known `www.mp3.com` Web site. Once there, click the **Stations** link. (**Channels** provides similar service on a subscription basis.) Click one of the station types (music, sports, and so on) and then one of the individual items. For example, click **Music** and then click **Space Radio**. You're prompted to play Space Radio on either a high-speed or low-speed link. (Ground control to Major Tom, you're out of tune.) Click the low-speed link if you're using a modem for your Internet connection or are on a heavily loaded high-speed connection — for example, if all your colleagues are listening to Space Radio, too. If you have a better-than-a-modem connection and no one is hogging your bandwidth listening to Art Bell, go crazy and click the high-speed connection link.

Netscape Navigator uses the mpg123 MP3 player by default when it encounters an MP3 connection. Sometimes it's difficult to get it to work correctly. If that's the case, right-click the link and save it as a file. The next time that you want to access that particular audio feed, you can open the file directly from your application without going through a browser. (A streaming MP3 file has a m3u extension.)

m3u files are metafiles similar to ram files, containing information on the actual connections that are used to play the audio stream. Start any the xmms MP3 player by clicking the GNOME Main Menu button and choosing Programs➪Multimedia➪xmms. When xmms starts, it automatically opens the Load File window. Click the m3u file and then the OK button. xmms starts playing the audio stream.

Crime and punishment: Napster and MP3.com

The well-known — some may say infamous — Napster software provides a mechanism for people to share their MP3 music files over the Internet — something the major record companies are decidedly unhappy about.

Napster consists of two parts. The first is a common database of people who are willing to share their music; the second is each user's Napster client, which provides an interface to the database and a communications channel between any two people who link up. MP3.com, similar to Napster in concept, is also under similar fire by record companies. A number of pending cases aim to shut the Napster down and make MP3 pay a fortune in damages. Is Napster evil? Is MP3.com? The record companies and some artists think so. So far Napster has only been used to transfer music, but there's no reason why you won't be able to transfer data — books and such — via the same mechanism in the future, bringing other types of media giants into the fray.

It'll to be interesting to see how the companies like Napster fare in the digital age. Certainly, this technology is going to change the way music and other information is distributed. Legal or not, Napster and/or its clone sites are likely to continue to operate. Will we see individual CDs sold as they are now in a few years? Probably. Once the music industry figures out that they can make more money by distributing their libraries over the Internet, and Internet connections become much faster (than is possible with modems), then the distribution methods will likely change very quickly.

Note: Unfortunately, the Napster software only runs on Windows and Mac platforms. The curious can check out this phenomenon at www.napster.com.

Going Hollywood with RealPlayer

RealPlayer 7 plays streaming video in addition to audio. You can connect to video streams in the same way as you do with audio streams (this process, including installing and setting up RealPlayer, is described earlier in this chapter).

RealPlayer — and streaming media in general — is undeniably an exciting technology that makes your Red Hat Linux system a television set as well as a radio! But what video can you play? The following two sections give you a good head start on finding streaming video content to check out.

Finding video at Real.com

A good place to start looking for video is Real's home page at www.real.com, where you can find a lot of cool features. The lower half of the page shows numerous links to content that it provides or gives access to. Figure 11-9 shows the links that were current when this book was written. Following is some of the cool stuff you can find at Real.com:

✔ **Movie trailers:** There's always a link to a featured trailer on the Real Audio home page. You can click the **more trailers** link on the Real.com home page to see a list of the current trailers. Click one and you go to another Real Audio Web page that contains a link to the video stream, as well as information about the movie. Figure 11-10 shows a Web page for Almost Famous (Dreamworks SKG).

Broadband and narrowband links are provided to the movie's video clips. Broadband refers to Internet connections that are very fast. Broadband connections can be classified as any connection faster than a 56 Kbps modem. Click the **Broadband** link if you are connected to a network with a fast connection (such as a DSL or cable modem connection); otherwise click the **Narrowband** link.

Netscape Communicator fires up RealPlayer. Your RealPlayer then connects to the video stream for that clip, buffers several seconds of the clip, and starts playing it. It's sure a lot more fun watching movie trailers all day than working! (As the warning goes, don't try this at work. We are professional, experienced slackers — er hackers — and know what we're doing. You may get into trouble if you're not careful.)

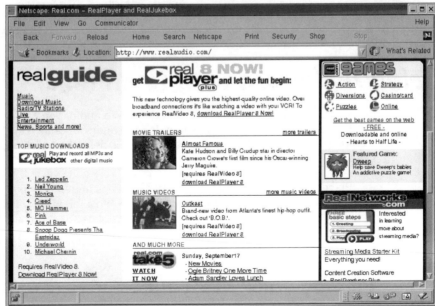

Figure 11-9:
The lower half of Real's home page.

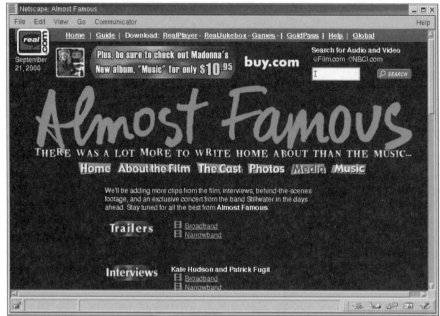

Figure 11-10:
A Web page
Link to a
movie
trailer.

✔ **Music videos:** Right below the movie trailers on the Real.com home page are links to music videos. There's always a link to a featured video displayed on the Real Audio home page. You can go look at other videos by clicking the **more music videos** link.

✔ **Video archives:** The archives that Real Audio provides are a lot more fun than the current list. You have the choice of viewing a large library of old or older movies. To find the archives, click the **more trailers** link on the Real.com home page. On the left side of the screen, there is a **Vintage** link that takes you to the archive. You can select from many great pictures. Figure 11-11 shows a snippet from *West Side Story*, 1961.

The movies listed on the Vintage page are all a year (or two or three years) old. You can have fun looking through all the movies that you did see — or didn't.

Another fun repository of video clips that you can use gtv to view is at the following URL, where you can even find video clips of everyone's favorite pals Wallace and Grommet:

```
http://wwwzenger.informatik.tu-
        muenchen.de/persons/paula/mpeg/index.html
```

Figure 11-11:
A clip from
*West Side
Story.*

✔ **News clips:** If you want topical information you can get news clips from numerous news organizations. For example, from RealPlayer7, choose File➪Open Location. Enter the following URL into the text box:

```
http://channels.real.com/vram/single?programs=16
```

The current headlines from Fox News are then displayed in RealPlayer 7. You can access the news of the day as if you tuned into the five o'clock news on TV.

✔ **Cable programming:** Some cable TV channels — especially the fun ones — are starting to provide some of their programming on the Internet. For example, from RealPlayer, choose File➪Open Location. Enter the following URL into the text box and press the Enter key:

```
http://channels.real.com/vram/single?programs=44&&tcode
```

The Comedy Central video page appears presenting a collage of recent video clips, such as their in-depth coverage of the 2000 Olympics as shown in Figure 11-12.

RealPlayer goes through a clip of each show; you can also click any one of the shows and watch its clip immediately.

Figure 11-12:
Comedy
Central's
Olympic
coverage.

Finding streaming video from other sources

Other than Real.com and stumbling across content, probably the best way at this early stage of multimedia Web fun is to search the Internet for all things video and MPEG. As of this writing, however, you're not going to find a whole lot of video content available on the Internet. But this dearth of content is bound reverse itself as access to high-speed Internet access becomes widely available and the big movie studios, and television networks, discover new ways to make money. (They'll realize pretty quickly that a lot of us want to watch our novellas (soaps) — what is bad Ignacio doing to poor Julisa on *Te Sigo Amando* today or who is eating rats a la mode on *Survivor* — on our computers at work each day. Sheesh, get with the times, guys!)

We think RealPlayer is a lot of fun and — more importantly — a preview of what you can expect to see more of. In the near future, there will be a wealth of programming available directly from the Web. No one knows who will be showing what and what the "what" will be. We can say with confidence that there will be a lot of it out there. Have fun!

Punching through firewalls

Firewalls are often necessary to fight the evils that lurks on the Internet, but they can really put a kink in your listening pleasure. The following two sections describe how to fight your way out through a firewall into the fresh streams of audio — and video — air.

Getting RealPlayer through your firewall

If your Red Hat Linux workstation sits on a network with a filtering firewall (see Chapters 5 and 6), then you don't need to modify RealPlayer. A firewall is used to prevent unauthorized access from outside — in most cases the Internet — your computer and/or network. The key is that the filtering firewall allows all outgoing TCP/UDP connections (ports), such as either of the ones we show you how to construct in Chapters 5 and 6. But if your network uses a filtering firewall that allows only specific connections, then you may have to modify RealPlayer. In such a case, it's likely that RealPlayer can find its way through the firewall if you tell it to use the HTTP protocol in place of the specialized PNA and RTSP; PNA and RTSP are protocols that are used to access RealAudio streams.

To configure RealPlayer so that it's not blocked by the firewalls described in Chapters 5 and 6, follow these steps:

1. **Start RealPlayer and choose View➪Preferences.**

   The Preferences window appears as shown in Figure 11-13.

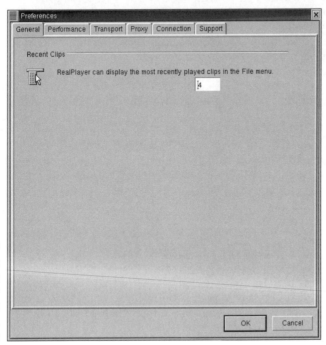

Figure 11-13:
The
RealPlayer
Preferences
window.

2. Click the Transport tab and then click the RTSP Settings button.

The Specify Transport window appears. By default, RealPlayer uses the TCP transport protocol to make its connections. TCP is another Internet protocol used to transport information over the Internet. In order for TCP to work, your Internet gateway/firewall generally has to be specifically configured to allow it.

3. Click the Use HTTP Only button and then click the OK button.

Specifying HTTP makes RealPlayer use that protocol for all of its connections. HTTP is almost universally used for browsing the Web. RealPlayer can make connections more reliably with HTTP. Figure 11-14 shows the window with the HTTP Only button activated.

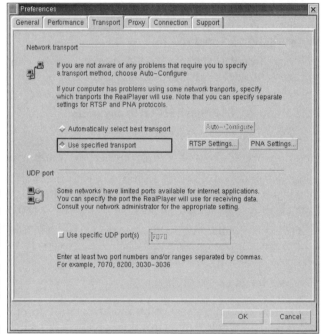

Figure 11-14: Telling RealPlayer to use HTTP instead of the RTSP protocol.

4. Repeat Seps 2 and 3 but click the PNA settings button instead in Step 2.

If you're using the IP-filtering firewall described in Chapter 5 to protect your Internet gateway, then you must use the `ip_masq_raudio` kernel module with it. The firewall script described in Chapter 5 loads that module. It's mentioned here because it is essential, and you should check that it is indeed loaded by running the `lsmod` program if you have trouble accessing video with RealPlayer.

Audio by proxy (using RealPlayer with your firewall)

If your Red Hat Linux computer and/or network are protected by a proxying firewall, then you need to tell RealPlayer about it. A *proxying firewall* is a system that is designed to protect your system from unauthorized outside access. To clue RealPlayer in about your proxying firewall, follow these steps:

1. **In RealPlayer, choose View⇨Preferences.**

2. **Click the Proxy tab.**

   From here, you can tell RealPlayer how to get through your firewall to the Internet. How you configure RealPlayer depends on your firewall. This subject is far too large to approach in depth here, but there are a few simple things you can do that should allow you to get out of your local network through the firewall.

   First you need to tell RealPlayer the location of your proxying firewall. Many proxys allow HTTP through the standard port 80. This is a good place to start.

3. **Click the Manually Configure HTTP Proxy option.**

   The Proxy Server text box appears.

4. **Type the network address of your proxy server in that window.**

   For example, if your proxy server address is `proxy.paunchy.net`, as shown in Figure 11-15, then that is what you type. If the proxy uses a port other than 80, then change the value; in most cases this is not necessary.

   Having a proxy firewall that provides proxys for the PNA and RTSP protocols is unusual. If you do have one, then you can type its address in the Use PNA Proxy and Use RTSP Proxy text boxes.

5. **Click OK and try to use RealPlayer.**

If you can not access an audio stream after modifying RealPlayer, then go back to the Preferences window and click the Transport tab. Click the RTSP button and the Specify Transport window appears. RealPlayer tries to use the TCP transport protocol to make its connections. Your firewall — either proxy or filtering — may not allow that, so you should click the Use HTTP Only option. Repeat the process for the PNA settings.

This tells Real Audio to only use the common HTTP protocol instead of PNA and RTSP. HTTP is less efficient than PNA and RTSP, but is still better than nothing. Click OK to return to the Preferences window. Click OK again and try to make your connection.

**Figure
11-15:**
Configuring
RealPlayer
to use a
proxy
firewall.

If it still doesn't work, then go back to the Preferences window and click the Transport tab. Try to let RealPlayer figure things out for you. Click the Automatically Select Best Transport option and then click the Auto-Configure button. RealPlayer tries everything it can think of to get connected. If you're lucky, it figures out what to use. If not, then you must go back to the Proxy tab and make sure that you set the proxy server address correctly.

If you still aren't having any luck, consult your friendly system administrator and try to figure things out. If you manage your firewall yourself, then consider turning it off. Whether you want to risk that is up to you. Assess your system and determine what you need to protect. If you're running a bank, then you don't want to turn the firewall off. If you're a simple home user, then you can probably turn your firewall off briefly; you may want to temporarily disconnect the rest of your network from your Internet gateway.

Turn off your firewall and try connecting again. With no firewall, everything should work. If it doesn't, then your problem lies elsewhere. If it works, then try to modify your firewall to allow Real Audio connections (this discussion is outside the scope of this book). Good luck!

Chapter 12

Using Red Hat Linux Desktop Productivity Tools

Red Hat Linux is a great distribution with a large base of applications. But Red Hat Linux is also lacking a major desktop office suite, probably because they're monstrous programs and Red Hat wants to ship with less than 10 CD-ROMs (as do the publishers of this book!). Full office suites provide you with word processing, spreadsheet, and other high-level capabilities all within one suite of applications.

Major desktop-productivity suites such as StarOffice, Applixware, and WordPerfect Office are all available to the Linux world, moving Linux out of the back office and into the light of everyday use.

In this chapter, we discuss StarOffice, not Applixware, because StarOffice is free *and* was recently released as open source by Sun Microsystems! Which office suite is better is a question best left to personal taste and opinion. You can find a good comparison of Applixware and StarOffice in Issue 54 of the *Linux Journal* at www.linuxjournal.com/issue54/3080.html, by Fred Butzen, co-author of *The Linux Network* (IDG Books Worldwide, Inc.).

If you're interested in Applixware, which supplies pretty much the same desktop productivity functions as StarOffice, it's available from VistaSource at `www.vistasource.com`. Corel Corporation — the former king of DOS word processing with WordPerfect — also produces a full office suite like StarOffice or Applixware called WordPerfect Office 2000. For more information on this product, go to `www.corel.com` and click the <u>WordPerfect Office 2000</u> link. The word processor WordPerfect 8 is available alone for download from `www.corel.com/download`.

A StarOffice is Born

StarOffice is a desktop productivity suite that does nearly everything that Microsoft Office does, but for less. How much less? Well, 100 percent less because it's now 100 percent free. Sun Microsystems, Inc. recently purchased StarOffice and licenses it under the GPL/LGPL and SIISL licenses. What do all those letters mean? They mean F . . . R . . . E . . . E, and they also mean that Linux can integrate office productivity features from StarOffice now because the Linux and StarOffice share the GPL license. More information about the licenses can be found at the following URL:

```
http://www.openoffice.org/project/www/license.html
```

Not only is StarOffice free, but it is also very powerful, providing the user with the following functions:

- ✔ **Writer:** A full-function *what-you-see-is-what-you-get* (WYSIWIG) word processor. StarOffice comes with many functions that you expect — formatting, cutting and pasting, graphics, spell check, and more. It can also read from and write to Microsoft Word 97/2000 files.

- ✔ **Calc:** A full-function spreadsheet program used by Wall Street brokers. If you're familiar with spreadsheet software, then Calc should be straightforward to use.

- ✔ **Impress:** A graphics program with all the bells and whistles for creating presentations. You can also import and export PowerPoint documents.

- ✔ **Draw:** Your personal graphics tools for creating anything from a novice drawing to a masterpiece. This program provides your creative side with a tool for creating graphics.

- ✔ **Schedule:** This program helps you to organize your time. If you're like Paul, it's increasingly difficult to schedule quality coffee time. Schedule helps find the time.

- ✔ **HTML editor:** This application is pretty obvious in its purpose: building Web pages. You enter what you want on the screen and StarOffice saves it in HTML form. The process is as simple as that.

✔ **E-mail client:** This is a full-function e-mail client program that can read, write, and filter your e-mail for you. You probably want to stick with Netscape Communicator if only to minimize the number of software packages that you use. Nothing is wrong with this tool, but if you're like us and run the Netscape browser constantly, then you may as well use it for e-mail, too. Doing so provides you with fuller integration of your Web browsing and e-mail clients.

✔ **HTML editor:** StarOffice writer is also able to create HTML documents. HTML is the language of the Internet, and this function makes it really easy to create Web pages. HTML editor works the same as the word processor, but the text that you enter is saved in an HTML-formatted documents. Any HTML document that you save can be used as a Web page.

Okay, so StarOffice has a lot of great features. But how good are they? Can they get the job done? Well, while the last edition of this book was written in Applixware Words and edited with Microsoft Office, this one was written mostly in StarOffice. Applixware Words, you see, does not have the ability to use the Microsoft Word Track Changes mechanism (also known as revision marks, so you can see who's done what to a document). This makes it impossible to read all of your editor's many suggestions. As attractive as those suggestions may be on a Monday morning at 3 a.m. with a couple of hours to go before deadline, it's still necessary to be able to read those revision marks. When StarOffice released its new version — 5.2 — with Track Changes and the ability to save files in Word 97/2000 format, there was no competition, which is why this book was largely written and edited in StarOffice 5.2.

StarOffice also has the advantage of running nicely on less than top-of-the-line equipment, such as Paul's creaky old Cyrix P120 (equivalent to a Pentium I 90 – 120 MHz processor). Paul is definitely thrifty when it comes to buying computer equipment, but he appreciates not having to pay top dollar for a 1 GHz chip simply to write down a few words.

Getting StarOffice

StarOffice is freely available from Sun Microsystems, Inc. You can download it from their Web site or purchase a copy on CD-ROM for $10. To download it from the Web site, follow these steps:

1. **Log in as a regular user and start Netscape Communicator.**

We recommend you install StarOffice as a regular user, and that's what we show you how to do here. That's because you want to be able to use it without changing its file permissions and ownership. StarOffice can be difficult to use as a regular user if you install it as root.

2. **Go to** www.sun.com/staroffice/get.html.

3. **Under the heading Free Downloads! (see Figure 12-1), click the StarOffice 5.2 software link.**

   The StarOffice 5.2 Application Suite Web page appears.

4. **Click your language under the Linux (x86) column heading towards the top-left of the page.**

5. **Assuming this is your first time downloading StarOffice, click the Register button.**

6. **Type in the username and password that you want to use; then give Sun the story of your life by entering your name, address, and so on. Then click the Register button.**

   The next screen is for the lawyers.

7. **Click the Accept button and then click the Continue button.**

8. **The Sun Download window provides three different U.S. time zones from which to download: East, Central, and West.**

   There are also European and Asian zones. Select the zone closest to you and click the Download StarOffice 5.2, Linux, English (97.62MB) button.

   The Save As window dialog box appears.

Figure 12-1:
Sun Micro-
systems'
Get
StarOffice
page.

97.62MB is a lot of megabytes. If you're using a 56K modem, it should take several hours to download. Sun lets you download the file in pieces if you want, so that you don't have to download the whole monstrous file in one sitting. For this book we assume you download the one big file, which is much less complicated to deal with. The time needed to download StarOffice is worth it. Just think: You get a full-fledged word-processing, spreadsheet editing, database-ing, HTML-ing piece of software!

9. **Click the Save button.**

   The StarOffice installation file is saved to your home directory. You can then exit Netscape Navigator if you want.

How do you download something from the Internet if you haven't configured Linux to connect to the Internet? You could use another computer that is already connected to download the software. You can also go to Chapter 6, which gives you instructions for connecting to the Internet. After you connect, use the Netscape browser to go to the Sun Web site, and download the software as described in the preceding steps, or order StarOffice on CD from the following URL for $9.95 plus shipping:

```
http://www.sun.com/products/staroffice/5.2/buy.html#small
```

Installing StarOffice

After downloading StarOffice (the filename is `so-5_2-ga-bin-linux-en.bin`), you must install the program. To do so, follow these steps:

1. **Log in as root.**

   StarOffice comes stored in a self-extracting file. But before you can extract it, you must turn on its Linux execution privileges.

2. **Start the GNOME File Manager by clicking the GNOME Main Menu button and choosing Programs⇨File Manager.**

3. **Go to the directory where you saved the** `so-5_2-ga-bin-linux-en.bin` **file to.**

   Figure 12-2 shows the File Manager window.

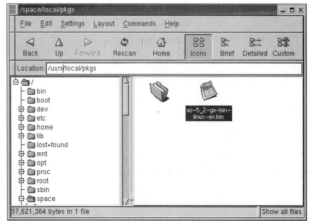

Figure 12-2:
The GNOME
file
manager.

4. **Turn on the Linux execution flag by right-clicking the file and then choosing Properties from the pop-up menu that appears.**

5. **Click the Permissions tab in the Properties window (see Figure 12-3).**

Figure 12-3:
Making the
StarOffice
installation
script
executable.

6. **Click the User button in the Exec column and then click the OK button.**

The file can now be executed by root.

You can manually change the file permission by running the following command from a terminal session:

```
chmod +x /home/login/so-5_2-ga-bin-linux-en.bin
```

The pathname that you supply depends on where you downloaded the demo to. The preceding instruction assumes that you downloaded StarOffice to your home directory. If you put it someplace else, or have a CD-ROM copy, then make the appropriate adjustments.

7. **Start the installation process by double-clicking the** `so-5_2-ga-bin-linux-en.bin` **file icon in the File Manager window.**

   StarOffice is powerful. It's also big. Depending on how fast your computer is, it may take a minute or two for the script to run and the installation process to begin. After it starts, the Welcome to the Installation window appears, as shown Figure 12-4.

8. **Click Next.**

   The Important Information screen appears.

9. **Read the oh-so-important information and click the Next button.**

   The next window takes care of the lawyers.

10. **Click Accept.**

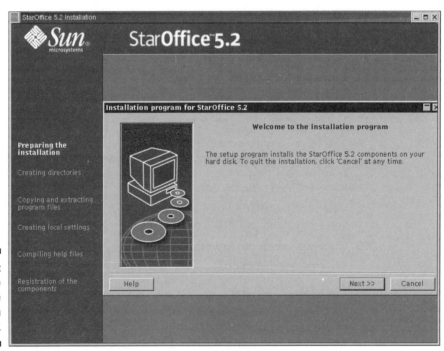

Figure 12-4: The StarOffice installation window.

11. (Optional) Enter your life's history in the Enter User Data window that appears and click Next.

Keep in mind that your user information is included in StarOffice documents that you create before you really do type your whole life's story in!

The Select Installation Type window appears.

You have three installation types to choose from. The standard one includes most of the StarOffice features, but it takes over 265MB of hard drive space. If you want to roll your own installation, select the Custom option. You're prompted in further windows to select the features to install. If you're tight for space, then select the Minimal install. We assume that you select the Standard installation here.

12. Click the Standard Installation option and then click Next.

The StarOffice setup program wants to install itself into your home directory. If you select the default, it creates the directory — for example, /home/lidia/Office52 — for you. We use the StarOffice default here.

13. Click Next.

You are prompted to let the setup program create the /Office52 directory in your home directory for you.

14. Click Yes.

A dialog box is opened that asks you if you want to run Java.

15. You do not need to run Java, so click the Next button.

The Start Copying screen appears. As each StarOffice module — for example the word processor — is installed, you are given short explanations of what they do. You are also shown a progress meter that displays the estimated time to completion.

When the installation process is finished, a window opens up thanking you for installing StarOffice.

16. Click the Complete button.

StarOffice is installed to your Red Hat Linux computer.

17. Click OK to continue.

You software is installed. You may encounter messages that tell you that certain secondary elements can't be installed for one reason or another. They shouldn't cause any problems for you, so just click the OK button.

The installation is finished, and you're shown the Installation Completed window. You now have a great word processing system — and more.

18. Click the Complete button.

Getting to Know StarOffice

If you're familiar with Microsoft Office, then you should be able to find your way around StarOffice. The look and feel is a little different, but the idea is the same. StarOffice is also morally superior to Office because it's free *and* open source. The following sections briefly describe some of the most common functions of StarOffice.

This section provides only a basic introduction to the things you can do with StarOffice. No, we're not lazy — it's just that it would take too much space to describe it all in detail. Please experiment with your own test documents and consult the online help for more information, or see *StarOffice for Linux For Dummies* by Michael Meadhra (IDG Books Worldwide, Inc.).

Firing up StarOffice

After you install StarOffice, you need to be able to start it up. You can create a GNOME applet launcher that starts StarOffice with a click of a mouse. To do so, follow these steps:

1. **Click the GNOME Main Menu button and choose Panel⇨Add to Panel⇨Launcher menus.**

   The Create Launcher Applet window appears, as shown in Figure 12-5.

Figure 12-5:
Creating an applet launcher window for StarOffice.

2. **Enter the name of the launcher icon in the Name text box.**

   For instance, type StarOffice.

3. **(Optional) You can enter a comment in the Comment text box.**

   The text that you enter is displayed over the icon when you place the mouse cursor over it.

4. **Enter the location of the StarOffice program in the Command text box. For example, type** /home/lidia/Office52/soffice **if that's where you installed it.**

   StarOffice supplies some images that can be used for the applet icon, but they're sorta wimpy. Instead, we use the normal GNOME icons; in this case, we select the GNOME tigrette.

5. **Click the OK button in the launcher window.**

   The new icon is inserted into the GNOME panel (the menu bar along the bottom of your screen).

6. **Click the new StarOffice launcher that you just created in the GNOME panel.**

   After thinking about life for a while, the StarOffice window appears, as shown in Figure 12-6.

The first time that you start up StarOffice, it prompts you to decide if you want to use the Internet. If you click Yes, it tries to find information about how you connect to the Net. With the default Red Hat Linux installation, StarOffice should find that you have Netscape. Click Netscape and then click Next. If you use Netscape Communicator to read e-mail from the Internet, click the Don't Use the Internet button.

The StarOffice window that is displayed is the launching point for all the StarOffice components and is referred to as the *Desktop*. StarOffice is technically also a window manager just like GNOME; it displays the individual applications that make up StarOffice. You can also show files and directories in the Desktop just like you do with GNOME or Windows.

The Desktop is organized by default to show the applications available to you from StarOffice. You can click the New Text Document icon, for example, and StarOffice opens up the Writer word processor with a new document for you.

The Desktop is really a file manager that you can access and use files and directories. The StarOffice Desktop default directory is Office52/user/desktop (Office52 is installed in /home/*login* by default, where *login* is your login name, so the full pathname is /home/*login*/Office52/user/desktop). Therefore, it displays the applications stored in that directory. Those applications are actually URLs that point to the actual applications; you can view the information about the URLs by right-clicking any of them and then clicking Properties in the submenu that pops up.

To demonstrate how the StarOffice Desktop works as a file manager, click the Up One Level button near the top-left of the screen (it looks like a yellow folder with an up arrow on it). The desktop displays the next directory up — /home/*login*/Office52/user. This directory contains mostly directories and is displayed as such. Keep moving up by levels and you eventually go to the root (/) directory.

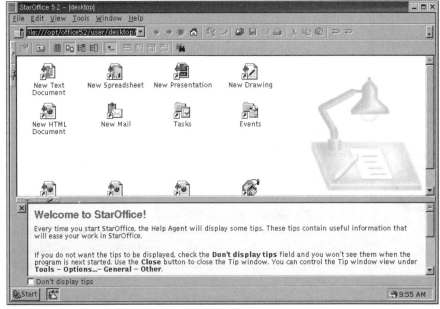

Figure 12-6:
The
StarOffice
desktop
window.

The desktop also has a menu bar displayed across the top of the screen. You can access all of its functions through this menu. The following list introduces the main menu functions. The layout and operation of the menu should be familiar if you are used to Microsoft Office:

✔ **File:** As you may expect, you can open, close, save, and otherwise manipulate StarOffice documents with the File menu. Writer files have the .sdw suffix. Other file formats, such as Microsoft Word 97 and HTML, must be imported and exported.

✔ **Edit:** Provides all the functions that you need to modify documents. Functions such as cut, copy, paste, and delete are all provided here. The functions that are active at any time depend on whether you are editing a document, spreadsheet, or presentation. For example, the cut, copy, and paste options are not active — can't be used — if you are not editing a document (like just after you start up StarOffice and have not opened any files).

You can also track changes just like with Microsoft Windows. Go to Edit➪Changes, and you can track changes on a character-by-character basis. You can display the changes or keep them hidden from view. Once you're satisfied with your edits, you can commit the changes and save only the finished document to disk. Pretty cool.

StarOffice also provides the Find and Replace function from the Edit menu. The Find and Replace feature enables you to find text strings and either replace them with another string or delete them. You can search forward or backward through a document. You can replace one instance or all instances.

✔ **View:** Displays or hides the various menu bars. You can have Words display its formatting characters and also increase or decrease the size — zoom in or out — of the text displayed on the screen. The zoom function enables you to make smaller fonts more readable without changing the document.

✔ **Insert:** Lets you insert special characters, objects, files, and macros into your documents. *Special characters* include various symbols that are not part of the normal character set. *Objects* include graphics, symbols, and figures. (You can create your own figures with Draw.) You can also insert macros and hyperlinks into your documents.

You can insert tables into documents with any number of rows and columns. Words can automatically adjust the row height, or you can do it manually. Choose Insert➪Tables and play around with it.

✔ **Tools:** Provides access to the spell-checker, thesaurus, and similar functions. The spell-checker and thesaurus are self-explanatory.

✔ **Window:** This menu provides control over how your Desktop looks. It can modify and move windows as well as provide other manipulation capabilities.

✔ **Help:** StarOffice provides pretty good online help services. Many are context sensitive. If you are editing a text document, click the Help menu to get access to information related to the Writer module.

For example, choose Help➪Help Agent, and the Help Agent window appears. The Help Agent provides assistance in several areas of interest to the new user, including the following:

- **Introduction to Writer:** Provides an introduction to the word processor.

- **Basics tips text documents:** All you ever want to know about reading, writing, and printing text documents.

- **Advanced tips:** Extends the previous basic text document tip to more advanced subjects.

- **Menus:** Describes how all of the StarOffice menus work together.

- **Toolbars:** Describes the toolbars that provides information and shortcuts.

- **Shortcuts:** Describes what key combinations can be used to perform various word-processing functions.

- **New stuff:** Describes what's new since the last StarOffice version.

- **Support:** Displays some brief information about getting support from Sun Microsystems.

Printing with StarOffice

Printing from StarOffice is a simple process once you have configured Red Hat Linux to use a printer. This section first describes how to configure a Red Hat Linux printer and then shows how to setup StarOffice to use that printer.

Configuring a printer that is attached to your Red Hat Linux computer is a simple process. All that you have to do is run the printtool configuration tool and enter the information about your printer. The following steps describe how to do it:

1. **Log in to your Red Hat Linux computer as root.**

2. **Attach a printer to your Linux computer's parallel (printer) port.**

   The parallel port is a 25-pin female connector on the back of your computer case. New computers usually label the parallel port with some kind of printer icon (altough sometimes it's hard to imagine how they come up with the symbol). If yours is not marked, then there's no harm in plugging your printer into the appropriate port. If you choose a non-printer port, it's probably a serial port and nothing bad can happen other than not being able to print. In that case, use trial-and-error to find the correct port.

3. **Start the printer configuration tool by clicking the GNOME Main Menu Button and choosing Programs⇨System⇨Printtool.**

   If you have not already configured a printer, printtool starts up with a blank screen.

4. **To add a printer, click the Add button.**

   The Add a Printer Entry window appears, as shown in Figure 12-7.

   If you're not on a network, you want to configure a local printer, which is the option selected by default.

5. **Click OK to install a local printer.**

   Because your printer is already connected, printtool detects and displays it.

Figure 12-7:
The Add a
Printer Entry
window.

6. **Click OK.**

   The Edit Local Printer Entry window appears, as shown in Figure 12-8.

   The default values for the printer name, spool directory, and file limit fields should all be acceptable. (You can choose any name for the printer that you want, but by convention, the default name is lp. You can assign multiple names to a single printer.)

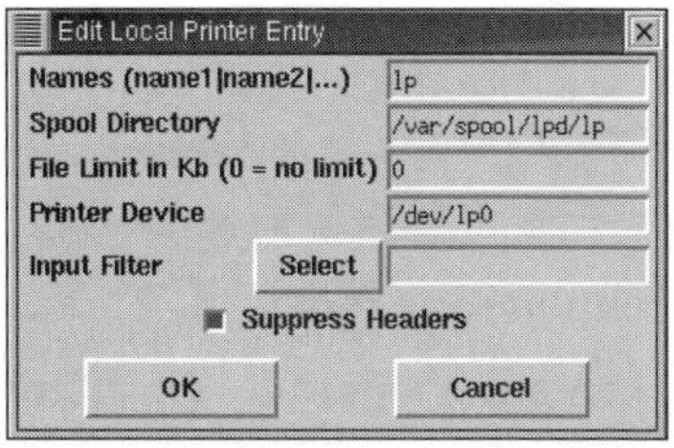

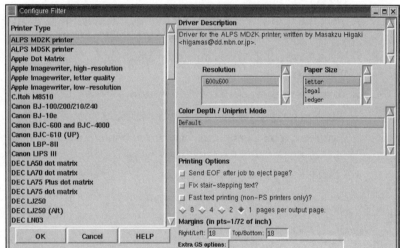

Figure 12-8:
The Edit
Local
Printer Entry
window.

7. If your printer port is detected, it should show up in the Printer Device field; if it doesn't, then choose the port yourself and then click the Input Filter Select button.

The Configure Filter window appears, as shown in Figure 12-9.

Figure 12-9:
The
Configure
Filter
window.

8. Highlight and select the printer type that you are using and click OK.

The control will be sent back to the Edit Local Printer Entry window.

9. Click OK.

You are sent back to the RHS Linux Printer System Manager window, where your new printer is displayed.

10. To test your new printer setup, choose Tests➪Print Postscript test page (you can also choose to print a plain text file).

The PostScript test file is printed.

Importing and exporting Office files

The File menu contains the Import and Export selections, from which you can import an office file from major office productivity suite formats, such as Microsoft Office and WordPerfect. To import a file, follow these steps:

1. **Choose File⇨Open.**

   The StarOffice File Manager window appears.

2. **Double-click any of the directories to browse the Red Hat Linux file system (directories are distinguished by orange file folder icons).**

3. **Click the file that you want to open.**

4. **Click the Open button.**

Now that you have a printer connected to your Red Hat Linux computer, you can print from StarOffice without any further configuration. StarOffice uses the Red Hat Linux printer configuration by default. Open a file that you want to print. From the StarOffice desktop, choose File⇨Print. You can choose to print the entire document, individual pages, or ranges of pages. It's quick and easy.

Introducing Your PalmPilot to Red Hat Linux

You can let Red Hat Linux pilot your personal digital assistant — PDA — for you. Red Hat Linux is a jack-of-all-trades and provides functions that let you use backup and synchronize your PalmPilot with it. This section describes how to increase your productivity with the help of Red Hat Linux and your PalmPilot.

The software to use PalmPilot with Red Hat Linux has been around for only a short time. The current version that is packaged with Red Hat Linux 7.0 is the first time that it has been really usable. It's a welcome improvement.

Before Red Hat Linux can talk to your Palm you have to install the pilot-link RPM package. To do so, log in as root, insert CD1 that came with this book into your CD-ROM drive, and run the following command:

```
rpm -ivh /mnt/cdrom/RedHat/RPMS/pilot-link*
```

Backing up and restoring your PalmPilot

The first thing you can use pilot-link for is to back up your PalmPilot databases to your computer. To do so, follow these steps:

1. **Log in as root.**

2. **Create a link to your serial port (COM1 in DOS/Windows terms) that's connected to your Pilot cradle by entering the following command:**

```
ln -s /dev/ttyS0 /dev/pilot
```

If your cradle is connected to the second port (COM2), then you would use the following command:

```
ln -s /dev/ttyS1 /dev/pilot
```

3. **Plug your Pilot cradle into your computer's serial port.**

The cable attached to your cradle has a female 9-pin (called a DB9) plug attached to it. Most, if not all, modern computers have a 9-pin male plug that connects to serial port one. That serial port is controlled by the /dev/ttyS0 Linux device (in the DOS/Windows world, it is COM1).

4. **Plug your PalmPilot into its cradle.**

5. **Enter the following command:**

```
pilot-xfer -b pilot.bak
```

Note that the name that you supply to the pilot-xfer program is arbitrary. You can create any name you want; the directory is created in the /root directory unless you give it another pathname, such as /home/myname/pilot.bak. The name refers to a directory where your Pilot's databases — address book, calendar, and so on — are stored.

The directory is created if it doesn't already exist.

6. **Press the HotSync button on the Pilot cradle and all the databases are copied to your Red Hat Linux computer.**

The pilot-xfer program displays the progress similar to the following code:

```
Waiting for connection on /dev/pilot (press the HotSync
        button now)...
Connected
Backing up 'pilot.bak/AddressDB.pdb'... OK
Backing up 'pilot.bak/DatebookDB.pdb'... OK
Backing up 'pilot.bak/ExpenseDB.pdb'... OK
...
```

You can restore the databases to the PalmPilot by reversing the process. Just type **pilot-xfer -r pilot.bak** and press the HotSync button on the cradle.

Synchronizing your calendar

The pilot-link package provides a mechanism for synchronizing your Pilot calendar to your Red Hat Linux computer. The pilot-link package provides a one-way mechanism for downloading your calendar into an ical readable file.

To download your calendar to your Red Hat Linux computer, follow these steps:

1. **Log in as any user.**
2. **Connect your Pilot cradle to your computer.**

   The read-ical program does the dirty work, writing the PalmPilot information into a file on your computer and overwriting whatever file is specified. You do, however, want to be careful not to accidentally overwrite your calendar file. Don't copy your Palm Pilot calendar database directly to your ical calendar filename; instead, copy it to a temporary file as in Step 3.

3. **To write to a temporary file, enter the following command:**

   ```
   read-ical ical.tmp
   ```

4. **Press the HotSync button on your Pilot cradle.**

   The information is copied into ical.tmp.

5. **Start ical by clicking the GNOME Main Menu button and choosing Programs⇨Applications⇨Ical.**

6. **Import the Pilot calendar into ical by choosing File⇨Include Calendar⇨ical.tmp.**

7. **Make a date.**

8. **Save your calendar.**

Before you can synchronize your calendar to your PalmPilot, you have to obtain another program. Unfortunately, the reverse of read-ical is not included with the pilot-link package. You must download and compile the syncal software package to transfer your Ical calendar information to your PalmPilot.

John Franks was kind enough to create a program to synchronize your calendar to your PalmPilot. He created the program in true Linux fashion — because he needed it. He also created a Web page to serve syncal at: http://hopf.math.nwu.edu/syncal.

To compile the `syncal` software, follow these steps:

1. **Log in as root.**

2. **Change to the standard Linux directory for storing source code by entering the following at a command prompt:**

   ```
   cd /usr/local/src
   ```

3. **Download the `syncal` program** from `http://hopf.math.nwu.edu/syncal/syncal-0.8.6.tar.gz`.

   By the time you read this, a newer version may exist. If so, adjust these steps as necessary.

4. **Unpack the `syncal` software package by entering the following command:**

   ```
   tar xvzf syncal*
   ```

5. **Go to the `syncal-0.8.6` directory by entering the following command:**

   ```
   cd syncal-0.8.6
   ```

6. **Compile the program by entering the following command:**

   ```
   make
   ```

7. **Copy the new program to the standard execution directory `/usr/bin` by entering the following at a command prompt:**

   ```
   cp syncal /usr/bin
   ```

8. **Log out as root and log back in as a regular user.**

9. **Update your Pilot's calendar by typing:**

   ```
   syncal
   ```

Check out your updated calendar on your PalmPilot. Pretty nice, eh? This is a very useful capability. If you're like us, you use your PalmPilot on a daily basis. Being able to use it with your Red Hat Linux workstation is especially handy.

Applications Galore!

The list of Linux applications is growing by leaps and bounds. Red Hat maintains a Web page for information on Linux applications — both commercial and open source. The address of that page is `www.redhat.com/appindex/index.html`.

You can find programs for every major area of interest on this page. The list is constantly growing and is a good indication of the overall health and future direction of Linux. The following two sections briefly describe a couple of the more powerful programs available for Linux that help ease the transition from Windows software for Linux users.

A Window on Linux

One really useful tool for Linux is Microsoft's Windows NT Server 4.0, Terminal Server Edition with Citrix's MetaFrame, which displays a full-featured Microsoft Windows NT desktop on your Linux computer. Applications actually run on a Windows NT server but are displayed on your Linux computer as an X window. You get a virtual Windows NT machine running on your Linux computer!

"Ack!" some of you may cry in disgust. "We don't need no stinking Windows!" And granted, most of what the average user needs to do can be done with Linux. But certain functions, like a company timesheet, can run only on a Windows computer. By using MetaFrame/Terminal Server, Paul does not need to have a second computer or to bug his coworkers. He simply fires up his MetaFrame client window, connects to the server, and has a Windows machine within his Linux computer. No muss, no fuss.

You can download Citrix's client program from its Web site at `www.citrix.com`. The company provides a basic Windows NT/Terminal server edition for demonstration purposes. The Web site offers full instructions, but this is a challenging endeavor. We mention it here to let you know that you can remotely run Windows applications from your Red Hat Linux computer.

Days of Wine and roses

Wine stands for *WINdows Emulator*. It converts Windows API functions into their X Window System equivalents. You can then run Windows executables on Linux. Pretty sweet!

The Wine home page address is `www.winehq.com`. This site contains not only the latest versions and updates, but also several FAQs. Wine is also somewhat challenging to use. We mention it here to provide you with the knowledge of what can be done with Red Hat Linux.

Part IV
Revenge of the Nerds

In this part . . .

1n the great tradition of slackers and procrastinators, we've left the real work for last. In this part, you find out about the basics of running a Red Hat Linux computer.

We start by describing Linux files and directories in Chapter 13. Chapter 14 introduces the Linux standard shell called BASH. We teach you how to manage disks and partitions in Chapter 15. The next chapter introduces you to the wonderful world of Shells and shell scripts. Chapter 17 progresses to the advanced world of script writing.

If you're to manage a Red Hat Linux box, then some serious attention is warranted, and given, in Chapter 18. It provides some detailed help in fixing computer problems. Networking is used as the backdrop for your troubleshooting apprenticeship.

Chapter 13

Filing Your Life Away

- -

In This Chapter

▶ Discovering the ins and outs of files and directories

▶ Finding your way through the Linux file system

▶ Moving around in the Linux file system

▶ Creating, moving, copying, and destroying directories and files

▶ Giving permissions and taking them away

- -

*I*n this chapter, you take your first steps through the Linux file and directory structure. Don't worry, Linux may live a structured life, but it's still very flexible. With a little bit of introduction, you'll understand the Linux way of life.

We also introduce you to file types, subdirectories, and the root — which is not of all evil — directory. You also are shown the way home — to your home directory, that is. After you're oriented with the Linux files and directories structure, we show you how to make some changes, such as how to copy and move files and directories, as well as how to destroy them.

Getting Linux File Facts Straight

Linux files are similar to Unix, DOS, Windows, and Macintosh files. All operating systems use files to store information. Files allow you to organize your stuff and keep them separate. For instance, the text that makes up this chapter is stored in a file; all the other chapters are stored in their own files. Follow the bouncing prompt as we make short work of long files.

If you need to brush up on how to decipher the code examples in this book, we give you the basics in the Introduction to this book.

Storing files

A *file* is a collection of information that is identified by a filename. Linux stores files in directories. Linux can store multiple files in the same directory as long as they have different names; Linux stores files with the same name in different directories.

Confused? An example may help. Suppose you get a grand idea and decide to keep it in a file named idea in your directory called /wonderful. Now suppose you've had a couple of pots of coffee and are having a very fertile day and come up with another idea. If you want to keep your second idea file in the /wonderful directory, you use a different name, such as /wonderful/ myidea2. (We hope your ideas are more original than our filenames.) You can also, however, keep the file in another location — called the /bizarre directory. If you decide to keep your second idea in /bizarre, you can call it idea, and the filename becomes /bizarre/idea. Linux sees this file and the /wonderful/idea file as different files. Remember, though, that each directory may contain only one file with the same name.

Wonderful or not, Linux filenames can be as long as 256 characters. They can contain uppercase and lowercase letters (also known as mixed case), numbers, and special characters, such as the underscore (_), the dot (.), and the hyphen (-). Because filenames can be made up of mixed case names, and each name is distinct, we call these names *case sensitive.* For example, the names *FILENAME, filename,* and *FiLeNaMe* are unique filenames of different files (such as Compaq's OpenVMS), but they are the same filename.

Although filenames technically can contain wildcard characters, such as the asterisk (*) and the question mark (?), using them is not a good idea. Various command interpreters, or *shells,* use wildcards to match several filenames at one time. If your filenames contain wildcard characters, you'll have trouble specifying only those files. We recommend that you create filenames that don't contain spaces or other characters that have meaning to shells. In this way, Linux filenames are different than DOS and Windows filenames.

Sorting through file types

Linux files can contain all sorts of information. The following five categories of files will become the most familiar to you:

- ✔ **User data files** contain information you create. User data files, sometimes known as *flat files,* usually contain the simplest data, consisting of plain text and numbers. More complex user data files, such as graphics or spreadsheet files, must be interpreted and used by special programs. These files are mostly illegible if you look at them with a text editor, because the contents of these files are not always ASCII text. Changing these files generally affects only the user who owns the files.

✔ **System data files** are used by the system to keep track of users on the system, logins, passwords, and so on. As system administrator, you may be required to view or edit these files. As a regular user, you don't need to be concerned with system data files except, perhaps, the ones that you use as examples for your own private startup files.

✔ **Directory files** hold the names of files — and other directories — that belong to them. These files and directories are called *children*. Directories in Linux (and Unix) are just another type of file. If you are in a directory, the directory above you is called the *parent*. Isn't that homey?

When you list files with the ls -l command, it displays a list of files and directories. Directory files begin with the letter d. For example:

```
[lidia@veracruz lidia]$ ls -l
drwxr-xr-x 5 lidia lidia 1024 Oct 9 2000 Desktop
drwx------ 2 lidia lidia 1024 Oct 9 2000 nsmail
```

✔ **Special files** represent either hardware devices (such as a disk drive, a tape drive, or a keyboard) or some type of placeholder that the operating system uses. The /dev directory holds many of these special files. You can see this directory by running the following command at a command prompt:

```
ls -l /dev
```

✔ **Executable files** contain instructions (usually called *programs,* or *shell scripts*) for your computer. When you type the name of one of these files, you're telling the operating system to *execute* the instructions. Some executable files look like gibberish, and others look like long lists of computer commands. A lot of these executable files are located in /bin, /usr/bin, /sbin, and /usr/sbin.

Understanding files and directories

If you live in the Windows world, you can think of a Linux file system as one huge file folder that contains files and other file folders, which in turn contain files and other file folders, which in turn contain files and . . . well, you get the point. In fact, the Linux file system is generally organized this way. One big directory contains files and other directories, and all the other directories in turn contain files and directories.

Directories and subdirectories

A directory contained, or *nested,* in another directory is called a *subdirectory*. For example, the directory called /mother may contain a subdirectory called /child. The relationship between the two is referred to as parent and child. The full name of the subdirectory is /mother/child, which would make a good place to keep a file containing information about a family reunion called /mother/child/reunion.

The root directory

In the tree directory structure of Linux, DOS, and Unix, the big directory at the bottom of the tree is called the *root* directory. root is the parent of all other directories — the poor guy must be exhausted — and is represented by a single / symbol (pronounced slash). From the root directory, the whole directory structure grows like a tree, with directories and subdirectories branching off like limbs.

If you could turn the tree over so that the trunk is in the air and the branches are toward the ground, you would have an *inverted tree* — which is the way the Linux file system is normally drawn and represented (with the root at the top). If we were talking about Mother Nature, you'd soon have a dead tree. Because this is computer technology, however, you have something that looks like an ever-growing, upside-down tree.

What's in a name?

You name directories in the same way that you name files, following the same rules. Almost the only way that you can tell whether a name is a filename or a directory name is the way that the slash character (/) is used to show directories nested in other directories. For example, usr/local means that local is found in the usr directory. You know that usr is a directory because the trailing slash character tells you so; however, you don't know whether local is a file or a directory.

If you issue the ls command with the -f option, Linux lists directories with a slash character at the end, as in local/, so you would know that local is a directory.

The simplest way to tell whether the slash character indicates the root directory or separates directories, or directories and files, is to see whether anything appears before the slash character in the directory path specification. If nothing appears before the slash, you have the root directory. For example, you know that /usr is a subdirectory or a file in the root directory because it has only a single slash character before it.

Home again

Linux systems have a directory called /home, which contains the user's home directory, where he or she can

✔ Store files

✔ Create more subdirectories

✔ Move, delete, and modify subdirectories and files

Linux system files as well as files belonging to other users are never in a user's /home directory. Linux decides where the /home directory is placed, and that location can be changed only by a superuser, not by general users. Linux is this dictatorial because it has to maintain order and keep a handle on security.

 Your /home directory is not safe from prying eyes. To be sure that your privacy is maintained, you need to lock your directory. (We tell you how in the "Granting Permissions" section.) But anyone logging in to your system as root (superuser) can see what's in your /home directory, even if you do lock it up.

Moving Around the File System with pwd and cd

You can navigate the Linux file system without a map or a GPS. All you need to know are two commands: pwd and cd. (These commands are run from the command line.) But you also need to know where you are to start with, hence the usefulness of the next section.

Figuring out where you are

To find out where you are in the Linux file system, simply type **pwd** at the command prompt as follows:

```
[lidia@veracruz lidia]$pwd
```

We receive the following response

```
/home/lidia
[lidia@veracruz lidia]$
```

indicating that we're logged in as lidia and are currently in the /home/lidia directory. Unless your alter ego is out there, you should be logged in as *yourself* and be in the /home/yourself directory, where *yourself* is your login name.

The pwd command stands for *print working directory.* Your *working directory* is the default directory where Linux commands perform their actions. When you type the ls(1) command, for example, Linux shows you the files in your working directory. Any file actions on your part occur in your working directory unless you are root. For security reasons that we won't go into here, the root user is not configured by default to be able to work on the current working directory. You can change this, but in general, the root user must explicitly specify the current working directory. For example, if you are root and are in the /etc directory, and you want to indicate the hosts file, you must type **cat ./hosts** instead of just **cat hosts**.

Type this command:

```
ls -la
```

You see only the files that are in your working directory. If you want to specify a file that isn't in your working directory, you have to specify the name of the directory that contains the file, as well as the name of the file. For example, the following command lists the passwd file in the /etc directory:

```
ls -la /etc/passwd
```

Specifying the directory path

If the file you want to read is in a subdirectory of the directory that you are in, you can reach the file by typing a relative filename. *Relative filenames* specify the location of files relative to where you are.

In addition to what we tell earlier in this chapter about specifying directory paths, you need to know these three additional rules:

- ✔ One dot (.) always stands for your current directory.
- ✔ Two dots (..) specify the parent directory of the directory you are currently in.
- ✔ All directory paths that include (.) or (..) are relative directory paths.

You can see these files by using the -a option of the ls(1) command. Without the -a option, the ls(1) command does not bother to list the . or .. files, or any filename beginning with a period. This may seem strange, but the creators of Unix thought that having some files that were normally hidden kept the directory structure cleaner. Therefore, filenames that are always there (. and ..) and special-purpose files are hidden. The types of files that should be hidden are those that the user normally does not need to see in every listing of the directory structure (files used to tailor applications to the user's preferences, for example).

Now specify a pathname relative to where you are. For example:

```
[lidia@veracruz lidia]$pwd
/home/lidia
[lidia@veracruz lidia]$ ls -la ../../etc/passwd
```

The last line indicates that to find the `passwd` file, you go up two directory levels (../../) and then down to `/etc`.

If you want to see the login accounts on your system, you can issue the following command from your home directory:

```
[lidia@veracruz lidia]$ ls -la ..
```

This command lists the parent directory. Because the parent directory (`/home`) has all the login directories of the people on your system, this command shows you the names of their login directories.

You have been looking at relative pathnames, which are relative to where you are in the file system. Filenames that are valid from anywhere in the file system are called *absolute filenames*. These filenames always begin with the slash character (/), which signifies root.

```
ls -la /etc/passwd
```

Changing your working directory

Sometimes, you may want to change your working directory because doing so allows you to work with shorter relative pathnames. To do so, you simply use the `cd` (for *change directory*) command.

To change from your current working directory to the `/usr` directory, for example, type the following:

```
cd /usr
```

Going home

If you type **cd** by itself, without any directory name, you return to your home directory. Just knowing that you can easily get back to familiar territory is comforting. There's no place like home.

You can also use `cd` with a *relative* specification. For example:

```
cd ..
```

If you are in the directory `/usr/bin` and type the preceding command, Linux takes you to the parent directory called `/usr`, as follows:

```
[lidia@veracruz lidia]$ cd /usr/bin
[lidia@veracruz bin]$ cd ..
[lidia@veracruz usr]$
```

Here are a couple of tricks: If you type **cd ~**, then you go to your home directory (the tilde ~ is synonymous with /home/username). If you type
cd ~<*username*>, then you can go to that user's home directory. On very
large systems, this command is useful because it eliminates the need for you
to remember — and type — large directory specifications.

Creating and Adding to Files with cat

Unlike cats, the cat command is simple, easy to use, and one of the most
useful Linux commands (sorry, Paul likes dogs and is allergic to cats). The
name cat stands for *concatenate,* meaning *to add to the end of.* The cat command does exactly what you tell it to and takes your input (mostly from the
keyboard) and outputs it to the screen. Real cats like to do what they want to
do and will not help display the contents of Linux files.

Make sure that you are *not* logged in as root when you go through this section and the sections that follow. Wait until you are thoroughly familiar with
this chapter before you log in as root and try the examples. Linux (for the
most part) doesn't have an *undo* function, although a change is in the works.

To find out what the cat command is all about, follow these steps:

1. **Make sure that you are in the /home directory.**

   To go home, click your heels . . . no, that's another book. Type **cd** at the
   prompt and then type **pwd**.

2. **Enter the cat command at the command prompt.**

   The cursor moves to the next line, but nothing else happens because
   cat is waiting for you to input something.

3. **Type Hi and then press Enter. Then type a few more lines.**

   Here's what we typed and what appeared on the screen:

   ```
   Hi
   Hi
   What?
   What?
   Whatever!
   Whatever!
   ```

   Everything you type is repeated on the screen after you press Enter. Big
   deal, you say? We explain why this is useful in a moment.

4. **To get out of the cat command, press Ctrl+D (if you're not at the
   beginning of a line, press Ctrl+D twice).**

Most Unix and Linux people write Ctrl+D as ^D, which means *end of file* (EOF) to Linux. When the `cat` command sees ^D, it assumes that it's finished with that line and moves to the next one. If ^D is on an empty line by itself, the `cat` command has no other input to move to and thus exits.

We promised that we'd explain the usefulness of the `cat` command. We always try to keep our promises, so here goes. You can use the following two symbols to save the output of the `cat` command to a file; the final symbol reads the content of a file and sends it to the `cat` command:

- ✔ > is known as *redirection of standard output.* When you use it, you tell the computer, "Capture the information that normally goes to the screen, create a file, and put the information into it."

- ✔ >> is known as *appending standard output.* When you use this symbol, you tell the computer, "Capture the information that would normally go to the screen and append the information to an existing file. If the file doesn't exist, create it."

- ✔ < is used to tell the computer, "Take the information from the specified file and feed it to *standard in* (also known as *standard input*), acting as though the information is coming from the keyboard."

In this example, you use the `cat` command to create a file by redirecting the output of the `cat` command from the screen to the filename you want:

1. **At the command line, type** cat > **followed by the name of your file. Then type your heart out.**

   Here's what we typed:

   ```
   [lidia@veracruz lidia]$ cat > dogfile
   Hi again
   Dogfish. Dogleg. Dog days.
   veracruz. Dogfight. Doggone.
   ```

   Everything is repeated to the file called `dogfile` rather than to the screen. Linux created `dogfile` for us because the filename didn't already exist.

2. **When you finish typing, just press ^D on an empty line.**

   You're right back at the Linux prompt.

Are you wondering whether the `cat` command did what you wanted? You can check by using the `cat` command and the filename again:

```
[lidia@veracruz lidia]$ cat dogfile
Hi again
Dogfish. Dogleg. Dog days.
veracruz. Dogfight. Doggone.
[lidia@veracruz lidia]$
```

This time the `cat` command took the file off the disk and put the output to *standard out* (also known as *standard output*), which in this case is your computer screen.

If you think of something else you want to add to the file, you can use the append symbol (>>) with the filename. Linux adds whatever you type to the end of the filename. Returning to `dogfile`:

```
[lidia@veracruz lidia]$ cat >> dogfile
Dog-eared. Doggerel.
```

Use the `cat` command to concatenate files or concatenate input to either the beginning or the end of the file. It is the only command created to do this. You can also use the >> symbol to add data to the *end* of a file.

You can use the >> symbol with many Linux commands. For example:

```
cat file1 file2 file3 file4 >fileout
```

joins file1, file2, file3, and file4, putting the results in fileout. In the following:

```
sort file1 >>file2
```

the `sort` command sorts the contents of file1 and appends it to a (perhaps already existing) file2. If file2 doesn't exist, the system creates file2 and then puts the sorted output into it.

When you finish, be sure to end the session with ^D.

Manipulating Files and Directories

Linux has many ways to create, move, copy, and delete files and directories. Some of these features are so easy to use that you need to be careful: Unlike other operating systems, Linux doesn't tell you that you are about to overwrite a file — it just follows your orders and overwrites!

We said it once, but we'll say it again: Make sure that you are *not* logged in as root when you go through these sections.

Creating directories

To create a new directory in Linux, you use the `mkdir` command (just like in DOS). The command looks like this:

```
[lidia@veracruz lidia]$mkdir newdirectory
```

This command creates a subdirectory under your current or working directory. If you want the subdirectory under another directory, change to that directory first and then create the new subdirectory.

Create a new directory called `santa_cruz`. Go ahead, do it:

```
mkdir santa_cruz
```

(Can you tell where we would rather be right now?)

Now create another directory called work:

```
mkdir work
```

And then change the directory to put yourself in the `santa_cruz` directory:

```
cd santa_cruz
```

Now create a file under `santa_cruz` called `radman`, by using the `cat` command (see "Creating and Adding to Files with cat," earlier in this chapter):

```
cat >radman
Once upon a time there lived a handsome prince.
^D
```

Now create another file:

```
cat >jewels
Once upon a time there lived a beautiful princess.
^D
```

And one more:

```
cat >moody
The handsome prince and beautiful princess had a dog named
          Moody.
^D
```

Now you have some files to work with.

Moving and copying files and directories

The commands for moving and copying directories and files are `mv` for move and `cp` for copy. If you want to rename a file, you can use the move command. No, you're not really moving the file, but in Linux (and Unix), the developers realized that renaming something was a lot like moving it. The format of the move command is

```
mv source destination
```

With your example files from the preceding section, you can move the file named `radman` to a file named `bryant` by executing the following command:

```
mv radman bryant
```

This command leaves the file in the `santa_cruz` directory but changes its name to `bryant`. So you see the file was not really moved, but just renamed.

Now try moving the `bryant` file to the `work` directory. To do that, you have to first move the file up and then move it into the `work` directory. You can do it with one command:

```
mv bryant ../work
```

Note that the destination file uses the .. (or parent directory) designation. This command tells Linux to go up one directory level and look for a directory called `work`, and then put the file into that directory with the name `bryant`, because you did not specify any other name. If you instead did this:

```
mv bryant ../work/supersalesman
```

the `bryant` file would move to the `work` directory named `supersalesman`. Note that in both cases (with the file maintaining its name of `bryant` or taking the new name `supersalesman`), your current directory is still `santa_cruz`, and all your filenames are relative to that directory.

Strictly speaking, the file still has not really moved. The data bits are still on the same part of the disk where they were originally. The *file specification* (the directory path plus the filename) that you use to talk about the file is different, so it appears to have moved.

In early versions of Unix, you were not allowed to use `mv` to move a file from one disk partition to another; you could only copy it by using the `cp` command. Linux allows you to use the `mv` command to move a file anywhere. Normally, `mv` leaves the data in place and just changes the file's name or the directory where the name is placed. But when the file is moved across disk partitions (for example, from `/usr` to `/home` in a lot of Linux systems), the data is copied to the new disk partition, the new name is put in place in that partition's directory structure, and the name and file's data are removed from the old disk partition.

Copying a file does move some data. The syntax is

```
cp source destination
```

Look familiar? It's the same syntax you use for the move command.

Now make two copies of the jewels file. Because you can't have two files of the same name in the same directory, you have to think of a new name, such as jewels2. (Hey, we're writing this early in the morning. How creative can we be?)

```
cp jewels jewels2
```

If you want a copy of a file but in a different directory, you can use the same filename. For example, suppose you want to copy a file called moody to the ../work directory. You can keep the name moody because its full pathname has work in it instead of santa_cruz:

```
cp moody ../work
```

As you can see, the pathname specifications for files are similar from command to command, even though the file contents and commands are different.

Removing files

The command for removing, or deleting, a file is rm. If you've been following along in our little story, the handsome prince now has two beautiful princesses (jewels and jewels2) in the santa_cruz directory. As most people know, this is probably one too many princesses, so get rid of the second one:

```
rm jewels2
```

You have removed the extra file from the current directory. To remove a file from another directory, you need to provide a relative filename or an absolute filename. For example, if you want to expunge moody from the work directory, you would type the following:

```
rm ../work/moody
```

You are allowed to use wildcards with rm, but please be careful if you do so! When files are removed in Linux, they are gone forever — kaput, vanished — and can't be recovered.

The following command removes *everything* in the current directory and all of the directories under it that you have permission to remove:

```
[lidia@veracruz lidia]$rm -r *
```

To lessen the danger of removing a lot of files inadvertently when using wildcards, be sure to use the -i option with rm, cp, mv, and various other commands. The -i option means *interactive,* and it lists each filename to be removed (with the rm command) or overwritten (with the mv or cp command). If you answer either y or Y to the question, the file is removed or overwritten, respectively. If you answer anything else, Linux leaves the file alone.

Removing directories

You can remove not only files but also directories. If you are still following along with the story about the handsome prince and his princess, you now have two directories in your home directory that are taking up a small amount of space. Because you are finished with them, you can delete them and recover that space for other tasks.

First, return to your home directory:

```
[lidia@veracruz lidia]$ cd
```

Now remove the santa_cruz directory:

```
[lidia@veracruz lidia]$rm -rf santa_cruz
```

This command removes the santa_cruz directory and all files and directories under it. Note that this is just the rm command with options for recursively and forcefully. (*Recursively* means to keep going down in the directory structure and remove files and directories as you find them. *Forcefully* means that the file should be removed if at all possible; ignore cases where rm may prompt the user for further information.)

Another command specifically for removing empty directories is called rmdir. With rmdir, the directory must be empty to be removed. If you attempt to remove the work directory without first deleting its files, the system displays the following message:

```
[lidia@veracruz lidia]$ rmdir work
rmdir: work: Directory not empty
[lidia@veracruz lidia]$ rm -rf work
```

Granting Permissions

Files and directories in Linux have owners and are assigned a list of permissions. This system of ownership and permissions forms the basis for restricting and allowing access to files. File permissions can also be used to specify whether a file is executable as a command and to determine who can use the file or command. Ownership and permissions are important to know because even if you are the only one who uses your system, some commands and databases are owned by other users, including root (the superuser). Permissions on these files either allow or disallow you, the general user, to update these files.

Using the ls command with the -l option allows you to see the file's permissions, along with other relevant information, such as who owns the file, what group of people have permission to access or modify the file, the size of the file or directory, the last time the file was modified, and the name of the file.

First, create a file with the touch command. The Unix and Linux communities use the touch command for many things, one of which is to create a little zero-length file:

```
[lidia@veracruz lidia]$ touch partytime
[lidia@veracruz lidia]$ ls -l partytime
-rw-rw-r-- owner group 0 Oct 31 16:00 partytime
```

The -rw-rw-r-- are the permissions for the partytime file: The owner is you, and the group is probably you but may be someone or something else, depending on how your system is set up and administered.

You may be wondering how you can become an owner of a file. Well, you are automatically the owner of any file you create, which makes sense. As the owner, you can change the default file permissions — and even the ownership. If you change the file ownership, however, *you* lose ownership privileges.

To change the ownership of a file or a directory, use the chown command. (Get it? chown — change ownership.) In general, you have to be root to do this.

Suppose you've decided to settle down and lead a more contemplative life, one more in line with a new profession of haiku writing. Someone else will have to plan the weekend sprees and all-night bashes. So you give up ownership of the partytime file:

```
[lidia@veracruz lidia]$chown root partytime
```

This command changes the ownership of partytime to root. If you want to change it back, you can use the chown command, but you have to do it as root.

Files and users all belong to *groups*. In the partytime example, the group is users. Having groups enables you to give large numbers of users — but not all users — access to files. Group permissions and ownership are handy for making sure that the members of a special project or workgroup have access to files needed by the entire group.

To see which groups are available to you on your system, take a look at the /etc/group file. To do so, use the more command. You see a file that looks somewhat like this:

```
root::0:root
bin::1:root,bin,daemon
...
nobody::99:
users::100:
floppy:x:19:
.....
your_user_name::500:your_user_name
```

where *your_user_name* is the login name you use for your account. Please remember that the file won't look exactly like this, just similar. The names at the beginning of the line are the group names. The names at the end of the line (such as root, bin, and daemon) are user-group names that can belong to the user-group list.

To change the group that the file belongs to, log in as root and use the chgrp command. Its syntax is the same as that of the chown command. For example, to change the group that partytime belongs to, you would issue the following:

```
[lidia@veracruz lidia]$chgrp newgroupname partytime
```

Red Hat assigns a unique group to each user. For instance, when you add the first user to your system, that user gets the user ID and group ID of 500. The next user receives the user ID and group ID of 501, and so on. This gives you a lot of control over who gets what access to your files.

Making Your Own Rules

You, as the owner of a file, can specify permissions for reading, writing to, or executing a file. You can also determine who (yourself, a group of people, or everyone in general) can do these actions on a file. What do these permissions mean? Read on (you have our permission):

✔ **Read permission** for a file enables you to read the file. For a directory, read permission allows the ls command to list the names of the files in the directory. You must also have execute permission for the directory name to use the -l option of the ls command or to change to that directory.

✔ **Write permission** for a file means you can modify the file. For a directory, you can create or delete files inside that directory.

✔ **Execute permission** for a file means you can type the name of the file and execute it. You can't view or copy the file unless you also have read permission. This means that files containing executable Linux commands, called *shell scripts,* must be both executable and readable by the person executing them. Programs written in a compiled language such as C, however, must have only executable permissions, to protect them from being copied where they shouldn't be copied.

For a directory, execute permission means that you can change to that directory (with cd). Unless you also have read permission for the directory, ls -l won't work. You can list directories and files in that directory, but you can't see additional information about the files or directories by just using an ls -l command. This may seem strange, but it's useful for security.

The first character of a file permission is a hyphen (-) if it is a file or d if the file is a directory. The nine other characters are read, write, and execute positions for each of the three categories of file permissions:

✔ Owner (also known as the user)

✔ Group

✔ Others

Your partytime file, for example, may show the following permissions when listed with the ls -l partytime command:

```
-rw-rw-r--
```

The hyphen (-) in the first position indicates that it is a regular file (not a directory or other special file). The next characters (rw-) are the owner's permissions. The owner can read and write to the file but can't execute it. The next three characters (rw-) are the group's permissions. The group has read-only access to the file. The last three characters (r--) are the others' permissions, which are also read-only.

[-][rw-][r--][r--] illustrates the four parts of the permissions: the file type followed by three sets of triplets, indicating the read, write, and execute permissions for the owner, group, and *other* users of the file (meaning *everyone else*).

You can specify most file permissions by using only six letters:

✔ **ugo,** which stands for — no, not a car — user (or owner), group, and other

✔ **rwx,** which stands for read, write, and execute

These six letters, and some symbols such as = and commas, are put together into a specification of how you want to set the file's permissions.

The command for changing permissions is chmod. The syntax for the command is

```
chmod specification filename
```

Change the mode of partytime to give the user the ability to read, write, and execute the file:

```
chmod u=rwx partytime
```

That was easy enough, wasn't it? What if you want to give the group permission to only read and execute the file? You would execute the following command:

```
chmod g=rx partytime
```

Note that this last command does not affect the permissions for owner or other, just the group's permissions.

Now set all the permissions at once. Separate each group of characters with a comma:

```
chmod u=r,g=rw,o=rwx partytime
```

This command sets the user's permissions to just read, the group's permissions to read and write, and the other's permissions to read, write, and execute.

You can set the permission bits in other ways. But this way is so simple, why use any other?

Chapter 14

Bashing Your Shell

- -

In This Chapter

▶ Discovering the bash shell

▶ Experimenting with wildcards

▶ Using bash history to find files

▶ Banging around to find files

- -

*I*magine that you are in a foreign country, for instance New Mexico, (Estados Unidos de Norte America), and don't know the language (English and Espanōl), so you hire an interpreter to accompany you. You tell the interpreter what you want to do and where you want to go. Assuming that nothing goes wrong with your flight, the interpreter then decides what steps to take (hire a taxi or take the subway, for example) and in what order. When you to talk to people, the interpreter translates your statements into that country's native language. Sorta simple in concept but you need to do your homework first to make it work right.

Shells (also known as *command interpreters*) do much the same thing. They take the English-like commands that you type in, gather resources (such as filenames and memory), and supply lower-level statements to the computer to do what you want.

Bashing Ahead!

bash is the Red Hat Linux default shell. The first thing that you need to do is to give bash a platform. You can do that by starting a terminal emulation program such as the GNOME terminal that is provided by the GNOME window environment. A terminal emulator program simulates the old-style terminals that were used for many years to interact with computers.

You can start the GNOME terminal emulator program by clicking the icon that looks like a computer screen on the GNOME main panel, as shown in Figure 14-1.

The GNOME terminal appears, as shown in Figure 14-2.

Figure 14-1:
The GNOME
terminal
icon in the
GNOME
main panel.

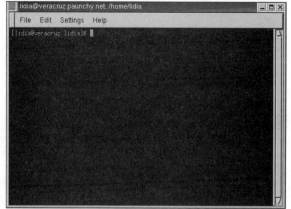

Figure 14-2:
The GNOME
terminal
screen.

You should see the `bash` shell prompt in the GNOME terminal window. Your shell prompt should look something like this:

```
[lidia@veracruz lidia]$
```

The most important element of this *prompt* is the $ at the end of the line, which is the shell's method of saying, "Okay, I'm finished with the last thing, so give me something else to do." The information contained within the square brackets ([ ]) tells you who you are logged in as, the name of the computer that you are logged in to, and the last part of the directory that you are in; for instance, if you are in your home directory, /home/me, the *me* part of the directory is displayed.

If you are logged in as root or have become a superuser through the use of the `su(1)` command, the $ is replaced with a # sign, which indicates that the user is root or otherwise has become a superuser.

To make sure that your default shell is the `bash` shell rather than one of the other shells, type the following:

```
[lidia@veracruz lidia]$ bash
```

After you press Enter, Red Hat Linux gives you one of two responses. If `bash` wasn't installed properly, you see the following:

```
command not found
```

If you didn't install your own Linux system, you should find the person who did and throttle him within an inch of . . . no, no. You should find the person who installed your Linux system and kindly ask them to help you use the `bash` shell as your default shell.

When you log in to a Red Hat Linux computer, you are assigned a shell to use. The shell is specified in the `/etc/passwd` file. The root user, for instance has a line in the `passwd` file that looks like this: `root:x:0:0:root:/root:/bin/bash`. The segment `/bin/bash` tells Red Hat Linux where to find the shell to use for the user.

A shell for all seasons

When Ken Thompson and Dennis Ritchie first started writing Unix, they wanted to investigate lots of new ideas in using computers. One of the ideas they explored was making the human interface to the computer changeable and adaptable to the specific needs of the application.

This human interface (or more specifically, what humans interact with most) is typically called a *command interpreter* because it looks at each command as it is typed and converts it into something the computer can follow as an instruction. Most computer systems back then had the command interpreter built into the operating system, which meant the user couldn't change it. (DOS is constructed this way.) The Unix developers wanted to separate the command interpreter from the rest of the operating system. Because the functionality desired was both a command interpreter and a complete environment, it was called a *shell.* The first command interpreter for Unix was called the Bourne shell, often abbreviated as `sh`.

Later, when Unix escaped from Bell Labs and fled to the University of California, Berkeley, the developers decided to extend the shell. They made it more of a programming language and included some features found in the C language. The resulting shell was the C shell, abbreviated `csh` (pronounced "sea shell," of course).

Both the Bourne shell and the C shell existed for many years. The Bourne shell version was available on both System V and Berkeley-based systems. The C shell was used only on Berkeley systems — AT&T was paranoid about having a shell on its system that was created by long-haired college students. The researchers at Bell Labs fought to add the C shell, and eventually it was ported to System V, too.

Next, enter GNU, a collection of software based on Unix and maintained by the Free Software Foundation. (GNU, by the way, stands for GNU's Not Unix.) The GNU project decided it needed a shell free of royalty restrictions. Unfortunately, at the time, the C shell was still under restrictions from AT&T. So the GNU folks decided to create their own royalty-free, GPLed shell. Their new shell would be compatible with the Bourne shell, incorporate some of the C shell idea, and have some interesting new features. They called their shell `bash`, for Bourne Again SHell.

(continued)

(continued)

Meanwhile, innovation stirred at AT&T. David Korn, a researcher there, merged the best of the Bourne shell, C shell, and any other shells he could find, and made the resulting shell even better for programmers by implementing several programming features. The most notable addition was *functions* (which helps to divide large shells into smaller, easier-to-maintain ones). His shell was named the Korn shell (abbreviated ksh). Eventually, this shell also developed graphical features and was adopted by the Open Software Foundation folks as part of their Common Desktop Environment (dtksh).

As the price of computers dropped and freely distributable versions of Unix (netBSD, FreeBSD, and Linux) made their way across the Internet, new shells evolved from the old ones and other shells started to appear, such as

- **tcsh:** A C shell with filename completion and command-line editing

- **ash:** A System V – like shell

- **zsh:** Like ksh, but with built-in spelling correction on the command-line completion, among other useful features

- **pdksk:** A public domain reimplementation of the Korn shell

So why do we have all these shells (and shell-like languages)? They are examples of how separating the command interface from the operating system can allow the language to grow and improve. They are also examples of how specialized languages can be combined with other shells and programs to do really powerful work. If one shell existed, under the control of one person or organization, innovation would probably take much longer.

If you're lucky, you see the following:

```
[lidia@veracruz lidia]$
```

Geez. Linux didn't seem to do much. It did, though. You're definitely in the bash shell and ready to see its power.

If you're logged in as superuser or root (a # appears at the end of your shell prompt), change over to a nonsuperuser account. No examples in this chapter require superuser privileges. And because you're experimenting with shells, limiting potential damage is a good idea. Remember, it's not called *superuser* for nothing.

Commanding Linux with bash

A *command* is just program that you run in order to get something done. For instance, you use the ls command to list files and the mount command to make a floppy or CD-ROM drive accessible. Linux provides a rich and varied set of standard commands that you use to manage your system.

Issuing commands can be simple or complicated. That's because Red Hat Linux is a powerful operating system and can do just about anything that you want it to. We introduce some Red hat Linux commands in this chapter.

Commands can contain one, two, or all three parts, but the first part — the command name — must always be present:

- ✔ The command name.
- ✔ Options to the command (telling the command how to change its actions for a specific execution).
- ✔ Input or output files, which supply data or give the command a place to put output data, respectively.

I command you!

To see how the three parts of a command work together, suppose you type the following Linux command at the shell prompt:

```
ls -l *
```

When bash looks at that line, it performs the following steps:

1. bash creates a new environment for the ls command to be executed in and determines what should be *standard input* and *standard output* to the command. Standard input is normally the keyboard, and standard output is normally the video screen. (You find out more about environments in a moment.)

2. bash expands * to match all the filenames in that particular directory. By *expanding* the filenames, we mean that certain special characters are used to indicate groups of filenames. When these characters are used, the computer sees what filenames match up with these special characters and supplies the filenames to the command, instead of the special characters.

   For example, suppose that you have the files ert, wert, uity, and opgt in your current directory. If you type

   ```
   ls -l *
   ```

   to the ls command, it looks like you typed

   ```
   ls -l ert opgt uity wert
   ```

Note that the shell puts the names in alphabetical order before giving them to the command.

3. Next, bash searches the PATH environmental variable looking for a command called ls. The PATH variable holds the names of directories that contain commands you may want to execute. If the command you want is not in the list, you have to explicitly tell the shell where it can find the command by typing either a complete or relative pathname to the command.

4. bash executes the ls command in the new environment, passing to the command the -l argument and all the filenames it expanded, due to the use of the * character in the command.

5. After ls runs, bash returns to the current environment, throwing away all the side effects that occurred in the new environment, such as an environmental variable changing its value.

In Step 1, we mentioned the *environment.* A shell operates in an environment just like humans live and work in an environment. We expect to have and use certain things in our human environment. Suppose you leave your office for a few days, and someone else steps in to use it. At first, this newcomer uses your environment as you arranged it. The person probably appreciates the fact that the phone works, office supplies are in the desk, and so on. But after a while, the newcomer starts moving and changing things, and maybe even drinking decaffeinated coffee out of your coffee mug! When you come back from your trip, everything is changed. You can't find things easily, and green stuff is growing in the bottom of your mug. Wouldn't it have been nice if that person had left the office (your environment) exactly as you had arranged it?

bash creates an environment for commands to operate in. When a new command is executed, bash creates a clean copy of the environment, executes the command in it, and then throws away that environment, returning to the environment it started with.

Now look at a more complex example than just the one command ls -l *:

```
cd /usr/lib
ls -l * | more
```

In this case:

1. bash creates a new environment for the ls command to be executed in and determines what should be the input (called *standard input* in technical jargon) and the output (called *standard output* in nerd-speak) to the command. You can call this new environment child number 1; the old environment is its parent.

2. bash creates another new environment for the more command to be executed in, called child number 2, and determines what should be input and output to the more command. Because the pipe | symbol is used between the ls -l * command and the more command, the output of

the `ls -l *` command is sent to the input of the `more` command. The output of `more` is sent to the output of the parent `bash` shell. The parent shell is the one into which you have been typing commands and information, and the output of that original `bash` shell is the screen.

3. `bash` expands `*` to match all the filenames in that particular directory, as before.

4. Next, in the child 1 environment, `bash` searches the PATH environmental variable looking for a command called `ls`. The same process occurs for the `more` command in child number 2.

5. `bash` executes the `ls` command in the child number 1 environment, passing to the command the `-l` argument and all the filenames it expanded, due to the use of the `*` character in the command.

6. `more` sees the output of `ls -l *` as its input, and puts its output to the screen.

7. After `ls` runs, `bash` returns to the parent environment, throwing away all the side effects that occurred in the child number 1 environment.

8. `more` sees the end of its input from `ls`, puts the last of its data out to the screen, and terminates.

9. `bash` returns to its parent environment, throwing away all the changes that `more` may have made to the child number 2 environment.

The original `bash` shell is called the *parent,* and the two new environments that `bash` created are called *children,* or *child number 1* and *child number 2.*

Putting the output of one into the standard input of the other, as demonstrated with the command

```
ls -l * | more
```

is called *piping.* The `|` symbol is called — you guessed it — the pipe symbol.

Piping: Oh Danny Boy, the pipes. . . .

Many Linux commands generate a lot of output, and if it all went to standard output as output to the screen, without some type of control, it would scroll past. For example, type the following:

```
ls -al /etc
```

This command lists all the files in your /usr directory. Because this directory holds a truckload of files, the information scrolls down your screen faster than you — or any Evelyn Wood graduate — can read it. You can, however, correct this.

With a process called *piping,* Linux uses the output from one command as the input for another. It's not as confusing as it sounds. In the last example, you had too much information — or *output* — to fit on one lonely screen. You can take that information and put — or *input* — it into a program that divides the information into screen-sized pieces and then displays them.

To do this, you use the `more` command, which is an appropriate name for this tool. You *pipe* the list command's output to the `more` command. But how do you pipe? You use the | character on your keyboard. We bet you were wondering what the heck that key was for. Type the command as follows:

```
ls -al /etc | more
```

Linux doesn't care if spaces surround the | character, but you may want to use them for clarity and to get in the habit of including spaces because they are important at other times.

When you press Enter, the information appears one screen at a time with the word *More* appearing at the bottom of each screen except the last one. To move to the next screen, press the spacebar. When you finish with the last screen, the `more` command takes you back to the Linux prompt. The `more` command can do even more. When the screen halts with the word *More* appearing at the bottom, you can type some commands to the `more` program:

- **q** to get out of the `more` command without wading through all those screens
- **h** to see a list of all commands available in the `more` command

Note that if you press Enter after one screen at a time, Linux shows you the next entry in the list, not the next screen.

Note that some commands to the `more` program (such as the b command) don't work when you're piping input into the program, as opposed to using `more` with a file.

Everyone makes mistakes. Everyone changes his mind from time to time. For those reasons, you need to know how to delete text from the Linux command line. If you want to start over, press Ctrl+U to remove everything you have typed on the command line — if you have not yet pressed Enter. The Backspace key erases one character at a time. The left- and right-arrow keys move the cursor along the line of characters without erasing; when you get to the place you want to change, use the Backspace key to erase mistakes and retype changes. In most cases, the up- and down-arrow keys jump the cursor back and forth through the last few commands.

Linux sometimes uses a command called `less`, which duplicates the functionality of the `more` command. Originally, the `less` command was designed to be more robust than the `more` command, but the `more` command caught up and they are now almost the same. Some Linux systems display text with the less command instead of the more command, which most Unix programs use.

The less and more commands have two apparent differences. One, the less command requires a q command to get back to the Linux prompt, even when you are at the end of the last page. Two, the more command always says *More* at the bottom of a screen, whereas less has just a : character at the bottom of the screen to indicate that it's waiting for you to input the next command.

Regular expressions: Wildcards and one-eyed jacks

If you had to type every filename for every command, Linux would still be useful. But something that makes Linux more useful is the capability to use a few special characters — called *metacharacters*, *pattern-matching characters, wildcards*, or *regular expressions* — to supply filenames. Just as you can substitute wildcards for any card of your choice in a poker game, Linux pattern-matching characters can be substituted for filenames and directory names, much like DOS wildcards.

Three of these special pattern-matching characters follow:

- ✔ * (asterisk)
- ✔ ? (question mark)
- ✔ \ (backslash)

The asterisk matches at least one character in any filename. For example, * matches the following filenames:

> a
>
> acd
>
> bce
>
> moody

You'll probably use * the most in the command ls -l*.

The question mark matches any single character. The string of characters a?c, for example, matches the following:

> abc
>
> adc
>
> aac

afc

a9c

The question mark and the asterisk can be helpful for identifying a particular type of file, if you're careful about naming your files. For example, text editor files usually have the .txt extension, and Microsoft Word files have the .doc extension. Linux doesn't care what the name of a file is, but some programs work only with a particular type of file.

Now suppose you followed the convention of naming all your text files with the .txt extension, and you want to see all the text files in a directory. You can use the ls command like this:

```
ls -l *.txt
```

The screen displays all the files in this directory with the .txt extension. Notice that we didn't say that the command shows you all text files or that it shows only text files. If you want to name a graphics file with a .txt extension, Linux happily obliges you. For your own sanity, however, be diligent in naming files. Some programs (such as those that create audio files or picture files) strictly enforce a naming convention on files they create, but Linux itself doesn't care.

What do you do if the * is part of the filename you're trying to match? How can you tell the shell that you want only the file that contains *, and not all the other files? The backslash character prevents the shell from interpreting the * as a metacharacter and expanding it — in Linux terminology, the backslash *escapes* the meaning of the special character. For example, hi*est matches a file named *hightest,* but hi*est matches only the *hi*est* filename.

If you want to delete the file hi*est, then enter the command:

```
rm hi*est
```

The * expands to mean any character or characters (actually, * can also mean zero, or no characters) and the file is removed. You can also explicitly delete the file by using the following command:

```
rm hi\*est
```

The backslash tells the shell to treat the asterisk as a character and not to expand it to mean zero or more characters.

Although more regular expression characters are available, the ones listed in this section are enough for you to work with for a while.

Tweaking Linux commands with options

Most Linux commands are flexible and can be modified to perform special tasks. You can use two devices to alter a command: command options and standard input and standard output redirection. You find out about command options first.

You can use *command options* to fine-tune the actions of a Linux command. We introduce the ls command earlier in this chapter so that you can see the results of actions taken on the file system. To see how its options work, in the next example, try out the ls command several times, with different options.

Use the mkdir command to make a new directory called vacation and then use the cd command to change your working directory to that new directory:

```
[lidia@veracruz emptydirectory]$ mkdir vacation
[lidia@veracruz emptydirectory]$ cd vacation
```

At the Linux prompt, type ls as follows:

```
[lidia@veracruz vacation]$ ls
[lidia@veracruz vacation]$
```

That didn't do much, did it? It seems as if the account has no files. You may need an option. Try the -a option and see what happens:

```
[lidia@veracruz vacation]$ ls -a
.  ..
[lidia@veracruz vacation]$
```

Remember to type the commands and options exactly as shown. For example, the ls -a command has a space between the command and the option, and no space between the hyphen and the letter *a*.

Notice the two files (they're actually directories, but in Linux all directories are just files) that the ls command displayed. What? All you see are dots? Well, the single dot represents the directory you are in; the double dot represents the parent directory, which is typically the one above the directory you're in. (Linux creates these filenames and puts them into the directory for you. If you just installed your directory, all you have are files that begin with a period.)

Next, create a few additional files in the vacation directory, by using the touch command:

```
[lidia@veracruz vacation]$ touch file1
[lidia@veracruz vacation]$ touch .dotfile
```

Now if you use the same `ls` command (without the -a option), you see the following:

```
[lidia@veracruz vacation]$ ls
file1
[lidia@veracruz vacation]$
```

And if you redo the `ls` command with the -a option, you get this:

```
[lidia@veracruz vacation]$ ls -a
... .dotfile  file1
[lidia@veracruz vacation]$
```

The `ls` command by default doesn't list files that begin with a period. By adding the -a option, you modify the action taken by `ls` to print every filename whether or not it begins with a dot.

The `ls` command has many options, and you can use more than one at a time. Want to see how? Modify the-a option by adding l to it. The command line becomes

```
[lidia@veracruz vacation]$ls -al
 total 5
drwx------ 3(username)(groupname)(filesize) Jul 04 14:33 ./
drwxr-xr-x 6 root    root    (filesize) Jul 04 22:15 ../
-rw-rw-r-- 1(username)(groupname)(filesize) Jul 04 11:30
           .dotfile
-rw-rw-r-- 1 (username)(groupname)(filesize) Jul 04 17:40
           file1
```

As you can see, instead of just listing the filenames, the l option shows a more detailed listing of files. If long listings don't fit on a single line, Linux just wraps them to the next line.

Most of the time, Linux doesn't care about what order you type the options and therefore considers `ls -al` and `ls -la` to be the same. Multiple option choices aren't available with all commands, however, and work only with commands that have single letters to specify their options.

The `ls` command lists files in alphabetical order as the default, but you can tailor the output. For example, `ls -alt` displays the files in order by date and time, with the most recent first; `ls -altr` reverses that order.

Letting bash's memory make your life easier

`bash` has a good memory. By default, `bash` remembers your last 500 commands. That function is very useful because it allows you to recycle your work. Several ways exist for recalling your past work, and this section describes how to do so.

Editing commands at the command line

One of the most useful bash features is *command-line editing,* which is the capability to change parts of a command line without having to retype the entire command. Suppose you type the following line:

```
[lidia@veracruz lidia]$ ls -l * | more
```

You actually meant to use the less command, not the more command, but you pressed Enter anyway.

You groan. You press Ctrl+C to halt the command. You would really like to reexecute the command, changing *more* to *less,* without having to type the entire command. Easy. Just do the following:

```
[lidia@veracruz lidia]$ ^more^less
```

This line resubmits the command to bash with more changed to less, as follows:

```
ls -l * | less
```

Output appears. If you have to stop the less command, press Q.

Note that the shell redisplays the first command with the change, and then the command is reexecuted. How does the shell know about the first command? History. bash remembers all the commands you have typed (to a certain extent) and allows you to edit and resubmit them. Awesome.

We say "to a certain extent" because bash remembers only a certain number of commands, depending on a parameter in the environment. After bash holds that many previous commands, it throws away the oldest ones as you type in newer ones. Normally, this parameter is large (perhaps 1,000 commands), so bash essentially remembers every command that you enter (We can't imagine ever wanting to be able to recall more than the last thousand commands that we entered).

Bang-bang!

The fact that the shell remembers the command lines you type is useful for reexecuting commands at a later time. Simple *reexecution commands* are represented by exclamation points. In computerese, an exclamation point is called a *bang,* and two exclamation points are called — you guessed it — *bang-bang.*

Here are two key ways to use the exclamation point:

- !! reexecutes the last command.
- !<partial command line> reexecutes the command line that started with *<partial command line>*.

Here's an example. Type **!cat** on the command line as follows (*cat* is the *<partial command line>* mentioned in the preceding list):

```
[lidia@veracruz lidia]$ !cat
```

bash searches backward through the previously executed commands in this session, looking for the first occurrence of a command line that starts with the letters *cat*. After the program locates the command, it is reexecuted.

A little timid about this? Perhaps your memory of which command you typed and when is a little faulty. Add :p to the command line to see what history finds. The command looks like this:

```
[lidia@veracruz lidia]$ !cat:p
cat /etc/passwd
```

To run the command that !:p found, enter bang-bang, like this:

```
[lidia@veracruz lidia]$ !!
```

While using history to find and reexecute command lines, you can also make additions to the command line. Starting from the beginning with our example, if you type the following:

```
[lidia@veracruz lidia]$ cat /etc/passwd
```

the file /etc/passwd is output to standard output, which in this case is the screen.

When you reexecute the preceding command by typing !!, you can also send the output to the sort command by using the pipe symbol:

```
[lidia@veracruz lidia]$ !! | sort
cat /etc/passwd |sort
[lidia@veracruz lidia]$
```

Linux pulls the /etc/passwd file from the disk and passes it to standard output, feeds it into the standard input of sort, and then outputs it to the screen in sorted fashion.

The bash shell also makes use of the up-arrow and down-arrow keys to reuse commands. The up-arrow key sequentially returns commands starting from the most recent. The down-arrow key, not surprisingly, goes forward in time. This is bash's most convenient feature.

This history command displays all the commands that you have used up to the Red Hat default of 1,000. You can use the history command to perform a sort of archaeological dig. For instance, if you want to see all the commands of a certain type that you have used, then you can pipe the output of the history command to the grep filter. To find all the times that you have entered the `ls` command, you can use the command: `history | grep ls`.

Several shells (such as `csh`, `bash`, `tcsh`, and `zsh`) have this type of simple editing, but `bash` also has more elaborate editing.

Back to the future

Linux offers a handy tool for rerunning long commands that you've already entered. Press Ctrl+P, and the display scrolls though the commands that you've entered, one command at a time in reverse order, showing the most recent command first. When the command you want appears on the screen, just press Enter to run it.

Recalling file names

Suppose your mind has been wandering, and although you do remember that a file in /etc contains passwords, you can't remember whether the file is in /etc/passwd, /etc/password, or whatever. You may want the command interpreter to choose the proper spelling of the filename for you, rather than type what you think it may be.

You can first list the files in the /etc directory, and then use `more` to view the specific file you want to see (/etc/passwd):

```
[lidia@veracruz lidia]$ ls /etc/pass*
/etc/passwd
[lidia@veracruz lidia]$ more /etc/passwd
```

Or you can use a shortcut with `bash` by pressing the Tab key after you think you have a unique match:

```
[lidia@veracruz lidia]$ more /etc/pass<TAB>
```

The shell automatically expands the name of the file to /etc/passwd and then hesitates to see whether you want to accept the command:

```
[lidia@veracruz lidia]$ more /etc/passwd
```

When the shell automatically expands a filename and then hesitates, waiting for you to confirm a command by pressing the Enter key, this action is known as *command completion*. Now you can press the Enter key to execute the command.

But wait! What happens if you have two files, one /etc/passwd and the other /etc/password? When you press the Tab key, the system rings the bell, and the name doesn't expand. Press the Tab key a second time, and bash shows you all the possible expansions of that argument. If a huge number of expansions result, bash warns you:

```
#Press tab twice after typing the first line below.
[lidia@veracruz gifs]$ ls p
There are 255 possibilities. Do you really
wish to see them all? (y or n)
```

Chapter 15

Becoming a Suit: Managing the Red Hat Linux File System

*M*anaging the Linux file system is not a complex job but it is an important one. You have the responsibility of managing the Red Hat Linux file system and ensuring that users (even if you're the only user) have access to secure, uncorrupted data. You are the manager — yes, a suit — of your file system.

This chapter introduces you to managing your Linux file system. Consider yourself a management trainee.

Mounting and Dismounting

Red Hat Linux, and other Unix-like operating systems, use files in ways that are different from MS-DOS, Windows, and Macintosh operating systems. In Linux, *everything* is stored as files in predictable locations in the directory structure — Linux even stores commands as files. Like other modern operating systems, Linux has a tree-structured, hierarchical, directory organization called a *file system*.

All user-available disk space is combined in a single directory tree. The base of this system is the *root directory* (not to be confused with the root user), which is designated with a slash, /. A file system's contents are made available to Linux by merging the file system into the system directory through a process called *mounting.* This is just like mounting a horse except that no horse is involved.

File systems can be mounted or dismounted, which means that file systems can be connected or disconnected to the directory tree. The exception is the *root file system,* which is always mounted on the root directory when the system is running and cannot be dismounted. Other file systems may be mounted as needed, such as ones contained on another hard drive, a floppy disk, or a CD-ROM.

Mounting an MS-DOS file system

The following steps show you how to mount a file system. With a few simple clicks, you can become master of your own domain.

1. **Log in as root. Insert an MS-DOS formatted floppy into the drive.**

2. **Click the the Main Menu Button and choose Programs⇨System⇨ LinuxConf.**

   The Linuxconf window appears, as shown in Figure 15-1.

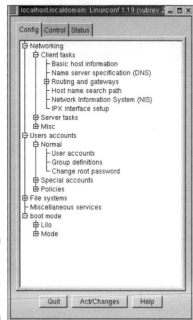

Figure 15-1:
The
Linuxconf
dialog box.

3. **Click the File Systems button.**

   The Filesystem configurator window appears, as shown in Figure 15-2.

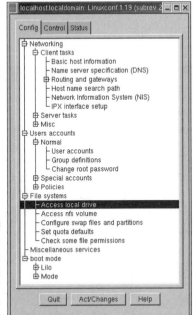

Figure 15-2:
The
Filesystem
configurator
window.

4. **Click Access Local Drive.**

   The Local volume window appears, as shown in Figure 15-3.

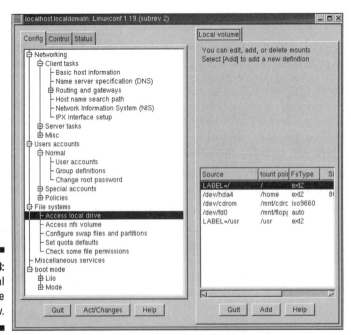

Figure 15-3:
The Local
volume
window.

5. **Click the Add button.**

The Volume specification window appears, as shown in Figure 15-4.

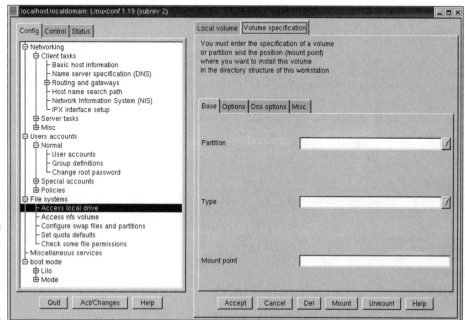

Figure 15-4:
The Volume specifi-
cation
window.

6. **Type** /dev/fd0 **in the Partition text box.**

You are not limited to mounting MS-DOS floppy disk file systems (the floppy is used because it's an example that is likely to be available to you if you're using your entire hard drive for Red Hat Linux.) You can mount the MS-DOS/Windows partition on your hard drive if you have set your computer up as a dual-boot system. All you have to do is substitute the /dev/fd0 device file with whatever your Windows partition uses. For instance, you may use the device file /dev/hda1 if you have Windows installed on the first partition of your IDE hard drive.

7. **Click the button to the right of the Type text box and select msdos from the drop-down list box.**

8. **Type** /mnt/floppy **in the Mount Point text box.**

You can also use these instructions to mount a CD-ROM. For instance, you can try mounting CD1. In that case, instead of specifying the /dev/fd0 device file in Step 6, you use /dev/cdrom instead. In Step 7, choose the iso9660 or msdos file system depending on what type of CD you have — the Red Hat Linux CDs are iso9660. Finally, use /mnt/cdrom as the mount point in Step 8.

9. **Click the Accept button and the MS-DOS-formatted floppy file system configuration is saved.**

    Accepting the configuration changes the /etc/fstab file. The fstab file stores the mounting information for storages devices, such as your hard drive and CD-ROM, attached to your Red Hat Linux computer. Canceling the configuration leaves the file as it was. If you make no changes, you can click Cancel.

10. **Next click the Mount button.**

    A simple dialog box opens and you are prompted to continue. Click Yes to continue and No to stop the mount process.

11. **Click Yes.**

    Your disk is mounted. (If mounting fails for any reason, a status window with the pertinent information appears. You can return to the previous menu by clicking the OK button.)

Mounting provides a good example of the difference between Linux and MS-DOS/Windows. If you use a floppy or CD with Windows, you just insert it into the drive and immediately have access to it. With Linux, you must insert the floppy into the drive and then explicitly mount it. Sounds complicated? Not really. Red Hat Linux and GNOME are configured to automatically start the process that mounts your floppy or CD when you insert it into the drive. We've presented the manual method here to show you how the process works.

You can use the preceding steps to mount any other file systems. For instance, if you install Red Hat Linux on a hard drive along with Windows, you can mount the Windows partition. Use Steps 6, 7, and 8 to specify the Windows partition. Specify the appropriate Windows partition, type, and mount point.

You can manually mount the floppy by running the following command from a bash shell.

```
mount _t msdos /dev/fd0 /mnt/floppy
```

A directory that is used as a mount point is just like any other directory — it can store files and other directories. But any files or directories stored in a directory used as a mount point is not visible or usable until the file system mounted on that directory is unmounted. (For more on unmounting files, see the "Unmounting file systems" section later in this chapter.)

Configuring file systems

The preceding section describes how to mount a file system. But those instructions assume that you're mounting a vanilla — your average PC — system. You can, however, specify other options. You can choose different options by clicking the Options tab in the Volume Specification window.

Here's a short description of each option:

- ✔ **Read-only:** The partition is mounted as read-only. You can not write to the file system.

- ✔ **User mountable:** When set, any user in addition to root can mount the partition. This is useful when regular users must be able to mount devices such as CDs and floppy disks.

- ✔ **Mountable by device owner:** A regular user that owns the device file (for instance, /dev/fd0) can mount the file system.

- ✔ **Not mount at boot time:** Red Hat Linux does not automatically mount the file system when it boots.

- ✔ **No program allowed to execute:** A regular user is not allowed to execute files found on a file system. You may want to allow a regular user to mount a device (like a CD), but not execute programs on them for security reasons.

- ✔ **No special device file support:** The device files found in the /dev directory are created with very specific permissions in order to enhance system security. This option prevents other, nonsecure device files from being used to mount a file system.

- ✔ **No setuid programs allowed:** This is a very important security feature. When an executable Linux file has its setuid bit set, it can be run by a regular user who belongs to the same group. If root owns the file, then whatever that file does is done with all the power of root. Files with setuid permission often present big security holes. Setting this option prevents any files found on the file system from exercising their setuid privileges.

- ✔ **User quota enabled:** This enables Linux quotas to be exercised. Quotas allow limits being set on what resources individual users can access.

- ✔ **Group quota enabled:** This enables quotas to be set for groups.

Unmounting file systems

Unmounting a Linux file system is a little simpler than mounting one. Because the file system is already mounted, you don't have to specify any options or other information. You just have to tell LinuxConf to unmount.

Be careful though. You never want to mount a hard drive-based file system like /, /usr, or /home. That sends your Red Hat Linux computer into never-never land. You must, however, unmount removable drives, like a CD-ROM or floppy disk, before removing them. You can also safely unmount a Windows partition because Red Hat Linux doesn't use it for any system-based purpose — you only mount a Windows partition when you're using that operating system.

To unmount a file system, follow these steps:

1. **Log in as root.**

2. **Click the Main Menu button and choose Programs⇨System⇨ LinuxConf.**

   The Linuxconf window appears.

3. **Click the File Systems button.**

   The Filesystem configurator window appears.

4. **Click Access Local Drive.**

   The Local volume window appears.

5. **Click the file system that you want to unmount.**

   The Volume specification window appears.

6. **Click the Unmount button.**

   The Unmount file system window appears.

7. **Click Yes.**

   An Unmount success window appears.

8. **Click OK.**

   Your file system is unmounted. You can now remove your floppy disk or CD.

You can run the `eject` command from a `bash` shell to eject a CD from its drive. You have to unmount the CD first, and then enter the `eject` command. Otherwise, to eject a CD, you must unmount it and then press the eject button on the CD-ROM drive. In either case, you can not eject the CD until you've unmounted it.

Sending Corrupted File Systems to Reform School

You can corrupt file systems by turning off your computer without properly shutting down Red Hat Linux. Corruption can also occur via a driver error or a hardware crash. The type of corruption that occurs when you incorrectly turn off your computer is generally not serious. You shouldn't push fate, however, and avoid even mild corruption.

The `fsck` utility checks Linux file systems. `fsck` reports errors and makes some repairs. Normally, the `fsck` program is called automatically when your system boots. Therefore, if your system crashes, `fsck` runs on all file systems that were mounted when the system crashed.

You can run `fsck` manually — as opposed to having the boot process run it automatically. In some cases, you must run it manually because it needs to prompt you during the process. Please note that the `fsck` utility can't help if you have corrupted data in a structurally intact file. Also, remember that except for the root file system, `fsck` runs on only unmounted file systems. You must make sure that the system is in single-user mode to use `fsck` on the root file system.

Here's the syntax for the `fsck` command:

```
fsck (options) filesystem
```

`filesystem` names the block special file where the file system resides. If `filesystem` is omitted, the `fsck` utility checks all the file systems listed in the `/etc/fstab` file configuration file. If the `fsck` utility finds any errors, it prompts you for input on what to do about the errors. For the most part, you simply agree with whatever the program suggests.

The `fsck` command has the following options:

- ✔ -p   Preen the file system. Perform automatic repairs that don't change the contents of files.

- ✔ -n   Answer no to all prompts and only list problems; don't repair them.

- ✔ -y   Answer yes to all prompts and repair damage regardless of how severe.

- ✔ -f   Force a file system check.

Many people run the `fsck` command with the -y option. If you run `fsck` with the -p option, Linux performs some steps automatically. Lost files are placed in the `lost+found` directory, zero-length files are deleted, and missing blocks are placed back on the list of *free blocks,* which are blocks still available for filling with data, among other things.

Adding More Drive Storage

Sooner or later, you're likely to want to add more hard drive storage to your Linux system to hold more programs, to hold more data, or to enable more users to log in. You usually increase drive storage by adding one or more drives at a time; each drive can have one or more drive partitions.

The drive partition is Linux's basic file storage unit. First, you create the file systems on the drive partitions, and then you combine the file systems to form a single directory tree structure. The directory tree structure can be on one drive or spread across many.

You can define drive partitions when adding a new drive or sometime later. In most cases, Linux defines drive partitions during the original Linux installation. You may divide a drive into one, two, four, or more partitions, each of which may contain a file system or may be used as a swap partition. Swap partitions allow very large programs or many small programs to run even if they take up more memory than you have as RAM in your computer. The total of all your swap partitions and RAM is called *virtual memory*.

After you create a drive partition, you must create a file system. The file system occupies a single space on the drive that has a unique block special file (device) name. This unique name accesses the file system regardless of whether the data is stored on all or only part of a physical drive or is an aggregation of multiple physical drives.

Adding a Disk Drive

The first step to increasing your drive space is to add a new disk drive. The following tasks are required to add a drive to your system (regardless of whether the drive is SCSI or IDE) and make it accessible to users:

 ✔ Attach the disk drive to your computer system.

 ✔ Provide a suitable device driver for the drive's controller in Linux. Completing this task may mean rebuilding the kernel of the Linux operating system (see Chapter 14 for details).

 ✔ Define at least one partition.

 ✔ Create the block special files for the partition(s).

 ✔ Create a Linux file system(s) on any partition(s) to be used for user files.

 ✔ Enter the new file systems into /etc/fstab, the configuration file.

 ✔ Mount the file systems (you may have to make a directory for a mount point).

The following sections guide you through the process of configuring a hard drive, a floppy drive, and a CD-ROM drive after they are physically installed.

Configuring a hard drive

The business of adding a hard drive to your microcomputer can be broken down into two steps:

 ✔ Physically adding the hard drive
 ✔ Logically making Linux aware of it

The first step is beyond the scope of this book, because your drive may be either IDE or SCSI, and the setup of the physical drive is dependent on the rest of the hardware in the system. We suggest that you consult the hardware manual that came with your system or have a computer reseller install your new hard drive. The Linux system is complicated by the fact that several operating systems — such as DOS, Linux, and SCO Unix — may share the same hard drive.

 To complete all the steps necessary to install and configure your new drive, you must know the total formatted drive capacity and the number of heads and cylinders, among other details. You can usually find this information in the documentation or from the manufacturer.

You may want to keep a record of the data from the partition table (as displayed by fdisk), such as

- Partition numbers
- Type
- Size
- Starting and ending blocks

Installing a drive

After the drive is attached to the system, Linux should recognize it when you boot. To review the booting messages in a slower fashion than they're displayed, use the dmesg command. If you added a new IDE drive, look for the mention of a new hdx drive, where the *x* is replaced with the letter *b, c, d,* or *e.* This information tells you that your kernel saw the new hard drive as it booted, and rebuilding the kernel is not necessary in order to add this drive. Likewise, if you're adding a new SCSI disk drive, you see a boot message indicating a new disk drive that has the designation sdx, where the *x* is a letter. In the IDE or SCSI case, you may see other messages with additional information.

The messages for an IDE drive may look like this:

```
hdb: HITACHI_DK227A-50, 4789MB w/512KB Cache,CHS=610/255/63
```

And sometime later, a message appears that looks like the following, which describes the existing partitions on the new drive (if any):

```
hdb: hdb1 hdb2 < hdb5 hdb6 hdb7 hdb8 >
```

A SCSI disk drive has messages that look like this:

```
SCSI device sdb: hdwr device= .......
  sdb: sdb1
```

If you see these messages, the kernel has seen your new drive, and you don't have to rebuild the kernel to use the new drive.

The Linux distribution on the companion CD-ROM features block special files for each of eight IDE disks (had – hdh) with nine partitions each (1 – 9). Linux also has block special files for seven SCSI hard drives (sda – sdg), which can have eight partitions each (1 – 8). In addition, Linux has a block special file for a SCSI CD-ROM (scd) with eight partitions (0 – 7). If you have lots of drives, or if your Linux distribution doesn't have enough block special files for your drive, you may have to create one or more additional block special files for the device, like this:

```
cd /dev; makedev sdg
```

This command creates the block special files for SCSI drive 7. Note that in both IDE and SCSI drives, the letters and drive numbers correspond: *a* is for the first disk, *b* is for the second disk, and so on.

If you add a SCSI disk drive with a lower ID number than one you already have, the new disk drive takes on that number. Suppose you have SCSI disk drives with hardware ID numbers of 0, 2, and 3. Linux gives these drives the names sda, sdb, and sdc, respectively. You make your partitions and your file systems, and create your entries in /etc/fstab to show where you want the file systems mounted. Now you get a new disk drive and set the hardware ID number to 1. When you reboot, the new disk drive gets the sdb designation and the disk drives with ID numbers of 2 and 3 are renamed to sdc and sdd, respectively. You must now, at the very least, change your /etc/fstab table. For this reason, we recommend adding SCSI disk drives to your system, starting with ID 0 and working up the number chain, with no gaps in the numbering.

Partitioning a drive

After you've created block special files, you can use fdisk to partition the drive. The command to call this utility is /usr/bin/fdisk. For example, if you want to invoke fdisk for partitioning the first IDE drive, you type the following command:

```
fdisk /dev/hda
```

Using fdisk is not too difficult; you can partition the drive fairly easily. We don't discuss it in this book though.

Making the file system

Every drive partition is simply an empty space with a beginning and an end. Unless the partition is being used for swap space, you have to put some type of file system on the partition before it can become useful. The mkfs (for make file system) command is used to create the file system on the partition. Normally, the file system is a native Linux file system, which at this time is called ext2. The Linux version of mkfs has been nicely streamlined and requires hardly any input. To create a file system on the disk drive partition sda1, for example, you type the following command:

```
mkfs -t ext2 /dev/sda1
```

Or, for an IDE drive, type this command:

```
mkfs -t ext2 /dev/hda1
```

If you want to create an MS-DOS file system on the drive partition, you use this command:

```
mkfs -t msdos /dev/sda2
```

You can continue to execute mkfs commands to create file systems for every partition on your new drive. Or you can leave some partitions without file systems (for future use), as long as you remember to perform the mkfs command on them before trying to attach them to your file system by using the mount command or the /etc/fstab table.

Congratulations! Your drive has been physically added to your system and partitioned, and you've added file systems to it. Now the drive is ready to join the rest of the file system — simply use either the mount command or the /etc/fstab file, which we describe earlier in this chapter.

Chapter 16

Revving Up the RPM

. . . .

In This Chapter

▶ Introducing RPM

▶ Finding out what RPM does

▶ Installing, updating, removing, querying, and verifying software with `gnorpm`

▶ Comparing RPM to `tar`

. . . .

This chapter introduces the Red Hat Package Manager (RPM). Red Hat, Inc. developed RPM in conjunction with another Linux distributor, Caldera Systems. It provides a mechanism for installing, updating, and removing software automatically. Without RPM, Linux would be not be where it is today and is a big reason why Red Hat is the de facto Linux distribution leader.

Introducing RPM

One of the primary reasons that the Red Hat Linux distribution became popular was that it added value for its customers. One such area was the Red Hat Package Manager (RPM). When Linux distributors, such as Red Hat, create a system like RPM, they provide value to their customers and make Open Source software profitable. The first Linux system that we used professionally required us to install all the software via the tape archive system (`tar`), and it was a bear to modify. RPM, on the other hand, accelerates like crazy as you wind out its engine and yet is quite easy to manage.

All the software that was installed during the Red Hat installation process is stored in RPM form. The `/mnt/cdrom/RedHat/RPMS` directory contains all the RPM packages. You can also install, update, or uninstall software. As of this writing, RPM is the most popular system for installing, modifying, and transporting Linux software.

The package-management concept has been around for quite a while, with all the major Unix vendors supplying their own systems. The idea is to distribute software in a single package and have a package manager do the work of installing or uninstalling, and managing the individual files. The Linux world has benefited greatly from this system that simplifies the distribution and use of software.

Taking a Look at What RPM Does

RPM performs three basic functions: installing, upgrading, and removing packages. In addition to these functions, it also can find out all sorts of information about installed and yet-to-be installed packages (and it also washes windows). Here's a brief rundown of each function:

- **Installing packages.** RPM installs software. Software systems such as Netscape have files of all types that must be put into certain locations in order to work properly. For example, under Red Hat, some of the Netscape files need to go into the /usr/bin directory. RPM does that organizational stuff automatically. Not only does RPM install files into their proper directories, but it also does such things as create the directories and run scripts to do the things that need to be done.

- **Upgrading packages.** RPM can update existing software packages for you. Gone are the days when updating a system was worse than going to the dentist. RPM keeps track — in a database of it's own — of all the packages that you have installed. When you upgrade a package, RPM does all of the bookkeeping chores and replaces only the files that need to be replaced. It also saves the configuration files that it replaces.

- **Removing packages.** The package database that the RPM keeps is also useful in removing packages. RPM goes to each file and uninstalls it. Directories belonging to the package are also removed when no files from other packages occupy them.

- **Querying packages and files.** RPM can also give you a great deal of information about a package and its files. You can use the query function to find out the function of a package and what files belong to it. It can also work on the RPM packages themselves, regardless of whether they have been installed.

- **Verifying packages.** Installed packages can be validated. RPM can check an installed package against a checksum (a computered fingerprint) to see if and how it has been changed. This feature is very useful for security reasons. If you suspect that a file or system has been hacked, you can use RPM to find out how it has changed.

Using GNOME RPM

Red Hat Linux provides a great tool called GNOME RPM for working with RPM packages. GNOME RPM, also called `gnorpm`, is a graphical tool that provides all the functions for managing RPMs. It's like putting automatic transmission on a car — GNOME RPM does the shifting for you.

Well, GNOME RPM does the shifting for you but you still have to drive it. But enough car talk. GNOME RPM provides easy access to RPM functions such as install, upgrade, uninstall, query, and verify. The following sections describe how to use GNOME RPM to rev up your RPM.

Starting GNOME RPM

To start GNOME RPM, click the Main Menu button and choose Programs➪ System➪ GNOME RPM. If you're not logged in as root, then you must either type the root password when prompted in the Input window (see Figure 16-1) or else run it in unprivileged mode. If you run in nonprivileged mode, you can use the query and verify functions but you can not install, upgrade, or uninstall packages. Typing the root password causes the GNOME RPM window to appear, as shown in Figure 16-2.

Figure 16-1:
The Input window prompts you for the root password.

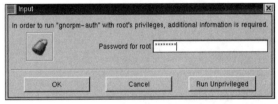

GNOME RPM displays all the Red Hat RPMs that are uninstalled on your system by default. The individual packages are organized into groups such as Amusements, Applications, and so on. Click the plus [+] sign to the left of each group folder icon to see the contents of the packages. For example, clicking Applications➪Multimedia shows you all of the multimedia packages that are not installed on your system as shown in Figure 16-3.

This may be a Dummies book but you, of course, are no dummy. It's obvious what the GNOME RPM buttons, displayed along the top of the GNOME RPM window are used for. The following sections describe how to use them for their intended function.

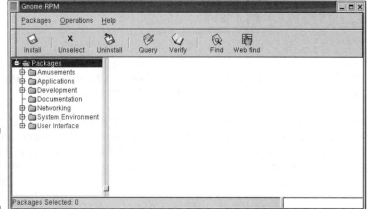

Figure 16-2:
The GNOME
RPM main
window.

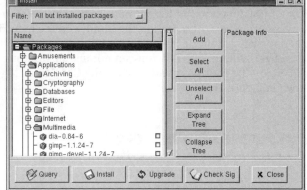

Figure 16-3:
The
uninstalled
Multimedia
group
packages
window.

Installing an RPM package from a CD-ROM

When you install your Red Hat Linux system, all the software that is copied to your hard drive from the CD-ROM comes from RPM packages. When you want to add additional software from the companion CD-ROM or an RPM repository such as www.freshmeat.net, or Red Hat itself at www.redhat.com, you can do so by using the Install button. To install an RPM package from a CD-ROM, follow these steps:

1. **Insert CD1 that came with this book in the CD-ROM drive.**

2. **Start GNOME RPM by clicking the Main Menu button and choosing Programs⇨System⇨GnoRPM.**

   If you're not logged in as the root user, then you're prompted to enter the root password in the Input dialog box that pops up (refer to Figure 16-1). Only root can install RPM packages.

3. **Type the root password into the dialog box.**

4. **Click the Install button.**

   GNOME RPM reads the CD-ROM and displays the RPMs, organized by group. By default, GNOME RPM displays uninstalled packages.

5. **If you want to display other types of packages you can click the Filter button at the top of the Install window and change to another option.**

   For example, you can display all of the RPM packages on CD1 by selecting the All Packages option, as shown in Figure 16-4.

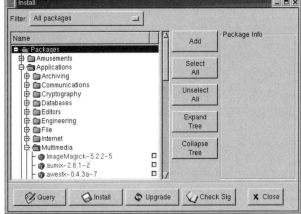

Figure 16-4:
The Install window with the All Packages filter selected.

6. **Select a package or packages from the groups.**

   For example, you can click Applications, click Communications, and then click the `pilot-link` package (which reads the digital audio directly from a CD), as shown in Figure 16-5. (If you double-click a package that is not yet installed, then it is automatically installed.)

7. **The Installing window appears to provide the status of the process while it occurs.**

   After the package finishes installing, you can connect your PalmPilot and download/upload address books, calendars, and submarine games to your heart's content (Chapter 12 describes the process in detail).

Figure 16-5:
Selecting a
package for
installation.

Installing an RPM package from the Internet

What happens if you want to install a package that is not on one of this book's CD-ROMs? GNOME RPM provides for that by enabling you to automatically search the Internet for RPM packages and install them! This is pretty cool since in the old days of, say 1999, you had to search the Internet with your browser, sort through myriad search results for the one that matched what you actually wanted, download the file(s), and then use the `rpm` — the manual version of `gnorpm` described later in this chapter — command to install it. That long process is now greatly simplified. To install an RPM package from the Internet, follow these steps:

1. **Insert the Red Hat Linux CD1 disc in the CD-ROM drive.**

2. **Start GNOME RPM by clicking the Main Menu button and choosing Programs⇨System⇨GnoRPM.**

3. **If you're not logged in as the superuser, then you're prompted to enter the root password in the dialog box that pops up. Only root can install RPM packages. Type the root password.**

4. **Click the Web Find button.**

   GNOME RPM goes out onto the Web and downloads a file from `www.redhat.com/RDF`. (You need to be connected to the Internet for this to work.) This file stores a list of all the RPM packages that Red Hat knows about. The Rpmfind window appears, as shown in Figure 16-6.

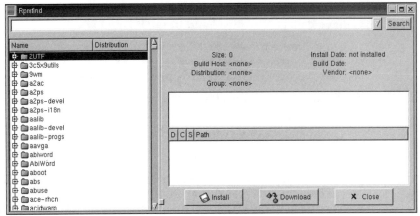

Figure 16-6:
The Rpmfind
window.

5. **Use the mouse to move up and down the list of available packages. Click the package that you want to install. Alternatively, you can enter a word in the text box at the top of the screen, click the Search button, and the package is found for you (if it exists).**

   Check out the `rplay` package, for example. This is a streaming audio package being developed under the GNU Public License — any one can use the package and redistribute it as long as they don't put any additional restrictions on it. `rplay` isn't quite ready for prime time yet, but we expect it to be useful in the future. Clicking `rplay` causes its various versions to appear.

6. **When you click a specific package, the information about it appears in the subwindow on the right side of the screen as shown in Figure 16-7.**

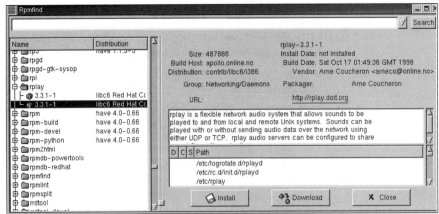

Figure 16-7:
Information
about a
package is
displayed.

7. **You can either download the package, in order to install it later, or have** gnorpm **download and install it automatically.**

   If you choose the former, click the Download button and then install it after it's downloaded. Otherwise, click the Install button and gnorpm does the work for you; it also provides a progress screen along the way.

8. **When you finish installing packages, click the Close button to exit the window.**

   You can play around with your package after installation. It's as simple as that!

If you like to roll your own, you can use the rpm command to install packages. The -i parameter indicates that an installation is to take place. You can also have rpm run in verbose (a lot of information) mode by using the -v option. (Note that you can combine options into a single group — for example -i -v can become -iv). To add the package, type the following command:

```
rpm -iv /mnt/cdrom/RedHat/RPMS/pilot-link*
```

You can upgrade a package that already has been installed on your system. Follow the instructions in the previous sections that describe installing RPMs from a CD-ROM and the Internet. Click the Upgrade button instead of the Install button and the existing package is upgraded.

Removing an RPM package

You may want to remove an RPM package. RPM packages are good residents on your computer because they lend themselves to easy removal. gnorpm permits you to remove packages via the uninstall function. To remove an RPM package, follow these steps:

1. **Start GNOME RPM by clicking the Main Menu button button and choosing Programs⇨System⇨GnoRPM.**

2. **If you're not logged in as the root user, the Input dialog box pops up and you're prompted to enter the root password, which you should do.**

3. **The GNOME RPM window opens up. Click any of the package groups and then any of the subgroups. The individual packages are displayed.**

4. **Click on the package that you want to remove — like that in Figure 16-8 — to select it.**

5. **Click the Uninstall button.**

   The Continue Removal window appears to confirm the removal process.

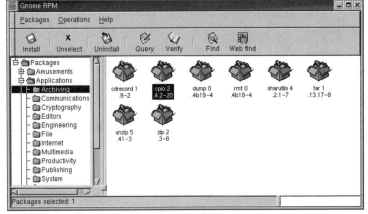

Figure 16-8:
Selecting a
package to
remove.

6. **Click Yes to remove the package.**

   Clicking No simply returns you to the main GNOME RPM window with no harm done.

7. **When you finish removing packages, click the Close button to exit the window.**

If you remove a package and realize that you didn't want to, then you have — in most cases — done very little harm. The beauty of installing everything on your Red Hat Linux computer from RPM packages is that you can easily reinstall any package.

Even if you remove the Linux kernel — the heart of your Red Hat Linux computer — you can still recover. As long as you don't turn off or reboot your computer, no harm occurs. That's because the kernel is running in memory (RAM) at all times. You can also reinstall most other packages without consequences. If only that were true for other things in life.

You access the uninstall function via the RPM erase option (-e). For example, the following command removes the Samba software from :

```
rpm -e samba
```

Sometimes, however, other package files occupy the same directories of the package that you want to delete. In these cases, you get a message saying that the directory cannot be deleted because it is not empty.

Getting information about an RPM package

After installing a package — for example, pilot-link —, you can find out information about the contents of the package by using the `gnorpm query` function. To use this function, follow these steps:

1. **Start GNOME RPM by clicking the Main Menu button and choosing Programs⇨System⇨GnoRPM.**

    You do not have to enter the root password when prompted in the Input window. GNOME RPM allows the non-root user to query packages.

2. **Click the Run Unprivileged button (sometimes it's necessary to click the button three times before it understands your desire) if you don't intend to install, upgrade, or uninstall a package.**

    The RPM package groups appear on the left side of the window.

3. **Click the group folder icon on the left side of the window.**

    The icon expands to show you the subgroups that contain the individual packages.

4. **Click a subgroup and then the package to be queried.**

    For example, choose Applications⇨Communications⇨Pilot-link.

    You can also use the Find button at the top of the page to locate packages to be queried. If you want to query uninstalled packages that reside on the CD-ROM, then insert the disc and wait for it to be mounted.

5. **After you select a package, click the Query button at the top of the window.**

    Information appears about when and where the package was created, what it does, and what files it contains, as shown in Figure 16-9.

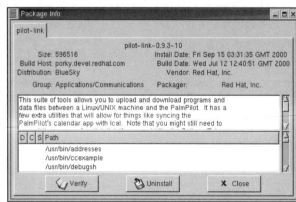

Figure 16-9:
The GNOME
RPM
window.

You can perform a query manually. The `rpm` command can return information about an RPM package. You can use the command as follows:

```
rpm -qi howto-html
```

By varying the query options, you can also list the files in the package, list all installed packages, and so on. Consult the RPM man page for more information.

Verifying RPM packages

You may need to verify that an installed package is what it says it is. You may, for example, think that a package isn't working correctly. Whatever your reason, `gnorpm` provides a `verify` function. To use this function, follow these steps:

1. **Start GNOME RPM by clicking the Main Menu button and choosing Programs⇨System⇨GnoRPM.**

2. **You do not have to enter the root password when prompted in the Input window.**

   GNOME RPM allows the non-root user to query packages.

3. **Click the Run Unprivileged button (sometimes it's necessary to click the button three times before it understands your desire) if you don't intend to install, upgrade, or uninstall a package.**

   RPM package groups are shown in the left half of the `gnorpm` window.

4. **Click the group folder icon and then the subgroup icon.**

   The individual packages icons are displayed.

5. **Click the package to be verified and click the Verify button at the top of the screen.**

   GNOME RPM checks the fingerprint of every file that belongs to the package against a known copy. Progress appears in the Verifying Packages window. When the program finishes, it displays information about what — if any — differences between the known and existing fingerprints exist. Figure 16-10 shows a sample window.

The Verifying Packages window tells you if any files in a package that have been changed or don't exist. It lists any changes in the files that belong to the package. For example, the first time that you add or delete a user account, the `/etc/passwd` file is modified.

The `rpm` command can also verify information about installed packages and their files. This is a very useful system administration tool. For example, if you're in doubt about the configuration file — suppose you accidentally removed the `/usr/bin/pilot-clip` file, then you can run this command:

```
rpm -V pilot-link
```

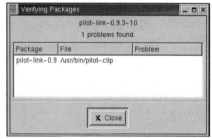

Figure 16-10:
The GNOME
RPM
Verifying
Packages
window.

The pilot-link RPM package keeps a `checksum` and compares the state of the installed files against it. The command returns

```
missing      /usr/bin/pilot-clip
```

which shows you that the `pilot-clip` file has been removed.

Modifying GNOME RPM defaults

You can modify the GNOME RPM defaults by choosing Operations⇨Preferences from the GNOME RPM window as shown in Figure 16-11. The following list shows some of the primary functions that you can alter:

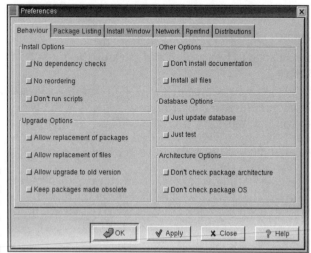

Figure 16-11:
The
Preferences
window.

✔ Behavior

✔ Package listing

✔ Install window

    ✔ Network

    ✔ Rpmfind

    ✔ Distributions

The following sections describe some of the more interesting and useful functions in each of the main systems.

Behaviour

The individual files that make up an RPM package often can simply be copied to their respective directories. Sometimes, however, more work is required. For example, some RPM packages require that a script be run after the files are copied to complete the installation. The following options are available in the GNOME RPM Install Options section of the Preferences window:

✔ **No dependency checks on installations:** To work correctly, some packages require that other packages be installed. RPM normally checks to see if all such packages — dependencies — exist before installing. You can, however, turn off that check if desired.

✔ **Don't run scripts:** RPM runs scripts, when they exist, after installing the software contained in a package. You can turn that off by selecting this option.

✔ **Don't reorder packages:** Sometimes you need to change the order that packages are installed. Another package may need to be installed first to satisfy a dependency.

✔ **Upgrade Options defaults:** You should never need to change these options.

✔ **Don't install documentation:** You can choose not to install README, docs, and other files by selecting this option.

✔ **Install all files:** Clicking this option installs all the files in a package.

✔ **Just update database:** This option updates the RPM database file but does not install any files.

✔ **Just test:** This option sees if the package can be installed. When you use this option and select a package to be installed, for example, then the process is started but nothing is installed.

✔ **Don't check package architecture:** Most RPM packages are dependent on the type of processor that your computer uses. For example, the packages on the Red Hat installation CDs shipped with this book can be used on Intel-based computers only.

✔ **Don't check package OS:** GNOME RPM does not check the operating system (OS) that the package is set to use.

Package listing

This is a really difficult set of options to understand. You can display packages as icons or as a list. Decisions, decisions.

Install window

Gnome RPM color-codes the packages that it displays based on their status. Older packages are gray, current ones green, and new ones blue. You can change those colors to your taste.

Gnome RPM automatically looks to your CD-ROM drive to find packages. The default directory is `/mnt/cdrom/RedHat/RPMS`. You can change that by clicking the Install Window tab in the Preferences window and editing the Default File Selection Dialog Path text box shown in Figure 16-12.

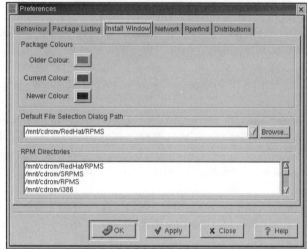

Figure 16-12:
The Default File Selection Dialog Path text box.

GNOME RPM also has a list of secondary directories to search when the Red Hat installation CD is not mounted. The secondary paths are listed in the RPM Directories window. The first entries show common CD-ROM directories, while the last ones point to your hard drive. You can change those entries to point to other locations.

Network

If your Red Hat Linux workstation is on a network that uses a proxying firewall, then you have to configure GNOME RPM to work with it. (A proxying firewall is a device that prevents unauthorized people from connecting to your network.) You can configure GNOME RPM to use a proxying firewall by choosing Operations⇨Preference. When the Preferences window opens, click the Network tab and the window shown in Figure 16-13 appears.

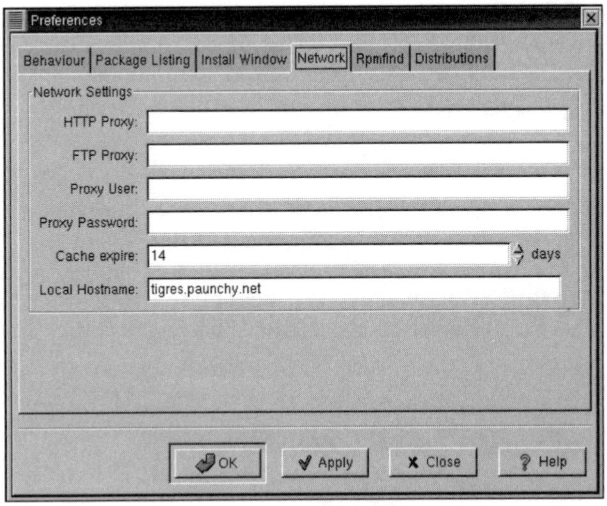

Figure 16-13:
The GNOME
RPM
Network
window.

You must type the host name of the proxy in the HTTP Proxy field. The host name looks something like myproxy.mynet.com, as shown in Figure 16-14. Sometimes packages are downloaded by FTP, and you may need to type the host name of the FTP Proxy in the corresponding field. If your proxying fire- wall requires a username and password, then type them in the Proxy User and Proxy Password fields.

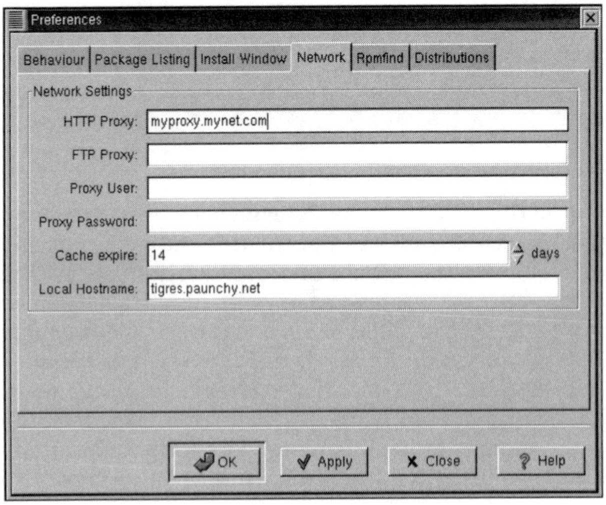

Figure 16-14:
The firewall
information.

GNOME RPM keeps a cache of download sites that you've accessed. You can change the length of time that it saves this information by changing the cache expire entry. Finally, GNOME RPM lists your local hostname in the field by that name. You rarely need to change your hostname.

Rpmfind

The Rpmfind window, shown in Figure 16-15, controls RPM find and download capabilities. The default server is located on Red Hat's Web site. This may change over time or other (better?) servers may pop up. Well, you have the power to change it here by changing the location to which your downloads are saved. One common location to save RPM packages is the `/usr/local/src` directory.

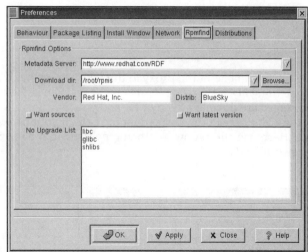

Figure 16-15: The Rpmfind window.

Until the advent of the RPM (and the Debian package manager on Debian Linux systems), Linux software was only distributed by `tar` archives, which are sometimes referred to as tarballs or more descriptively, hairballs. The `tar` file storage mechanism stores one or more files in a single file in a `tar` format. A `tar` file has the file suffix of `.tar`; if the `tar` file is compressed, it has a suffix like `.tgz` or `.tar.gz`. Using the `tar`-based distribution system is sufficient if your software does not change often and you are young. But when you need to upgrade or change software, or work with complex software systems, it becomes quite difficult to work with. Rather than spending your life spitting up hairballs, systems like RPM greatly simplify your life.

Chapter 17

Scripting Your Act

● ●

In This Chapter

▶ Writing a simple shell program

▶ Writing a not-so-simple shell program

▶ Finding out about multitasking

● ●

*A*fter you get the hang of working from within a shell, you can branch out to writing shell scripts. And when you're good at it, you can move to Hollywood and find fame and fortune. You probably never suspected that you could gain so much from purchasing a Linux book.

The bash shell that comes standard with Red Hat Linux provides you with a powerful programming environment. Shell programming is also referred to as writing scripts or scripting. Scripts are typically used to perform repetitive administrative tasks. This chapter describes how to get started in the exciting world of writing scripts. Send your dues to the Screen Actor's Guild right away!

Starting Out with a Simple Shell Script

Chapter 14 introduces the world of the interactive bash shell. You can use bash to manually run commands and applications. After a while, you may notice that you're typing certain commands over and over again. We're sure you'd prefer to run all those commands together rather than giving yourself carpal tunnel syndrome. Well, you can cut down on your orthopedic surgeon's bills by writing your own scripts.

The rest of this section describes how to create shell scripts, which contain a series of commands that are executed every time you type the name of the script as a command. First you create a simple shell script and later you create a more complex one.

Suppose you want to periodically generate a report, showing who owns the login accounts. You can simply print the /etc/passwd file, but that file has a lot more information in it than you need. Plus, you're an organized person and prefer to format the report yourself rather than use the password file's layout.

First, look at the following entry in the passwd file:

```
jorge:x:500:500:RH Linux dude:/home/jorge:/bin/bash
```

Each grouping of characters between the colons is called a *field*. For example, the first field in the example — jorge — is the username of the account. For the report, you want to display only the first and fifth fields. We use the cut command here to surgically extract the desired fields. The man page for cut shows that the way to construct the command is as follows:

```
cut -f 1,5 -d: /etc/passwd
```

The *man pages* are terse but complete descriptions of commands. To get to the man page for the cut command, type **man cut** on the command line.

You use the -f option to specify the fields you want printed — in this case the first and fifth fields. The -d option specifies what delimiter — a colon (:) in this case — is used to format the report. The preceding command spits out all the usernames in the passwd file that are formatted like this:

```
root:root

...

jorge:RH Linux dude
```

Creating a pipeline

You can filter the output of the cut command to display only the lines containing a specific string with the grep command. For example, the grep jorge command filters out, or blocks, everything fed to it that does not contain the string jorge.

But how do you use the two commands together? The answer is to use plumbing. Linux and bash enable you to pipe information generated by one command to the input of another. The pipe symbol, |, takes the output of cut and feeds it to grep. The following commands work together with pipe to produce what you want:

```
cut -f 1,5 -d: /etc/passwd |
    grep jorge
```

cut takes the first and fifth fields of every line in the /etc/passwd file and feeds it to grep. grep filters out everything but those lines that have the text string jorge. Because only one line contains the string jorge, the output looks like this:

```
jorge:RH Linux dude
```

Next make the output a little more readable by changing the colon delimiter to a dash with a space on either side. The stream editor sed is your ticket to formatting happiness. You can send the output of the cut and grep commands to sed with the following command:

```
cut -f 1,5 -d: /etc/passwd | sed -e 's/:/ - /'
```

Note the single quotes around `s/:/ - /`. These quotes instruct the shell to think of the entire string of characters as one *thing,* and present the string to the sed editor as the thing that -e has to work with. Without the single quotes, the shell would conclude from the blanks in the string that three different things are in that string of characters: s/:/, -, and /. In shell statements, unquoted blank space (called *white space*) is considered a separator.

You're now ready to start putting the bits and pieces together into a script that gives you the information you want along with some nice window dressing. You want some type of header that states the subject of the report and the date. You can use the echo command (for the header) and the date command (for the date):

```
echo Report of logon names and users on the Linux system
date
echo =======================================
cut -f 1,5 -d: /etc/passwd | sed -e `s/:/ - /'
```

You should add the line #!/bin/bash to the beginning of all scripts in order to assure that they run consistently across all Linux platforms. That line forces the computer to use the bash shell to run the script.

These four lines are not difficult to type, but having to remember them and retype them each time you run the report is a nuisance. We like to save time whenever we can, and our memory cells seem to be dropping like . . . ah, we forget. For those reasons, we want to use our favorite text editor to type the lines in a file.

Our favorite editor is vi, but then we're techie nerds. You can use a more humane editor like gedit by clicking the Main Menu button and choosing Programs➪Applications➪gedit. In the gedit window that appears, type the following text:

```
echo Report of login names and users on the Linux system
date
echo =======================================
cut -f 1,5 -d: /etc/passwd | sed -e `s/:/ - /'
```

Choose File➪Save As. In the Save As window, type the filename **get_user_info** in the Selection text box.

Next you must tell Red Hat Linux to execute the `get_user_info.sh` file. To do this, you must set the execute flag as follows:

```
chmod +x get_user_info
```

For more on permissions, check out Chapter 13.

Now type

```
./get_user_info
```

and you see your report run before your eyes! Type

```
./get_user_info | more
```

and you see that your `get_user_info` program acts like any other program. It pipes output to other programs, including the printer (if you have one available to your system):

```
./get_user_info | lpr
```

But notice that for your program, you have to type `./` in front of the filename. If you don't include `./`, you get the following message:

```
bash: get_user_info: command not found
```

You receive this message because your current directory, where the `get_user_info` shell script resides, is not in the list of directories contained in the PATH variable. If you type the following:

```
echo $PATH
```

you should see a line that looks something like this:

```
/usr/bin:/bin:/usr/X11R6/bin:/usr/local/bin:/opt/bin:home/jor
        ge/bin
```

A colon separates each *path* of a directory, so Linux searches for valid commands in these directories (in order): `/usr/bin`, `/bin`, `/usr/X11R6/bin`, and so forth. The directory that is most interesting to you is probably at the end of the line. It should be something like `/home/your user name/bin`. If you create that directory, you can place your own scripts and programs there and execute them without explicitly specifying the path. The following command creates your personal `bin` directory:

```
[zoot@veracruz zoot]$ mkdir ~/bin
```

Move your `get_user_info` file into your personal `bin` directory by typing:

```
[zoot@veracruz zoot]$ mv get_user_info ~/bin
```

Now you can execute the `get_user_info` script just like you can any other program:

```
[zoot@veracruz zoot]$ get_user_infoReport of login names and
          users on the Linux system
Fri Aug  4 21:34:44 MDT 2000
==========================================
root - root
bin - bin
daemon - daemon
adm - adm
lp - lp
sync - sync
shutdown - shutdown
halt - halt
mail - mail
news - news
uucp - uucp
operator - operator
games - games
gopher - gopher
ftp - FTP User
nobody - Nobody
xfs - X Font Server
gdm -
rpcuser - RPC Service User
mailnull -
paul -
zoot - RHLinux user

[zoot@veracruz zoot]$
```

You just wrote a program. It's a simple program, but as far as Red Hat Linux is concerned, it's as much a program as any other.

In many cases, shell scripts are more efficient than writing many lines in a traditional compiled language like C. Shell scripts are fairly easy to write, understand, and change. Even experienced programmers use them every day instead of writing more complex programs in other languages. Systems administrators couldn't survive without scripting languages such as shell.

Moving On to More Flexible Shell Scripts

The program in the previous section always works on the same file, which is hard-coded into the script. The rest of this chapter shows how to create more flexible shell scripts that can generate different filenames as needed and automatically adapt to being run on different dates.

Suppose you want to keep monthly copies of the passwd file and monitor the differences between them. You start by writing a program that copies the passwd file to another directory:

1. **Use your favorite editor to open up a new file in your home directory —**
   for example, /home/jorge/genreport.sh.

2. **Type the following into the** genreport.sh **file:**

   ```
   cat /etc/passwd > passwd`date +%Y%m`
   ```

   The genreport.sh script is simple. It copies the file /etc/passwd to standard output by using the cat command; the redirection symbol — > — sends the output into the specified file.

   Note that on the second line, you type two accent grave characters — ` — and not apostrophes — '. Think of an accent grave character as a backwards apostrophe.

   The script generates the filename by tacking a date onto the end of the string passwd. The date starts with the four-digit year and ends with the two-digit month. The date is generated by the date command.

   The date +%Y%m command outputs the year and month of the current date and generates the string 200007. The %Y tells date to output the four digit year. The %m generates the two digit month.

   If you're searching your keyboard for that accent grave character, you may find it under the tilde character (~).

3. **Don't forget to change the** generport.sh **file's permissions to make it**
   executable.

   Making a file executable means that it can be run as a program as in the following command:

   ```
   chmod u+rx /home/jorge/genreport
   ```

   Here the chmod command is used in a slightly different way than in its previous incarnation. The u+x makes the file executable by only the owner.

4. **Run the program by typing in the following command:**

   ```
   genreport.sh
   ```

   The script generates the file that contains the password information. The filename starts with the string passwd. The year and the month, two numerals each, are appended to the end of the file. For example, if you run this program in July of the year 2000, it produces a file with the name passwd200007 in the directory that you run it from.

5. Run the `ls  -l` **command and it displays the filename shown below.**

```
passwd200007
```

 Single commands that are not separated by a pipe symbol — that is, their standard output won't be fed to the standard input of the next command — may be placed on the same line and separated with a semicolon (;). This shortcut is useful in interactive mode because you don't have to press Enter and wait for a response; it seldom, however, saves any time in scripts. In scripts, putting commands on separate lines is better because they're easier to change later if necessary.

Suppose you run the program on the first day of the month over several months' time. You accumulate several copies of the `passwd` file, each with changes as login accounts are added and deleted.

Eventually the reports directory looks somewhat like this:

```
[zoot@veracruz reports]$ ls
passwd200007 passwd200009 passwd200011 passwd200001
passwd200008 passwd200010 passwd200012 passwd200002
```

To simulate running your `genreport` program over several months, follow these steps:

1. Create a directory called reports by typing the following command:

```
mkdir reports
```

This command creates a directory in your present working directory — pwd. Your `pwd` is whatever directory you happen to be working from. Your `bash` shell prompt shows your present working directory. For example, the last name in the prompt `[jorge@veracruz jorge]` is the pwd.

2. Execute the `genreport` **program once.**

3. Create seven copies of the report file for different months.

To do so, change the name of each new file to a different date. This action creates eight total files (the original and seven copies). The files have the same contents, but that's okay for now.

```
cp passwd200007 passwd200008
cp passwd200007 passwd200009
cp passwd200007 passwd200010
cp passwd200007 passwd200011
cp passwd200007 passwd200012
cp passwd200007 passwd200101
cp passwd200007 passwd200102
```

Just a few good commands

Shell programming depends heavily on the many hundreds of specialized programs that come with most Unix systems. Of these many hundreds, perhaps only 20 or 30 are used in day-to-day scripting, but the others are there just in case, and most, if not all, are documented in section one of the man pages.

Jon still remembers the day he began to feel comfortable with Unix (*long* before Linux was available). He was trying to do something with a shell script, utilizing the 20 to 30 commands he knew. Finally the thought occurred to him that although he was not sure that Unix had the command he needed, there was a strong probability that it did. So he started going through the manual pages looking for a command that may help. Sure enough, he found one. From that day on, he felt comfortable with Unix, even though he kept learning more about it every day. From time to time, he still goes through the reference pages of the manual, one by one, to find out about new commands and to refresh his memory on old ones.

Each of these commands typically does one thing very well, and you can put them together with pipes and other shell-script glue to solve a larger problem. Becoming familiar with them takes time and practice, but after you do that, your abilities expand a thousandfold.

---

4. **Write a shell script that shows you the accounts that were added and deleted from month to month.**

   One way to write this script is to create a program that allows you to supply the names of two of the files to see whether any accounts have been added or deleted. The second way is more automated: Have the program look through all the files to see whether any accounts have been added or deleted. Later in this chapter, you find out how to provide that level of automation.

Passing information to your shell with arguments

You can provide a shell script with extra pieces of information that can modify its action. Each piece of information is called an *argument.* Arguments follow a command and look something like this:

```
myscript arg1 arg2
```

The number of arguments depends on how you construct the script. The `arg1` and `arg2` arguments can be any value and are determined by how the script is written. For example, if you write a script to change the time — `changetime` —, you may supply it with the hour and minute like this: `changetime 10 32`. The arguments would tell the script to change the computer's time to 10:32.

1. **To illustrate how arguments work and how a script can use them, use an editor to create a small, simple shell script called** stuff **and put it in the your home directory:**

```
echo The zeroth argument $0
echo The first argument $1
echo The second argument $2
echo The third argument $3
echo The fourth argument $4
echo The number of expanded arguments $#
```

2. **Save the file.**

   Note that each line ends with either a number or the character (#) symbol, preceded by a dollar sign. These are special names inside the shell that will have values assigned to them, according to what you type on the command line as a command name and as arguments when you invoke the shell.

3. **Make the script executable by typing:**

```
chmod +x stuff
```

4. **Execute the** stuff **shell script that you just created by typing the following command:**

```
stuff
```

   The output should look like this:

```
The zeroth argument /home/zoot/bin/stuff
The first argument
The second argument
The third argument
The fourth argument
The number of expanded arguments 0
```

   Note that the zeroth argument (called $0) is the full pathname for the executed shell command. When executing the command name by itself on the line with no additional arguments or options, the zeroth argument is the only argument that receives information.

5. **Just for grins, supply a metacharacter on the shell command line as follows:**

```
stuff *
```

   The output looks like this:

```
The zeroth argument /home/zoot/bin/stuff
The first argument passwd199707
The second argument passwd199708
The third argument passwd199709
The fourth argument passwd199710
The number of expanded arguments 8
```

The bash shell expands the metacharacter — * — to include all the filenames in the current directory. bash actually generates a list of files and feeds it to the script. The Linux metacharacter often acts in a similar manner to the wildcard found in the Microsoft world. But there are significant differences. Describing metacharacters in detail is beyond the scope of this book. You can use the bash man page to find a good description of them.

The $# argument reports that eight arguments match the metacharacter. Only four of the filenames are printed, however, because you requested only four arguments — filenames in this case — in your shell script.

To see that eight arguments really are on the command line, type the following command:

```
echo *
```

The echo command echoes whatever follows it on the line. If you type echo Hi there and press the Enter key, Hi there appears on the next line. If you type the command line echo 5342 and press Enter, 5342 appears on the line.

But when you type echo * in your reports directory and press Enter, something different from * appears on the next line. What appears is the name of every file or directory in the reports directory. This happens because the bash shell sees the * as a regular expression and expands it to match every filename or directory name in the directory that does not begin with a period. That expanded line is then presented to the echo command.

The same thing happens to your stuff shell script or any other shell script that has a regular expression passed to it as an argument. The *shell* — not the command or shell script you invoke — expands the regular expression. Because you created eight filenames in the reports directory, you know that eight arguments are on the line (for the eight names in your directory) and not just the four you printed.

Now add the proper regular expansion to cover all the files called passwd2000xx; six exist:

```
[zoot@veracruz reports]$ stuff *2000*
The zeroth argument /home/zoot/bin/stuff
The first argument passwd.200007
The second argument passwd.200008
The third argument passwd.200009
The fourth argument passwd.200010
The number of expanded arguments 6
[zoot@veracruz reports]$
```

Only four files are returned in your four arguments $1 through $4 because the shell script asked for only four to be printed.

The final step causes metacharacter expansion of the 2001 years:

```
[zoot@veracruz reports]$ stuff *2001*
The zeroth argument /home/zoot/bin/stuff
The first argument passwd200101
The second argument passwd200102
The third argument
The fourth argument
The number of expanded arguments 2
[zoot@veracruz reports]$
```

Only two of the four arguments are filled. Likewise, the $# argument reports that only two files were expanded and placed on the command line.

Going with the flow

One series of commands is typically used only in a shell script to make decisions instead of on the command line (typed in one line at a time). These commands are *flow control,* or *conditional,* statements and are found in many computer languages in different forms. The simplest one in the bash shell language is if. The if statement is usually written as follows:

```
if list1
then
list2
fi
```

Or, for more complex conditions,

```
if list1
then
list2
[elif list3
then
list4]
{and so on...}
fi
```

Seems ugly, doesn't it? But it isn't too bad. Note that overall it begins with if and ends with fi, which is the backward spelling of if. Who says computer programmers have no sense of humor?

The *list* statements represent other shell commands, statements, and so forth that should be tested to see whether they are true or false *(list1 and list3)* or executed *(list2 and list4).*

So what are some examples of *list* statements? You see one in the next example, which is a test to see whether a file exists. In this case, the built-in function test -e sees whether a filename exists; if it exists, echo says so. You can try out this example on the command line without putting it in a shell. Make sure that you have spaces in front of and behind each left bracket ([) and right bracket (]). A small > appears after the first line, to indicate that the shell is expecting you to type some more:

```
[zoot@veracruz reports]$ if [ -e /etc/passwd ]
> then
> echo file exists
> else
> echo file does not exist
> fi
file exists
[zoot@veracruz reports]$
```

Now, to test to see whether the if statement can detect the passwd filename, type the name incorrectly:

```
[zoot@veracruz reports]$ if [ -e /etc/password ]
> then
> echo file exists
> else
> echo file does not exist
> fi
file does not exist
[zoot@veracruz reports]$
```

You can create other simple tests, such as

- ✔ -f for finding out whether a file exists and is a regular file, not a directory or device file

- ✔ -d for finding out whether a file exists and is a directory

- ✔ -r for finding out whether a file exists and is readable

In the manual pages, you can read more about tests to perform on filenames. You can even combine tests to check for many conditions at one time.

Putting your ideas together

Are you ready to put the concepts from the first shell script together with the concepts from the second shell script? The result is a program that selects two passwd files from different months and compares them. The program tests to make sure that all the filenames are typed correctly on the command line and then extracts the information from the files, compares them, and prints the differences, if any.

1. **Use a text editor to create a file called** `passdiff` **in your** ~/bin **directory, putting the following lines in it.**

Comments in the code below are preceded by the # character, which
tells the compiler to ignore the line. They do not affect the output of the
script. You do not need to enter them but they are good for providing
information about what the script does when you don't remember what
it does in the future.

```
### Shell comments start with a pound sign (#)
# on a line. Anything following a # is ignored
# by the shell and is used only by humans to
# understand what is going on in the script.
# Use comments liberally.
#
### if the number of arguments is not equal to 2
if [ $# != 2 ]
# then
then
# echo a usage message
echo Usage: passdiff file1 file2
# and exit with an error code of 9
exit 9
fi
### if the first argument is not a file
if [ ! -f $1 ]
# then echo message that the first argument is
# not a file
then
echo $1 is not a file
# and exit with an error code of 9
exit 9
fi
### Test the second argument the same way.
if [ ! -f $2 ]
then
echo $2 is not a file
exit 9
fi
### Now use the cut and sed statements, which we
# used before to create the logon-
# name/description. But this time, store the
# contents in files called /usr/tmp/get_user
# _info.?.$$ where the ? matches any digit
# and the $$ assumes the process number of the
# shell to create a unique filename. Two files
# with unique filenames will therefore be
# generated temporarily in /usr/tmp:
# get_user_info.1.processnumber and
# get_user_info.2.processnumber.
cut -f 1,5 -d: $1 | sed -e `s/:/-/' \
        >/usr/tmp/get_user_info.1.$$
```

```
cut -f 1,5 -d: $2 | sed -e `s/:/-/' \
        >/usr/tmp/get_user_info.2.$$
### There is a difference in Linux (as in most
# programming systems) between a single quote
# (that symbol below the double quote on a
# U.S. keyboard) and accent grave`, that symbol
# below the tilde (the squiggly thing) on a
# U.S. keyboard. In the following lines, the '
# symbol is a single quote, which turns off
# the shell's regular expression matching and
# allows the sed command to see the regular
# expression (if any).
### Use the diff command to compare the two
# files generated. diff creates output lines
# with a < symbol pointing to extra lines from
# the first file and a > symbol pointing to
# extra lines from the second file. The results
# are placed in a third temporary file created
# by using the process number as before.
diff /usr/tmp/get_user_info.1.$$
        /usr/tmp/get_user_info.2.$$ \
        >/usr/tmp/get_user_info.3.$$
### Now we echo whether or not there were any
# extra logon names echo password file $1 had
# these extra logon names: if there are any
# extra ones from the first file, print them to
# standard output:
### We have to use single quote marks around the
# `^<` argument to tell the shell script this is
# an argument to the grep command, and not a
# redirection symbol telling it to take the file
# of /usr/tmp/get_user_info.3.$$ and feed it
# through standard input.
grep `^<` /usr/tmp/get_user_info.3.$$
# Now we echo whether or not there were any
# extra logon names:
echo password file $2 had these extra logon names:
### if there are any extra ones from the second
# file, print them to standard output. (Note the
# use of single quotes in the line below.)
grep `^>` /usr/tmp/get_user_info.3.$$
# Remove all temporary files from /usr/tmp. The
# ? matches all three digits.
rm /usr/tmp/get_user_info.?.$$
# exit with a successful error code.
exit 0
```

2. **Remember to save the file. Change its mode to read and execute by typing the following:**

```
chmod u+rx ~/bin/passdiff
```

3. **Take the program for a test run by making some of the files in the reports directory different. Add one more line to** `passwd200008`, **as follows:**

```
ignacio::501:501:Malo patron de Arroyo
        Negro:/home/ignacio:/bin/bash
```

4. **Next add one more line to file** `passwd200010`:

```
bulldog::502:502:Yet Another Red Hat Linux
        User,,,,:/home/bulldog:/bin/bash
```

5. **Cross your fingers and test the program! Oops. Uncross your fingers and type the following:**

```
passdiff
```

You should see the following output:

```
Usage: passdiff file1 file2
```

6. **That was fun. The script told you that it expects the proper etiquette if it's going to perform for you. So now type the two** `passwd` **filenames as arguments:**

```
passdiff passwd200008 passwd20010
```

The script accepts the arguments but is still not happy:

```
pass20010 is not a file
```

7. **If you first don't succeed, try, try again. Type the two** `passwd` **file-names as arguments again:**

```
passdiff passwd200008 passwd200010
```

This time the script is happy and gives you what you want. You see the following output:

```
password file passwd.200008 had these extra logon names:
< ignacio - Malo patron de Arroyo Negro
password file passwd.200110 had these extra logon names:
> lencho - Henchman de Ignacio
```

Multitasking

When executing programs on a Linux system, being able to take advantage of its *multitasking* capabilities — that is, running multiple programs at the same time — is beneficial. This process is also called *job control*. Windows NT/2000 does this, Windows 9*x* seems to do it, and Unix systems have been doing it for almost 30 years. Most of this job control capability is due to the shell being able to launch background jobs and manage them.

For example, perhaps you have a task that will be running a long time, with little or no human input needed. When you start that task, all you have to do is put an & (ampersand) sign at the end of the line, and the job starts running in the background.

For example, if you start ical (a really nice graphical calendar program on the CD-ROM that comes with this book), you probably want it to run a long time, and yet you want to type other commands at the same time. (For more on the ical program, see Chapter 9.) To put ical into the background, you can start ical by typing the following command into a terminal emulator:

```
[zoot@veracruz zoot]$ ical&
[1] 2449
```

The number in brackets is the job number, followed by the process ID number. The *job number* is the number that the shell gives the ical program to keep track of the ical job. The *process ID number* is the number that the entire operating system uses to keep track of the ical program.

To find all the programs running under the shell you're currently using, you can use the jobs shell command, as follows:

```
[zoot@veracruz zoot]$ jobs
[1]+ Running        ical &
```

This information tells you that ical is job number 1, is running fine (thank you), is not waiting for any input from the console, and is having a great old time.

On the other hand, you can have another job (such as largejob) that you put temporarily into the background by simply putting the & at the end of the line:

```
[zoot@veracruz zoot]$ largejob &
```

Deciphering bash

Linux is known for its *cryptic* command names, error messages, and documentation. We prefer to think of the command names as *terse* — a lot of meaning in a small space. The man page on bash, however, is more than 60 pages long, with no examples and no cheery dialog to entertain you.

From that lengthy page count, you can surmise that shell programming involves a lot more than we can tell you in these few pages. Entire books have been written just on shell programming. What we show you in this book, however, should help you write a few short scripts to make your life easier.

When you type **jobs** as a command in this case, you see that `largejob` was stopped, waiting for input or for some other reason:

```
[zoot@veracruz zoot]$ jobs
[1]- Running            ical &
[2]+ Stopped (tty output)  largejob
```

You can bring `largejob` into the foreground by typing **fg %2** and giving it some more input, and then put `largejob` back into the background by pressing Ctrl+Z and typing **bg**. Whew. Here's how it looks:

```
[zoot@veracruz zoot]$ fg %2
largejob
zoot tries hard.
<CTRL+Z>
[2]+ Stopped             largejob
[zoot@veracruz zoot]$ bg
[2]+ largejob &
[zoot@veracruz zoot]$
```

You can have dozens or even hundreds of background processes. If they all accepted data from the keyboard at the same time, how would you know which program is receiving the data? Therefore, each program has to wait until you recognize it, bring it into the foreground, enter the necessary data, and then put it back into the background, where it blissfully keeps running until it terminates or again needs input from the keyboard (or standard input, as you have come to know it). Now you know why `largejob` was waiting to accept such valuable and timely input.

Chapter 18

Bringing in the Red Hat Repair Man: Troubleshooting Your Network

*T*his book is perfect and there's no way that anything described in it can ever go wrong. You'll be as lonely as the Maytag repairman if you expect trouble (the trouble is trouble never happens). Errata (corrections) are as outdated as a brick and mortar bookstore. This book makes setting up computers and networks so easy that you'll wonder why other people have so many problems! Blah, blah, blah, yada, yada, yada.

Well, maybe not. This guy named Murphy hangs out in both virtual and real bookstores. He's always jumping in just when things are starting to go well. The guy just can't keep his nose out of other people's business. This chapter is meant to smooth things out between you and Murphy in case he catches up with you.

It's the Tree's Fault, not Mine!

Troubleshooting is, as they say, more of an art than a science. Sometimes it's easy to see what the problem is and how to fix it. Other times it's not. The difficulty that you have fixing problems depends, of course, on how hard the problem is and how well you know your stuff. Obviously, the better acquainted you are with computers and Linux, the better you'll be at troubleshooting.

Every problem has a solution. Computers are cause-and-effect-based machines. When something breaks, or doesn't work, there's always a reason. The reason may not be easy to find but it exists.

But how do you find the cause? That's a million-dollar question. Getting a million bucks isn't easy unless you're willing to grind your teeth plotting against your fellow contestants for months on a desert island, purchase ten million Power Ball tickets or — believe it or not — work hard and work smart. Some people are willing to eat rats for the chance or are lucky enough to win the lottery, but most just have to work hard. Oh well.

Working hard is easy, but how do you work smart? That's where the idea of the fault tree comes in. The fault tree looks like an upside-down tree. The trunk of the tree represents the fault, or problem. The ends, or leaves, of the branches represent all of the possible causes. The fault tree is a conceptual aid that helps you to eliminate all but the cause of your problem. After that's done, solving the problem is virtually assured.

For example, Figure 18-1 shows part of a fault tree that points out what major subsystems you should look at. To find the solution to a problem, you need to systematically identify what's working. You work your way to what's not working, and then when you find it you usually solve your problem. The fault tree concept helps to formalize the process.

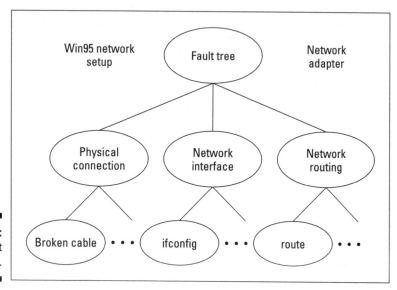

Figure 18-1:
The fault tree.

The blind leading the blind

Paul's colleague, Ken Hatfield, once said, "One of the side benefits from lots of troubleshooting comes from what I call the value of blind alleys. Most often in troubleshooting, you go down blind alleys, or in your tree example, the wrong branches of the solution tree. But in doing so, you learn something. In the future, when you encounter a different problem down the road, that previous blind alley may be the road to the solution." Well said.

Here's an example: Paul recently had a server that was having a lot of problems. The /var file

system had filled up, which caused some programs that used it to fail. When space on /var was freed up, most of the programs started to do their job again. But one program didn't work. Paul spent a long time trying to figure out why it didn't work even after the problem was fixed. As it turned out, this particular program's real problem was that its license had expired. He had not only walked down a blind alley but bumped into a wall and kept trying to go forward. D'oh!

Following are some of the possible faults:

✔ The first branch on the left involves problems with the physical connection: Do you have a network adapter? Is the cable connected properly to the adapter? If so, do you have a break in the cable? If so, then you have to fix or replace the cable.

✔ The second branch deals with the network interface configuration: Have you configured the IP address for your Ethernet adapter correctly? If so, is the netmask correct?

✔ The third branch helps decide if the problem exists with the network routing. Can your network packets be directed towards the correct network?

The fault tree helps you break down any big problem into simpler ones. By eliminating each simple problem one-by-one, you should eventually locate the root cause. The fault tree is a simple method for thinking a problem through.

The Fix Is In: Troubleshooting Your Network

One common problem involves getting your Red Hat Linux computer to work on a network. Not that you're having such problems after working through Chapter 6, but if the impossible happens and Murphy comes to visit, then this section should help out.

I is an enganeer

An experienced electrical engineer and Linux author once got really angry at a cable TV company. His cable service went dead in the middle of a Philadelphia Eagles game. They were losing, but the Eagles don't appear on TV much in Albuquerque. The cable company was called immediately. Well, the nice support person guided the poor engineer step-by-step through his own fault tree. First step: Is your VCR/TV turned on? "Yes, of course." Step two: Is the VCR button on your VCR toggled on? "Of course, ah, woops, no it isn't. Ah yes, it works now, thank you very much. Goodbye." D'oh! What was five years of electrical engineering school good for?

Your Red Hat Linux machine is the foundation of your network and must be set up correctly for anything to run. If it isn't working, or if you have some unusual setup (or Murphy is in a bad mood), you can check for several different causes.

We use the Red Hat Linux network as the troubleshooting example in this chapter. The Red Hat Linux network is one of the more difficult things to set up correctly because it not only depends on your Linux computer, but other computers as well. Suppose that your Red Hat Linux network is not working. Use the following sections as a simple fault tree that you can follow to troubleshoot your network.

Please see the Part of Tens chapters for insights into other problems. Chapter 20 describes how to find information about your Red Hat Linux computer; it also points out where you can get help. Chapter 21 discusses some of the simple, frequently encountered problems that people have with Red Hat Linux.

Checking Linux Networking

We describe the most likely problems in order from most simple to most complex. After cataloging the problems, we look at one of the branches of the fault tree to solve a problem.

Is the power turned on?

First verify that you turned on the power. Sounds simple, but hey, sometimes the simplest things go wrong.

Is your network cable broken?

Make sure that your network cables are not broken or cut. Check the connectors to make sure that they're okay.

Is your Ethernet hub or switch working?

Your Ethernet hub or switch should also be turned on. Ensure that the network cables are also connected securely.

If you're stuck in the Middle Ages (with me!) and are using that coaxial network cable called Thinnet — or 10base2 for Geeks — then you don't have to check an Ethernet hub/switch because there is none. Thinnet connects each NIC (computer, printer, and so on) to every other NIC on the subnet. In other words, each computer that is on a Thinnet cable is connected electrically to all the other computers in the network. Each computer sees all the network traffic on that cable. If any part of that bus is compromised, all traffic ceases. For example, if you disconnect the terminator at either end of the cable, all communication ends. The best way to troubleshoot that type of problem is to start at one end and work your way down the line. Try to get just two computers working together, then three, and so on. Eventually you'll find the problem.

Determining whether your network cable has been compromised requires addressing the following issues:

- If you're using Thinnet, make sure the "BNC" — Bayonet Nut Connector — connectors are securely attached.

- Look at the interface between the cable and Ethernet switch/hub — or the BNC connector if you are using Thinnet — to make sure they are in good physical contact. Sometimes the cable can pull out a little bit and break the connection.

- Look at the cable itself and make sure it hasn't been cut or crushed.

- If you're using Thinnet, make sure that each end of the cable has a 50ohm terminator attached to it. Thinnet must be terminated or else it will not work, just as it will not work if the cable is broken. The reason for this is that the radio frequency (RF) signal reflects from the unterminated end and interferes with the incoming signals. If you have a cable that you know is good, try substituting it. The idea is to eliminate as many segments that you are unsure about as possible. If you have just two computers in close proximity and you suspect a problem with the cable you are using, all you can do is try another cable. If the computers are far apart and rely on several segments or a long cable, try moving them closer together and using one short segment. If you have three or more computers, try getting just two of them working together. Then try adding another one. Proceed until you find the faulty segment.

Is your Ethernet adapter inserted correctly?

You have to have an Ethernet adapter to be connected to an Ethernet network. Make sure that your Ethernet adapter is plugged into your computer's system board — also known as a motherboard — snugly. Sometimes it's necessary to pull it out and then reinsert it. That process of pulling out an adapter and then plugging it back in is called *reseating*.

Is your network adapter configured correctly?

Sometimes a startup script is misconfigured, which causes the startup screen to go by without you seeing an error message. If that happens, login as root and from the shell prompt, type the command:

```
ifconfig
```

You see a listing of two different interfaces, as shown in the following code, or three interfaces if you have PPP configured. The program `ifconfig` tells the Linux kernel that you have a network adapter, and gives it an IP address and network mask. This is the first step in connecting your Linux computer to your network.

```
lo        Link encap:Local Loopback
          inet addr:127.0.0.1  Bcast:127.255.255.255
          Mask:255.0.0.0
          UP BROADCAST LOOPBACK RUNNING  MTU:3584  Metric:1
          RX packets:115 errors:0 dropped:0 overruns:0
          TX packets:115 errors:0 dropped:0 overruns:0

eth0      Link encap:10Mbps Ethernet  HWaddr 00:A0:24:2F:30:69
          inet addr:192.168.1.1 Bcast:192.168.1.255
Mask:255.255.255.0
          UP BROADCAST RUNNING MULTICAST  MTU:1500  Metric:1
          RX packets:16010 errors:18 dropped:18 overruns:23
          TX packets:7075 errors:0 dropped:0 overruns:0
          Interrupt:10 Base address:0x300
```

If you don't see the line containing `lo`, which is the loopback interface, or `eth0`, which is your network adapter, then your physical network connections have not been set up correctly. The loopback interface is not a physical device; it's used for the network software's internal workings. The loopback interface must be present for the network adapter to be configured.

If the loopback interface is not present, type the following command:

```
ifconfig lo 127.0.0.1
```

If the network adapter — generally an Ethernet card — is not present, type the following command:

```
ifconfig eth0 192.168.1.1
```

Because this is a class C network address, ifconfig automatically defaults to the 255.255.255.0 netmask. If you have an unusual netmask, which you shouldn't, type the following command:

```
ifconfig eth0 192.168.1.1 netmask 255.255.255.0
```

Type **ifconfig** and you should see your network adapter displayed correctly. If it's not, examine the manual page on ifconfig. You display this manual page by typing the following command and then pressing Enter.

```
man ifconfig
```

You can page through the document by pressing Enter to go line-by-line, pressing the spacebar to go forward one page at a time, pressing Ctrl+B to page backward, or pressing *q* to quit. The ifconfig man page shows a great deal of information on what and how ifconfig works. If you're still having problems, look at the Linux startup information by running the following command:

```
dmesg
```

You see the information that was displayed during the boot process. Look for your Ethernet NIC, which should appear after the Adding Swap line in the following code:

```
Freeing unused kernel memory: 60k freed
Adding Swap: 13651k swap-space (priority ?1)
Eth0:  3c509 at 0x310 tag1, BNC port, address ... aa,IRQ 11.
3c509.c:1.16 (2.2) 2/3/98
becker@cesdis.gsfc.nasa.govbecker@cesdis.gsfc.nasa.gov.
```

If you don't see your Ethernet adapter, then you may have a hardware problem. Check your adapter. Reseat it (take it out and put it back in) and see if it works. If not, then you probably need a new NIC. If you do see the NIC, then look inside the Linux kernel and see which devices it has. Type the following command to change to a special directory called /proc where process information is located:

```
cat /proc/devices
```

You should see a line with your network adapter listed. If you don't, then Linux doesn't know that it exists. If the NIC is Plug and Play (PnP) compatible, then that is often the problem. Linux frequently has problems working with PnP NICs. It's best to turn PnP off. Run the following program to see if you have a PnP NIC:

```
pnpprobe
```

If you see that your Ethernet NIC is PnP, then you can use the isapnp program to reconfigure it. isapnp is a difficult program to use — it's best to use the configuration program that comes with the NIC. In this case the 3c5x9cfg.exe, which runs under DOS, is used for configuring the 3Com 3c509 NIC. Use your NIC's configuration program and turn off PnP.

Try to run your Ethernet NIC again. If it still doesn't run, then you need to find out more information. You may have an interrupt or address conflict. Look at the list of interrupts and then the IO addresses of all the devices that the kernel knows about by typing the following commands:

```
cat /proc/interrupts
cat /proc/ioports
```

The IO address is the actual location in memory where the device — such as the network adapter — is accessed by the microprocessor (for instance, your Pentium chip). The interrupt is a way that the microprocessor is informed that it should stop whatever it's doing in order to process information that has arrived at the device that is sending the interrupt.

When your Ethernet adapter receives a packet, it sends an interrupt to the microprocessor that an event has occurred. Your Pentium stops what it's doing and processes the new information. Actually, the microprocessor interacts with Linux to do the processing.

Type **cat /proc/interrupts** to show both the interrupts and the IO addresses with which Red Hat Linux is familiar. The output should look like that in the following code:

```
 0:    378425    timer
 1:      1120    keyboard
 2:         0    cascade
10:     16077    3c509
13:         1    math error
14:     63652 +  ide0
```

Typing **cat /proc/ioports** shows the input/output ports that are used by Red Hat Linux to interact with the computer's devices. The following output shows the I/O ports used on this computer.

```
0000-001f : dma1
0020-003f : pic1
```

```
0040-005f : timer
0060-006f : keyboard
0080-009f : dma page reg
00a0-00bf : pic2
00c0-00df : dma2
00f0-00ff : npu
01f0-01f7 : ide0
0300-030f : 3c509
03c0-03df : vga+
03f0-03f5 : floppy
03f6-03f6 : ide0
03f7-03f7 : floppy DIR
```

Look for your network adapter. In this case, it's the 3c509. No conflicts exist, or it would not be working. If a conflict exists, you have to reconfigure the adapter. Run your Ethernet NIC configuration program and set the adapter's parameters in its EEPROM. Older adapters may have jumpers or little switches called DIP switches to set. If you think you have to do this, remember to write down all the other devices' interrupts and IO addresses so you don't end up conflicting with something else.

You also may be using a kernel that does not have networking installed. (This is unlikely in the newer versions of Red Hat Linux because the Linux kernel will automatically load networking — and other modules — on demand. But it's still informative to go ahead and look at these files in order to gain an understanding of how Linux works.)

Display the networking devices by typing the following command:

```
cat /proc/net/devices
```

The following output shows that the kernel is configured for loopback (lo) and Ethernet interface (eth0). The loopback interface is used only for internal networking. If you don't see the Ethernet interface, you may have an unsupported network adapter or a defective or misconfigured one. The Red Hat Linux kernel, by default, automatically loads modules as they are needed. You can look back at the results of your boot process by using the dmesg command. Look for a message that says delaying eth0 configuration. That most likely means that Linux was not able to load the network adapter module or the adapter isn't working.

Display the information about your devices by using the cat /proc/net/dev command:

Inter-face	Receive							Transmit			
	packets	errs	drop	fifo	frame	colls	carrier	packets	errs	drop	fifo
lo:	116	0	0	0		116	0	0	0		0	0
eth0:	16292	19	19	23	19	7245	0	0	0		54	0

Sometimes a network adapter will only work if you compile its driver directly into the kernel.

The next step is to make sure that your network routing is configured correctly. This is also a very easy thing to get confused. You don't need to set up routing outside your LAN yet, but Linux needs to know where to send packets on its own network. Look at your routing table by typing the following command:

```
netstat -r -n
```

You should see a listing of your routing table similar to the following code:

```
Kernel IP routing table
Destination      Gateway           Genmask          Flags   MSS
           Window  irtt Iface
192.168.1.0      0.0.0.0           255.255.255.0    U          0 0
           0 eth0
127.0.0.0        0.0.0.0           255.0.0.0        U          0 0
           0 lo
0.0.0.0          192.168.1.254     0.0.0.0          UG         0 0
           0 eth0
```

The destination is the location — IP address — that you want to send packets to; for example, the address 192.168.1.0 refers to my local network. The gateway is the address (computer or router) where the packets need to be sent so they can find their way to their destination. In the case where the destination is the local network, then the 0.0.0.0 means no gateway.

The *genmask* is used to separate the parts of the IP address that are used for the network address from the host number. The flags are used to indicate things like U for up and G for gateway. The metric is used as a measure of how far a packet has to travel to its destination (a number greater than 32 is considered to be infinite). The next two flags — Ref and Use — are not important for this discussion.

The Iface field shows what network interface is being used (eth0 refers to an Internet adapter and lo for the loopback interface; the loopback interface is used internally by the Linux kernel and you should not have any need to use it directly.) The information about each interface — the routing table — is displayed below the headings. For example, the first line tells Linux to send packets destined for addresses of 192.168.1.0 through 192.168.1.255 to the Ethernet adapter (eth0). The second line deals with the kernel's internal loopback interface. The third and last line, with the address of 0.0.0.0, is known as the default route. It defines where to send all packets that are not covered by a specific route.

You must have a route to the loopback interface (also referred to as lo), which is the127.0.0.0 address. If you're missing either or both parameters, you must set them. To set the loopback device — which must be set for the network adapter to work — type the following command:

```
route add -net 127.0.0.0
```

To set the route for the network adapter and your local network, type the following command:

```
route add -net 192.168.1.0
```

This route is assigned automatically to your network adapter. But if you want to assign it explicitly, type the command as follows:

```
route add -net 192.168.1.0 dev eth0
```

Type **netstat -r -n** to see your routing table. You should see entries for the loopback and the Ethernet. If you don't see a route to your network interface, try repeating the preceding steps. You may have to delete a route. To delete a route, type the following command:

```
route del 192.168.1.0
```

If the network adapter is configured correctly and the routing is correct, check the network. The best way to do this is to ping the loopback interface first and then the other computer. Type the following command, let it run for a few seconds (one ping occurs per second), and stop it by pressing Ctrl+C:

```
ping 127.0.0.1
```

You should see a response like the one shown in the following code:

```
PING 127.0.0.1 (127.0.0.1): 56 data bytes
64 bytes from 127.0.0.1: icmp_seq=0 ttl=64 time=2.0 ms
64 bytes from 127.0.0.1: icmp_seq=1 ttl=64 time=1.2 ms
64 bytes from 127.0.0.1: icmp_seq=2 ttl=64 time=1.1 ms
64 bytes from 127.0.0.1: icmp_seq=3 ttl=64 time=1.1 ms
?
--- 127.0.0.1 ping statistics ---
4 packets transmitted, 4 packets received, 0% packet loss
        round-trip min/avg/max = 1.1/1.8/4.6 ms
```

Each line shows the number of bytes returned from the loopback interface, the sequence, and the round-trip time. The last lines are the summary, which shows if any packets did not make the trip. This is a working system, but if you don't see any returned packet, something is wrong with your setup and you should review the steps outlined in the preceding paragraphs.

Next try pinging your Ethernet interface by typing:

```
ping 192.168.1.1
```

You should see a response like the following code:

```
PING 192.168.1.1 (198.168.1.1): 56 data bytes
64 bytes from 198.168.1.1: icmp_seq=0 ttl=64 time=2.0 ms
64 bytes from 198.168.1.1: icmp_seq=1 ttl=64 time=1.2 ms
64 bytes from 198.168.1.1: icmp_seq=2 ttl=64 time=1.1 ms
64 bytes from 198.168.1.1: icmp_seq=3 ttl=64 time=1.1 ms
?
--- 198.168.1.1 ping statistics ---
4 packets transmitted, 4 packets received, 0% packet loss
            round-trip min/avg/max = 1.1/1.8/4.6 ms
```

Is there another computer or network device with which to communicate?

Try to ping another computer — if one exists — on your network. Type the following command, let it run for 10 to 15 seconds, and stop it by pressing Ctrl+C:

```
ping 192.168.1.2
```

You should see a response like the following code:

```
PING 192.168.1.2 (192.168.1.2): 56 data bytes
64 bytes from 192.168.1.2: icmp_seq=0 ttl=32 time=3.1 ms
64 bytes from 192.168.1.2: icmp_seq=1 ttl=32 time=2.3 ms
64 bytes from 192.168.1.2: icmp_seq=2 ttl=32 time=2.5 ms
64 bytes from 192.168.1.2: icmp_seq=3 ttl=32 time=2.4 ms

--- 192.168.1.2 ping statistics ---
4 packets transmitted, 4 packets received, 0% packet loss

round-trip min/avg/max = 2.3/2.5/3.1 ms
```

If you get a continuous stream of returned packets and the packet loss is zero or very near zero, your network is working. If not, the problem may be in the other machine. Review the troubleshooting steps again in this chapter. Note that the ICMP is taking about 1 full millisecond (ms) longer to travel to the external computer than to the loopback device. That is because the loopback is completely internal to the Linux computer.

If you can't locate the problem and you're using a PPP connection to an Internet service provider (ISP), establish a PPP connection and try to ping the computer where you have your account. It's considered a security breach to continuously ping someone else's computer — and at least bad manners — so don't leave it running. Also, the ISP's firewall may not allow the Internet Control Message Protocol (ICMP) packets that ping uses. ICMP packets are the simplest type of packet defined in the Internet Protocol. They're used for doing simple things like a ping.

Chapter 19

Configuring X

Did you receive an error message during the installation, informing you that the X Window System (what we'll call X from now on) was not installed properly and that you had to install it later? Or was your video card or monitor not included in the supported hardware in Chapter 3. Perhaps you simply skipped configuring X in the first place. If so, this chapter is for you. Take solace in the fact that X is one of the trickiest parts of the Linux system to get working properly.

Discovering Your Hardware's True Identity

Before you start X, you need to find out information about your video controller card, monitor, mouse, and keyboard.

For your video controller card, you need to find out:

   ✔ The model number (and perhaps the video chip used)
   ✔ The amount of video RAM it has

You should be able to find this information in your system's documentation or by using MS-DOS or Windows, as described in Chapter 3. But now that you have Linux up and running, the next best method for finding that missing information is to run the SuperProbe program, which comes with most versions of Linux. We describe how to run SuperProbe in the next section.

Next you need to know the following about your mouse:

- ✔ The model number and manufacturer
- ✔ Whether it's a PS/2 bus mouse or a serial mouse

Again, your system's documentation should tell you, and often the bottom of the mouse offers some basic information.

A PS/2 mouse usually has a round connector on the end of its wire, or tail. A serial mouse has an oblong connector with nine holes. All varieties of PS/2 bus mice look the same to Linux. Different serial mice, however, have different characteristics. If you have a serial mouse, you need to know its model number and manufacturer, or whether it emulates some other well-known mouse.

Three-button mice work best with Linux, but you can get by with a two-button mouse. To X, holding down both buttons at the same time on a two-button mouse is equivalent to holding down the middle button of a three-button mouse, but only if the system is configured correctly. You can find out how to configure the mouse in Chapter 3.

Finally, you need to know about your monitor. Most monitor manuals have a table at the back with such information as:

- ✔ Horizontal sync range
- ✔ Vertical sync range
- ✔ Resolution
- ✔ Whether it is *multiscanning,* which means your monitor can run at several resolution rates

Older monitors, particularly VGA monitors that came with older systems, often aren't multiscanning. These monitors can be damaged if you try to use them at a higher resolution than VGA, which is 640 x 480.

Horizontal and vertical sync range numbers help X determine how to place the dots on the screen. The resolution number tells X how many dots can be on the screen horizontally and vertically. The 640 x 480 resolution is usually considered to be the worst, and 1,280 x 1,024 is usually considered to be the best for normal use. Strive for 800 x 600 resolution as a minimum and 1,024 x 768 as an ideal for most systems.

Higher video resolution uses more video memory (which is on the video card and therefore separate from the system memory), allows fewer simultaneous colors on the screen (for a given amount of video memory), and typically shrinks text on the screen, making it harder to see. On the other hand, using a higher resolution means that more information can be visible on the screen at one time for the same size monitor (even though the writing may be so small that you can't read it without new glasses). Some video cards can be upgraded to add more video memory, and some cannot.

Most newer monitors have built-in protection mechanisms to keep them from burning up in what is known as *overdriving,* but older monitors do not. Older monitors can literally catch on fire. Try to find the specifications for your monitor from the manual, from a dealer, or from the manufacturer's Web page.

If you hear noise from your monitor or smell burning components, turn off your computer immediately. If you think that the screen doesn't look right, press Ctrl+Alt+Backspace right away to stop X Server and then try a lower resolution. Otherwise, you can easily damage the monitor.

Running SuperProbe

In this section, we assume that you've booted your system and that it's in command-line mode (not a bad assumption if you're having problems running X). You may or may not have all the information needed to configure X. A final chance to gather information is to run the SuperProbe program, which is included on the accompanying CD-ROM.

You may be asking yourself, why didn't you have me run SuperProbe right off the bat? Well, SuperProbe is a great program, but it's not perfect. It may *hang* (make unresponsive) your system, forcing you to reboot. It may not give you all the information you need. It can even be fooled from time to time. Despite its drawbacks, SuperProbe is a good tool.

To run SuperProbe, follow these steps:

1. **Log in as** root.
2. **Change the directory to** /usr/bin/X11 **by typing** cd /usr/bin/X11.
3. **Execute the SuperProbe program in that directory by typing the following command:**

   ```
   SuperProbe
   ```

A lot of information spews from the program, followed by a rather frightening message:

```
WARNING - THIS SOFTWARE COULD HANG YOUR MACHINE.
      READ THE SuperProbe.1 MANUAL PAGE BEFORE
      RUNNING THIS PROGRAM.
      INTERRUPT WITHIN FIVE SECONDS TO ABORT!
```

Although SuperProbe can hang your machine, most of the time it doesn't. And even if it does, simply press the reset button on your machine or turn the power off and then on to reboot.

If SuperProbe does its job and does not hang your machine, it may come back with information like the following:

```
First video: Super-VGA
Chipset: S3 86C928PCI (PCI Probed)
Memory: 2048 Kbytes
RAMDAC: AT&T 20C491 15/16/24-bit DAC with gamma correction
     (with 6-bit wide lookup tables (or in 6-bit mode))
     (programmable for 6/8-bit wide lookup tables)
```

Awesome. This information tells you that your video board is made up of an S3 chip set (a lot of them are), is model number 86C928, and fits into the PCI bus. It has 2048K (2MB) of video memory and uses a RAMDAC made by AT&T. This last piece of information is not that helpful when used with the rest of the configuration programs, but write it down anyway. As you use this information about chips, be aware that sometimes the chips are known by nicknames. For example, the S3 86C928 may show up in the configuration programs as S3 928.

Running Xconfiguration

After you find out all about your video hardware, you're ready to start configuring X. We assume that you don't have X up and running. If it is up and running, you can skip the rest of this chapter.

The next step is to use a program called Xconfigurator. This program asks you a series of questions, such as the type of mouse, the type of graphics card, and the amount of video memory in your system. As you supply the answers, Xconfigurator builds a file that X Server uses later to communicate with your mouse, the video card, and the rest of the system. (Xconfigurator is the same program that the Red Hat installation system uses.)

Xconfigurator also tries to obtain information by probing the hardware. Sometimes the program is accurate, but it can make a mistake, particularly in older PCs, or with older video cards, or with serial mice. Therefore, you may have to supply information to the program. As Linux becomes more sophisticated in the methods it uses to probe hardware, and as hardware becomes more sophisticated in the information it can return to the operating system, fewer questions need to be asked. For now, though, you have Xconfigurator.

To run Xconfigurator program, follow these steps:

1. **Log in as** `root` **and and open a Terminal window by clicking on the GNOME Terminal icon on the GNOME panel at the bottom of the screen (it looks like a monitor).**

   Before you modify your current X Window settings, you should save the configuration file.

2. **Type in the following command to make a backup copy of XFree86 configuration file (**`/etc/X11/XF86config`**):**

   ```
   cp /etc/X11/XF86config /etc/X11/XF86config.bak
   ```

   The `XF86config` file stores the X Window System configuration information.

3. **Run the configuration program by entering the following command at the command prompt:**

   ```
   Xconfigurator
   ```

   Red Hat Linux 7 comes with the brand-spanking-new XFree86 Version 4 server. Xconfigurator does not always use the new server. You can force Xconfigurator to use it, however, by running the command shown below.

   ```
   Xconfigurator --preferxf4
   ```

   The `--preferxf4` command tells Xconfigurator to use the new XFree86 v4 system, if available.

4. **When the Welcome screen shown in Figure 19-1 appears, press the Enter key to continue.**

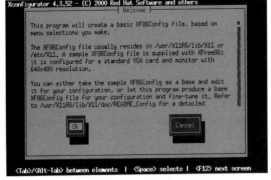

Figure 19-1: Selecting your graphics controller card.

5. **The PCI Probe Window opens, as shown in Figure 19-2.**

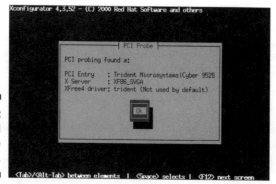

Figure 19-2:
The PCI
Probe
Window.

Xconfigurator is able to detect most PCI-based video controllers. In fact, you have very little choice other than to select the given PCI card when it does detect it. But that's not a problem because there's no reason why you'd want to use any other controller.

6. **If Xconfigurator detected your video controller, press the Enter key to continue and skip to Step 8. Otherwise, continue to Step 7 (and do not pass go, and do not collect $200!).**

   If you're using an older video controller, and Xconfigurator doesn't detect it, you're shown a list of manufacturers and models; choose your graphics card, Tab over to the OK button, and press Enter.

   Use the arrow keys to maneuver through the list. If you can't find a match, try the Generic VGA Compatible option as an alternative until you can find out more about your card. You can also select the Unlisted Card option, which appears at the end of the list. You are then asked whether you want different types of servers based on different chip sets. Not all video cards are specifically supported, and therefore, they utilize their chip sets to give them support.

   If you select the Unlisted Card option, VGA16 or SVGA is a good guess for most cards. The cards may not run at their maximum capacity, but at least they'll work.

   The Monitor Setup window appears, as shown in Figure 19-3. It shows all of the monitors that Xconfigurator knows about.

7. **Use the cursor keys to manuever through the list and select your monitor; if you find it, tab to the OK button and press Enter.**

   If the make and model isn't listed, then there are several generic options to select from. Use the PgDn key to jump down several pages to where the generic monitors are shown. The list starts with three generic LCD options, as shown in Figure 19-4; if you are using a laptop or a flatpanel LCD display, then select from these.

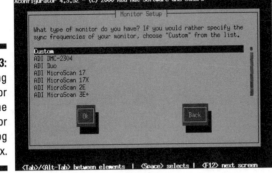

Figure 19-3:
Selecting
your monitor
from the
Monitor
Setup dialog
box.

Make your selection from the various monitor resolutions. In general, the higher the resolution that you can drive your monitor the better your graphics look. If you choose one that doesn't work, don't worry, you can always come back to this menu and make another selection.

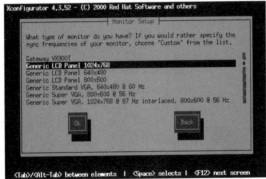

Figure 19-4:
The generic
monitor
settings.

After you select your monitor, the Video Memory window opens, and you are prompted to enter the amount of video memory available for X, as shown in Figure 19-5.

8. Xconfigurator highlights the memory value that it detects.

The amount of video memory that your video adapter has determines the resolution and number of colors that your monitor can display. Resolution is the density of pixels — the dots of light that make up your display — on your screen. The number of colors is the number of colors that each pixel can display.

The Custom/Generic monitor options

Xconfigurator gives you several generic monitor choices. You can use a generic monitor if your particular monitor is not found in the list of monitor. The following are descriptions of each setting:

✔ **Standard VGA:** This is the most basic resolution that you can use. It works in more circumstances than any other resolution but isn't significantly useful for getting work done. If you have trouble with the higher resolutions, then try this one — if only to find a starting point for getting to a higher one. Standard VGA is your safest bet.

✔ **Super VGA.** This is an intermediate resolution. It has a high enough density to get a reasonable-looking screen with which you can get work done. The resolution is also low enough to work on a large number of systems.

✔ **Generic Monitor that can do . . . :**These selections describe monitors that can display resolutions up to the given value.

✔ **8514 Compatible.** This setup is a leftover from ancient times. We rarely run into these monitors, but they may still exist in some numbers. If you have one, try it. Otherwise, don't bother.

✔ **Super VGA, 1024 x 768.** This is the highest resolution that you can get from the Custom setup. If your video card can handle it, you'll pack a lot of information onto your screen. Otherwise, try a lower resolution.

Figure 19-5:
The Video
Memory
screen.

If you don't know the amount of video memory in your video card, enter less rather than more in order to get X working. The less memory you tell X you have, however, the fewer colors at any given resolution you have available. After you get X working, you can go back and increase the memory.

9. **Select your memory amount, tab down to the OK button, and press the Enter key.**

The Clockchip Configurationwindow, as shown in Figure 19-6, appears. This is another leftover from the early days of video cards. In most cases, selecting the No Clockchip Setting (Recommended) option is best.

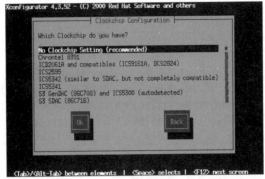

Figure 19-6:
The
Clockchip
Configura-
tion screen.

10. **The No Clockchip Setting (recommended) is selected by default, and because there should never be a need to enter any other value unless you know you have a reason to do so, tab down to the OK button and press the Enter key.**

    The Select Video Modes window appears, as shown in Figure 19-7.

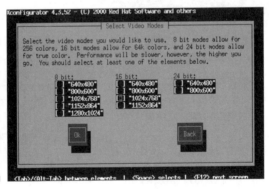

Figure 19-7:
Selecting
your
resolution
and colors
in the Video
Modes
window.

11. **In the Select Video Modes screen, select your monitor resolution.**

    You have the choice of one or more screen resolutions with 8, 16, or 24 bits of color. The higher the value of bits you select, the more colors you can see. But the number of colors takes up the memory on your video card. More memory is used as you go up in resolution, too.

    The lowest (8-bit) allows only 256 colors on the screen at one time. The 16-bit option allows for 65,535 colors, and 24-bit allows for over 16 million colors (also known as *true color*).

    To select the different resolutions, use the Tab and arrow keys to move among the choices, and use the spacebar to select and deselect entries. Select a reasonably high resolution/colors setting, and if it doesn't work, then back off to a lower setting until you find your maximum setting. (Alternatively, start low and work your way up.)

If you select more than one resolution at any one mode, you can switch between them after starting X Server by pressing Ctrl+Alt+Plus and Ctrl+Alt+Minus. If you have only one resolution at any one mode, pressing Ctrl+Alt+Plus does nothing.

12. **Select the resolution and color level of your display using the cursor keys (select the actual value by pressing the Space bar; the Space bar toggles any of the possible selections on and off) and then Tab down to the OK button and press the Return key.**

The Starting X screen, shown in Figure 19-8, is shown.

Figure 19-8:
You are prompted to test the X configuration in the Start X screen.

13. **Press the OK button to test your X configuration. If you press the Skip button, then no test is performed and you are prompted to finish the configuration, as described in Step 12.**

If X Server has been configured correctly, then a graphical — X — window appears with a small dialog box that asks you if you can see it. If you can see it, then everything is cool, and you should click the Yes button. You then see a dialog box asking you whether you want to have X start up when you boot your system. Select Yes if you want to do so. Finally, an informational window appears; click the OK button.

The final You're Done window is shown in Figure 19-9.

14. **Press the Enter key and you return to the shell prompt.**

If you still have problems, then start the entire Xconfiguration system again. You should also consult the HOWTO documents in the /usr/doc/HOWTO/ XFree86-HOWTO documents for more help.

Delving deep into color depth

Color depth, the number of colors your system can have active on the screen at any one time, is loosely a function of both the amount of video memory your system has and the screen resolution.

If your system has a small amount of memory (such as 1MB), your screen can have a resolution of 1,024 x 768 pixels (dots) with 256 colors (8 bits) on the screen at one time. If your system has 2MB, you can have 64K colors (16 bits) on the screen at the same time at the same resolution. If you have an older video board with a small amount of video memory but some additional video memory sockets, you may be able to upgrade the amount of video memory on the video card.

If you have only 1MB and want to see 64K colors on the screen at one time, you can reduce your resolution from 1,024 x 768 to 800 x 600 pixels. If you want true color (24 bits), you can set your resolution to 640 x 480 pixels. The picture that

you're viewing will take up more of the screen, but color depth versus resolution is a trade-off that you can make by choosing the right options.

When you want to display an image and the color depth is not correct, nothing drastic happens. The picture may look a little lackluster or not quite normal. X has an interesting capability to have virtual color maps, which allow the active window to utilize all the colors of the bits of color depth, even if other windows are using different colors. When this option is turned on (as it is with the Red Hat distribution on this book's companion CD), the various windows turn odd colors as your mouse moves from window to window, but the window that your mouse activates is shown in the best color available. With newer video cards and larger video memories, which allow for true color at high resolutions in every window, this option is less useful.

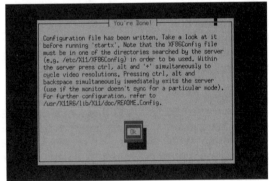

Figure 19-9:
The You're
Done
window.

Starting Your Xengine

Now you're ready to try out your new X configuration.

If you're already running X — have reconfigured it — then you can either reboot your computer or restart X. It's generally better and easier to simply restart it. To do this, press the Ctrl+Alt+Backspace keys at the same time. The screen goes black, flashes, takes a breath, flashes some more, and — if all goes well — returns with the new configuration.

If you're not running X, you can start it by entering the **startx** command at the command prompt.

If your new configuration doesn't work for some reason and the screen reverts to some unusable display, then something has gone wrong. It may be that you specified the video card incorrectly or that you answered some other question incorrectly. If you run into trouble, you can do several things:

- ✔ Rerun Xconfigurator. Hopefully, you can zero in on the correct configuration.
- ✔ Find out more detailed information about your video card and monitor by consulting manuals, documents, or Web sites.
- ✔ Find a newer version of XFree86 code from Red Hat at www.redhat.com or XFree organization itself at www.xfree86.org.
- ✔ Find an experienced Red Hat Linux guru to help you.
- ✔ Purchase another video adapter or monitor.
- ✔ Take a cruise to Fiji, where at the University of the South Pacific they have a really good computer science department in which everyone uses Linux.

If you try these solutions and still don't have X running, look around for a Red Hat Linux users' group at a local college or high school. Or perhaps a group of computer professionals in your area may help. If you call the local college computer science department, the folks there probably can help you find a student or staff member who uses Linux, has installed it on several types of machines, and can help you either figure out why your graphics system is not working or get a newer version of XFree86 that may support your video card.

If you feel strange going to these people to ask them for help, remember that they were once new to Linux, too, and probably had to struggle through an even more difficult installation. When you do go, remember to take *all* the accumulated information about your system that you have detected. It will save both you and them time and energy.

Finally, if your hardware is too new or proprietary, or if you have a notebook computer, you may want to buy a commercial X Server from Metrolink (www.metrolink.com) or Xi Graphics (www.xigraphics.com). Sometimes their codes work when XFree86 does not. Plus, if you buy an X Server, you can call the company's technical support line if you can't get it installed.

Finding out how X drivers are born

Your X programs come from code that was contributed to X project, which was first connected with Project Athena at the Massachusetts Institute of Technology. Later, the project became the main focus of the XConsortium, a nonprofit group established to develop Xtechnology.

Because the source code was freely distributable, a group of programmers from all over the world formed to give support to X Window code on low-end PC systems. They called themselves XFree86 based on the fact that their code was free and directed toward PCs, which were largely based on Intel x86 compatible processors.

Over time, they ported their code to freely distributable operating systems on other architectures. They did this — and continue to do this — for the love of programming. The XFree86 team

of programmers tries to give support to new video controllers as they come out. Unfortunately, giving this support is often difficult for several reasons:

- ✔ They have no relationship with the video controller manufacturer.

- ✔ The video controller manufacturer thinks that keeping the programming interface secret gives it an edge against its competitors.

- ✔ The video board is built into a larger system board.

- ✔ The video controller is simply too new.

Until support for new hardware is available, most people rely on SVGA compatibility mode to get the card to work.

If you knew all the issues involved in working with PC video hardware, you'd think it's fantastic that XFree86 developers can get it working at all (for more on XFree86, see the nearby sidebar). Even though XFree86 is freely distributable, you may want to make a donation to its development fund, which is listed at www.XFree86.org.

If your X Server is working and you want it to stop, press Ctrl+Alt+Backspace. You can then log off the root account. If you want to start X working again, log in to an account and type **startx**. X Server starts in a few moments.

Xterminating X

If you're accustomed to a Windows computer, having a section on shutting down the graphical interface may seem strange. After all, the Windows graphical interface is Windows — the GUI and the operating system are symbiotic. You can't run one without the other.

Red Hat Linux can run without running X. All you have to do is change the run level. The following steps show you how to do that:

1. **Log in as root.**

2. **Open a terminal emulator window.**

3. **Type the** `init 3` **command at the command prompt and press Enter.**

   X stops and you are returned to the command prompt.

You can also stop X in emergencies (say, if it freaks out) by pressing Ctrl+Alt+Backspace.

Part V

The Part of Tens

The 5th Wave   By Rich Tennant

"Think of our relationship as the latest version of Red Hat Linux— I will not share a directory on the love-branch of your life."

In this part . . .

Ah, the part you find in every *For Dummies* book: The Part of Tens. Here's where I get to rummage around and come up with ten of this and ten of that.

In Chapter 20, ten important places to find help are listed. You can use some of these sources also to enhance and widen your knowledge of Linux. There's no end to the things you can find out about Linux.

The ten most frequently encountered problems after people have installed Red Hat Linux are described in Chapter 21. If you have trouble that's not described in Chapter 18 — the network troubleshooting chapter — turn here first.

Chapter 20

Ten Sources of Help

By now, you're probably wondering whether any end exists to the amount of information and knowledge needed to run a Red Hat Linux system. The answer is yes; there is an end to the knowledge that you *need* to run a system well. But there's no end to the learning process if you want to understand how things work and interact. In this chapter, we suggest several ways to get additional training and support.

Books and More Books

When we started working with computers many years ago, the number of computer books about computers could fill one bookshelf, and they were mostly about the electronics of the hardware itself. Networking texts described the probability of two Ethernet packets colliding. We hardly ever saw books on computers in the popular press bookstores. Today, thousands of books on computers are available; most describe the software and its interactions, with the hardware taking a back seat. Books like the *...For Dummies* series aren't just for bookstores any more. You can find them in mass-market venues like Wal-Mart, for instance.

Perhaps you looked at other books before you bought this one and were intimidated by their use of technical terms. Or you thought them too general for what you wanted to do, and you wanted something more task-oriented. You may want to look over those books again because your knowledge level will be higher after reading this book. TCP/IP networking, compiler design, operating system theory, formal language theory, computer graphics, and systems administration training are all topics that you can study in greater depth when you have a Linux computer at your disposal.

Lots of books specifically about the Unix operating system are partially or completely applicable to Linux, such as books on Perl, a comprehensive interpreter. By getting one (or more) books on Perl and sitting down with your Linux system, you have both a new tool for doing your work and a new appreciation for a complete programming language. If you want to find out how to write Perl, you can just view the source code.

Linux HOWTOs

Don't forget about the Linux HOWTOs, which come on the commercial version of Red Hat Linux. You can obtain the disc by sending in the coupon included at the back of this book. These excellent guides to Linux are covered under the Linux Documentation Project — LDP — copyleft, which means you can print them.

School Days

Another way to find out more information about Unix and Linux is to take a course, perhaps at a local community college. Many colleges offer courses on Unix, and some have started using Linux to teach the Unix courses. You can do your homework on your system at home, or if you have a notebook (laptop computer), you can work anywhere. (Jon typed text for the first edition of this book in a hotel in Auckland, New Zealand, and updated text for the second edition in the United Airlines lounge in Chicago.) What we would have given during college for the chance to do computer projects sitting in the comfort of our own pub . . . er, dorm rooms. Instead, we had to sit in a room with a bunch of punch-card machines . . . well, never mind. We would have been much more comfortable and productive with a Linux system.

In the News

You can obtain additional information about the Linux operating system from the Internet. A facility called *Netnews* has tens of thousands of newsgroups, and each newsgroup covers a special topic. More than 30 newsgroups are devoted to Linux topics.

An ISP (Internet service provider) usually provides access to Netnews. You can use a text newsreader (such as `trn`, `tin`, or `pine`) or one of several Web browsers (such as the Netscape Communicator browser included on CD1 that came with this book) to read Netnews.

User Groups

User groups are springing up all over the country. Some are more active than others, but most hold meetings at least once a month. Some groups are Linux only; others are connected to a larger computer group — either Unix or a more general computer users association. User groups are a great opportunity to ask questions. User groups also tend to stimulate new ideas and ways of doing things.

You can find out if a Linux user group is in your area by checking with GLUE (Groups of Linux Users Everywhere), which is a service run by SSC (the publishers of the *Linux Journal*). GLUE is an automated map of user groups, and you can find it at the following address:

```
www.ssc.com
```

When you arrive at the site, click the **Resources** link, which takes you to the Linux Journal site. Then check out the Resources area there to find out where the user group closest to you meets.

No user group in your area? Then post a message at your local University or community college saying that you want to start one; other people in your area may decide to join you. Terrified at the thought of trying to start a user group? User group leaders often are not the most technically knowledgeable members but are simply good planners. They organize the meeting space, find (hound) speakers, send out meeting notices, locate sponsors, arrange refreshments (beer), and perform other organizational tasks. Sometimes being the leader seems like a thankless job, but when a meeting goes really well, it makes all the work worthwhile. So, as a newbie to Linux, you may not know a grep from an awk, but you still may make a very good chairperson.

Bring in the Cavalry

Some people want to be able to hire people to manage or fix their systems. This is what the commercial computer world calls *support*. Often, the place where you bought your computer — whether it's a store, a value-added reseller (VAR), or the manufacturer — provides the support.

Linux is criticized for not providing that same level of support. Although the number of hardware vendors that offers support is low, more and more people are well-versed in using Linux and are willing to offer some level of support, whether it be by e-mail, telephone, or on-site services.

The first group of people that offers support is the distribution makers. Red Hat Software, Inc. sells support contracts to their customers. These contracts range from e-mail support to telephone support. Red Hat, for example, recently introduced round-the-clock (24/7) support for a reasonable fee. Check out the Red Hat Web page (www.redhat.com) for more details.

Another group of people offering support is resellers of Linux systems. These people typically install Linux on hardware that you purchase from them. They will repair your system when it breaks, and help you with knotty problems (all for a fee).

The final group of people who offer support is the independent consultants who have learned about Linux and are now in the business of offering support for the system. You can find a list of consultants in a document called the Consultants HOWTO, which is available at the following address:

```
www.cyrius.com/tbm/usr/doc/HOWTO/Consultants-HOWTO
```

Once you become familiar with the resources that Red Hat Linux offers, you'll realize that it offers better support than most other proprietary systems. We find that consulting the HOWTO's or Usenet groups to solve problems and answer questions is easier than going through the traditional Help Desk route.

You can find a not-as-current copy of the consultants list on the *Red Hat Linux 7 For Dummies* documentation (CD3). You must send away for it with your coupon. You can also download the document from the Red Hat Web site.

Commercial Applications

Many Linux users are frugal (we prefer that term to *cheap*) and often want or need to use only freely distributable software. And in many cases, the freely distributable software is very good and does exactly what you want it to do. Other times, though, the software you want is available only as a commercial application.

Some Red Hat Linux users buy the latest and greatest hardware and want the same commercial applications on Linux that they have on their other operating systems, no matter what the price.

For commercial application vendors everywhere who may be reading this, we cannot stress enough that you should look at Linux just like *any other operating system.* You can sell your applications to a market that is not only appreciative but also believes, for various reasons, that its operating system should be *open.*

An example of functionality in the commercial world is Applixware Office by Applix, Inc. This office suite includes a word processor, a spreadsheet, a presentation package, a mail front end, an HTML authoring program, a graphical program for drawing pictures (usually to include in your presentation or paper), an application building program, and a scripting language that allows you to tie these and other programs together.

We wrote this book using Applixware Words and Sun Microsystems StarOffice. We chose to use these word processors instead of Microsoft Word because we could easily cut examples of code from the screen of our Red Hat Linux systems and paste them into the text of the book. We can also run the applications used as examples on the same machine. After finishing a chapter, we saved the chapter file in Rich Text Format (RTF) and e-mailed it to our editors. They used Microsoft Word and had no problem reading the material. Hey, the two worlds can get along.

Likewise, we use Applixware Presentation Editor to make presentations about Linux on Linux. When we talk about Linux at a show or a convention, we can demonstrate how to use X Window System while we have the presentation slides on the screen. If we used Microsoft PowerPoint, we would have to reboot the system into Linux to do the demo, an awkward approach at best. Applixware has many of the same functions as Microsoft products. Recent versions of Applixware Office can read and create PowerPoint output, and now we can run our systems truly FAT-free.

Visit Web Sites

A variety of Web sites are available for help. Some of these sites provide technical information, some provide news of about the Linux community, and others furnish a bandstand for the Linux community to voice its opinions. Here are some site that you may want to check out:

- **Linux International:** www.li.org
- **Linux Org:** www.linux.org
- **LinuxHQ:** www.linuxhq.com
- **Linux Today:** www.linuxtoday.com
- **Linux Documentation Project:** www.metalab.unc.edu/LDP/

- **Linux Now:** www.linuxnow.com
- ***Linux Journal, Linux Gazette, Linux Resources:*** www.ssc.com
- **Linux Focus:** www.linuxfocus.org
- ***Linux Weekly News:*** www.lwn.net
- **Slashdot:** www.slashdot.org
- **Freshmeat:** www.freshmeat.net
- **File Watcher:** www.filewatcher.org

This list is not exhaustive. You can find links to many more sites in some of the Web sites mentioned here.

Some of the lists offer opinions that are for mature audiences only. Most of the lists are moderated, and most of the opinions are mature, but people sometimes get carried away.

Attend Conferences

You can attend a number of conferences and trade shows to find out more information on Linux. All these shows are accurate as of the time we're writing this, but events may change. Where possible, we listed the more general Web addresses for these events. You may have to do a little Web surfing to find the next upcoming event. If you get stuck, try the Linux International Web site (www.li.org), which has an Events page that lists new events.

Linux Kongress

Linux Kongress is the oldest Linux event. Held in Germany every year, it's a technical conference with a small trade show. The Web site is www.linux-kongress.de.

Linux Expo

Linux Expo is held every spring in the Raleigh/Durham area in North Carolina. It's a technical conference, trade show, and all-in-all good time. In 1998, more than 2,000 attendees and numerous vendors attended. The Web site is www.linuxexpo.org.

USENIX/FREENIX

USENIX, a technical organization that has long supported Unix users, holds several technical conferences and small trade shows each year on various topics. A few years ago, a separate set of presentations, called FREENIX, was created for freely distributed operating systems such as Linux. If you're interested in a good technical conference that attracts Unix giants (such as Dennis Ritchie) or if you are a Linux developer, you may want to take a look at www. usenix.org.

CeBIT

CeBIT, the largest computer trade show in the world, is held yearly in Hannover, Germany. It often draws more than 600,000 people. Last year, Linux International (www.li.org) had a booth along with several other Linux vendors and drew more than 3,000 people. CeBIT is mostly a trade show, with very little (if any) conference sessions on Linux. To find out more about CeBIT, check out www. messe.de.

Comdex

For the past four years, Comdex has held a Linux Pavilion, made up of an ever-growing group of vendors who try to explain Linux to over 200,000 resellers, distributors, and other vendors. Comdex is held in the spring and fall in different U.S. cities. You can check out its Web site at www.comdex.com.

IDG's Linux World

Linux World is a new show with conferences that provides a venue for many commercial vendors. Its Web site is at www.linuxexpo.com.

Try to Help Others

After you've exhausted all avenues of help (or maybe even before), you should just try to figure it out yourself. Often, you'll find that the pieces fit together or that the software is not as difficult as you thought. Here are some tips:

> ✔ **If you are investigating a large software package, scan the documentation one time and then concentrate on the necessary topics.** Jon still remembers the first time he tried to learn groff, which is a powerful text-processing system. The documentation was daunting, and he thought he

would never learn the package. It turns out he was right — he never learned it. But he did learn enough to do a few simple things and that was all he needed to know. With those "few simple things" (less than 2 percent of the power of the package), he could write letters, create overhead slides, and do the necessary text processing. When he needed another command, he'd look it up in a reference book.

✔ **Create a small sample of what you want to do.** If you're working with a new command or part of Linux, create a small example of the one part of the command or software that you don't know, and see how that works.

✔ **Keep it small.** A friend of Jon's named Mike Gancarz wrote a book called *The Philosophy of Unix*. In this book, he talks about how Unix systems were created and programmed in the early days, utilizing lots of the small, cryptic (we prefer the word *terse*) commands that lurk below the glossy interface of X Window System. With these commands, you can create powerful programs called shell scripts or just use the commands one at a time to transform your data. The main tenet of his book is to keep things small and simple.

✔ **Remember that Linux is only a piece of code and your computer is only a machine.** So what if you make a mistake? You're probably running Linux on a machine that has only one user, you. That's the great thing about Linux: It runs on such inexpensive machinery that you can buy an old 486 computer with enough hard drive and memory in it to run Linux as a practice system, all for under $50. (Jon bought such a machine at a Ham Fest. It runs Linux very nicely.) So even if you have to reinstall your system due to some mistake you made, it won't disturb anyone else on your practice machine. You now know how to install Linux, so no one but you has to know when something goes wrong.

Our other suggestion is to help someone else. "What?" you say. "How can I help someone? I'm just a beginner in this field!"

We all started that way. No one is born with a knowledge of computer science. We all pick it up over time. The way to cement a thought or an idea, however, is to explain it clearly to someone else. Helping others install Linux on their PCs helps cement some of the concepts you've discovered. Another idea is to attend a Linux Install Fest, where lots of people go (with their machines) to install Linux. Here, not only do you get to help someone else, but you can also probably find out something from other attendees.

A main tenet of Linux is the word *open*. Linux is open and is best when shared.

Chapter 21

Ten Problem Areas and Solutions

● ●

● ●

*I*n any complex, technical situation, people end up having problems and issues that they need help with. The problems in this chapter were taken from a database of questions and answers created after hundreds of people installed the CD-ROMs. Some of these questions have been answered in the rest of the book, but because they still generate "what happened" questions, we repeat the information here.

I Can't Boot Red Hat Linux Anymore

Problem: You've installed Linux and everything is fine (naturally). Then one day you make a change to your Windows or Windows NT system, and Linux stops working. You no longer see the lilo boot prompt, so you can no longer specify that you want to boot Linux.

Solution: Various operating systems tend to think that they are the only operating system on the hard drive or on the system. Therefore, when they are installed or updated, they write things to an area of the system called the Master Boot Record (MBR). This process overlays the Linux boot loader (called LILO) and stops you from booting Linux. The best correction requires an ounce of prevention: Make an emergency boot disk, as we instruct you to do during installation. Keep this disk handy when you update your system (or during any other significant system event, such as repartitioning hard drives or rebuilding your kernel). Then if you make a mistake, you can boot the floppy, which will enable you to reboot your Linux operating system. When you've rebooted your system by using the boot disk, just log in as root and type **lilo** on the command line. This repairs the MBR by reinstalling LILO.

If you are installing multiple operating systems on a new machine, do yourself a favor and install Linux last. Otherwise, you have to keep reinstalling LILO.

My Hard Drive Numbers Have Changed Since Installation

Problem: Linux numbers hard drives each time it boots, calling SCSI hard drives names like sda, sdb, sdc, and sdd. Suppose that sda holds your Microsoft operating system, sdb holds the bulk of Linux, sdc holds your user files, and sdd holds your swap space. Now you add another hard drive and your user files are on sdd and your swap space is on sde. The new hard drive is called sdc but has nothing on it. What happened?

Solution: SCSI hard drives are lettered according to the SCSI IDs set on each hard drive. Linux names the hard drives by using this ordering scheme. If you insert a new hard drive into the SCSI bus with a SCSI ID that is lower than an existing hard drive, you rename all hard drives with a SCSI ID number above the one you just installed. It's best to start installing your SCSI hard drives with a SCSI ID of 0, 1, 2, and so on; then put other SCSI devices at the other end of the SCSI bus (SCSI IDs 6, 5, 4, and so on). Note that most SCSI controllers are set to SCSI ID 7 by default.

IDE hard drives are numbered according to the IDE controller they are on and whether they are a master or a slave on that controller. Therefore, adding a new hard drive to a set of IDE controllers will not change the existing names, as shown in the following two tables:

Controller	Hard Drive	Linux Name
ide0	master	hda
ide0	slave	hdb
ide1	master	hdc
ide1	slave	hdd

Controller	Hard Drive	Linux Name
ide2	master	hde
ide2	slave	hdf
ide3	master	hdg
ide3	slave	hdh

Controller designation	Controller priority
ide0	Primary controller
ide1	Secondary controller
ide2	Third controller
ide3	Fourth controller

My CD-ROM Isn't Detected

Problem: You're installing Linux, but it doesn't find your CD-ROM.

Solution: Most newer CD-ROMs are either EIDE (ATAPI) or SCSI, and most newer computer systems have enough support to see either the ATAPI CD-ROMs or the SCSI CD-ROMs, so CD-ROM support is not quite so much an issue as in the early days. In addition, some older systems and CD-ROMs are now supported.

Some early CD-ROMs pretended to be other devices (such as tape drives or floppies) to fool the computer system into using them, but these CD-ROMs were hidden from the detection system. If your system is one of these, don't despair: You can supply information to help Linux find your CD-ROM.

First look at the preceding section about hard drive numbering. This enables you to figure out the name that Linux would call your CD-ROM if Linux knew about it. If you have an EIDE/ATAPI CD-ROM, type the following line whenever you see the boot or lilo prompt while booting or installing your system:

```
linux hdX=cdrom
```

where *X* is the number your CD-ROM would have if it could be detected.

I Don't Know How to Remove LILO and Restore My MBR

Problem: You don't know how to replace the boot record that was on your system before you started installing Linux.

Solution: You can log in to Linux as root, and then type the following command:

```
lilo -u
```

Another solution is to boot MS-DOS or Windows 3.1, 95, 98, or NT to an MS-DOS prompt and type the following:

```
fdisk /mbr
```

I Can't Use LILO to Boot

Problem: You need to put Linux on a hard drive or a partition that is beyond the 1023rd cylinder, the second IDE hard drive, or the second SCSI ID number, or you need to do something else that will make it difficult for Linux to boot using LILO. Can you boot Linux in another way?

Solution: You can use a program called LOADLIN to boot from your MS-DOS or Windows system:

1. **Copy your configured Linux kernel to the C drive of your MS-DOS or Windows system.**

   The easiest way to do this is to install Linux, log in as root, and type the following:

   ```
   grep image /etc/lilo.conf
   ```

   A line similar to the following appears:

   ```
   image=/boot/vmlinuz-2.2.16-21
   ```

   This points to your compressed kernel, which in this example is located at /boot/vmlinuz-2.2.10-3.

2. **Copy the compressed kernel to a floppy disk, as follows:**

   ```
   mcopy /boot/vmlinuz-2.2.16-21 a:\vmlinux.gz
   ```

   The kernel name vmlinuz-2.2.16-21 refers to a specific version of the Linux kernel. Except for the /boot/vmlinuz- part, which remains constant, the name may be slightly different on your system.

A copy of LOADLIN comes with *Red Hat Linux 7 For Dummies* on CD1.

3. **Boot MS-DOS or Windows and put CD1 in your CD-ROM drive.**

4. **Go to the DOSUTILS directory and copy** LOADLIN.EXE **to your C drive.**

   If you are using MS-DOS or Windows 3.1, copy the LOADLIN16 file, which is the 16-bit version of the program.

5. **Copy the kernel image you just made on the floppy disk to your C drive.**

Now you can exit Windows and get to the MS-DOS prompt. You can then type the following (assuming your root partition is on partition /dev/hda5) to boot Linux:

```
C:\> loadlin vmlinux.gz root=/dev/hda5 ro
```

The ls Command Doesn't Show Files in Color

Problem: When running the ls command to show files in color, the command doesn't display files in color.

Solution: You have to edit the bashrc file in your home directory to add the following line to the end of the file:

```
alias ls='ls --color=auto'
```

Log off and then back in to reexecute your bashrc file (assuming you are using the bash shell), and ls shows different file types in different colors.

Linux Can't Find a Shell Script (Or a Program)

Problem: You type a command name, but Linux can't find the command, even if it's in the current directory.

Solution: When you type a shell or binary command name, Linux looks for the name in specific places and in a specific order. To find out what directories Linux looks in, and in what order, type the following command:

```
echo $PATH
```

You see a stream similar to the following:

```
/bin:/usr/bin:/usr/local/bin
```

These are the directories Linux looks in to find the command, program, or shell you want to execute. You may see more directories depending on your distribution or how your system administrator (if you have one) set up your system.

Now suppose you create a shell or a program called flobnob and want to execute it (and assuming you have set the permission bits to make flobnob executable by you). You have two choices (well, you have more than two choices, but I'm listing the safest ones). One choice is to type the following on the command line:

```
./flobnob
```

This tells Linux to look in this directory (./) and execute flobnob.

Your second choice is to move flobnob to one of the directories shown in the PATH variable, such as /usr/local/bin.

When I Start X Window System, I See a Gray Screen

Problem: You configured the X Window System, but when you log in as a general user (that is, not as root) and type **startx**, all you get is a gray screen with a big X in the middle. You wait a long time, but nothing happens.

Solution: First recognize that you may have to wait a long time for a slow CPU with a small amount of main memory (about 8MB). Some machines with small amounts of memory have required as long as 6 minutes to start X. But assuming that you are starting X on a machine with a faster CPU and more memory, you may have problems with permissions on your home directory. This is particularly true if X works when you are logged in as root (that is, as superuser) but not when you are logged in as a general user.

To correct this problem, log in as root and go to the home directory of the user who is having problems. For this example, suppose that the login name of the user is lupe. After you are in the user's home directory, issue the ls -ld command to see who owns that directory and what the permissions are on that directory:

```
cd ~lupe
ls -ld .
drwxrwx-- root bin 1024 Aug 31 16:00 .
```

Note that in this example, the directory is owned by root and the group ownership is `bin`, which does not allow `lupe` to have access to the directory structure inside the directory. Because the shells and terminal emulators that X needs require access to that directory structure, X can't fully work.

To correct this problem, use the `chown` and `chgrp` commands to change the ownership of the `/lupe` home directory to lupe and to change the group ownership of the lupe home directory to users:

```
chown lupe ~lupe
chgrp users ~lupe
```

Make sure you replace the `lupe` login name that we use in this example with the login name you are having difficulty with.

I Don't Know How to Make the X Window System Start at Boot Time

Problem: You don't want to have to log in to a command-line mode (such as DOS) and then type **startx**. Instead, you want to log in through X Window System.

Solution: We set up our machine so that it starts in nongraphical mode and then allows us to switch to X. (Many times, we only want to make a simple edit or look at something on the system, and logging in without X is simply faster.) If you like to see a graphical interface from the beginning, however, do the following. In the `/etc/inittab` file, change this line:

```
id:3:initdefault:
```

to this:

```
id:5:initdefault:
```

Save your changes and reboot. X starts at the end of the boot process, and you can then log in through the graphical interface. To go back to the old way of booting, change the line in the `/etc/inittab` file back to the following:

```
id:3:initdefault:
```

and reboot the machine.

I Never Seem to Have the Correct Time

Problem: When you boot Linux the time is wrong, so you set it with the date command. Then you boot Windows and its time is wrong, so you reset it. When you reboot Linux, its time is wrong again.

Solution: Most Unix systems keep their time by using Universal Time (also known as Greenwich Mean Time, or GMT), but Microsoft systems keep their time as local time. When you set the time in either system, you set the CPU clock to that version of the time. Then when you boot the other system, it interprets what is in the CPU clock differently and reports a different time.

Linux enables you to store and think of the clock as either GMT or local time. You make this choice when you install the system. To change your choice, follow these steps:

1. **Log in as root.**

2. **Type** timeconfig.

   The Configure Timezones dialog box appears. Set your system clock to GMT (Greenwich Mean Time) by selecting the Hardware Clock Set To GMT option at the top of the screen.

3. **Deselect the Hardware Clock Set To GMT option.**

   Highlight the option by pressing the tab key, if necessary. (Actually, you should be there when you activate the timeconfig command.)

4. **Press the spacebar to deselect the option. Press the tab key until you reach the OK button, and then press Enter.**

5. **Reset the time to the proper value by using the date command if you reboot Linux or through the Windows system if you boot Windows.**

Part VI
Appendixes

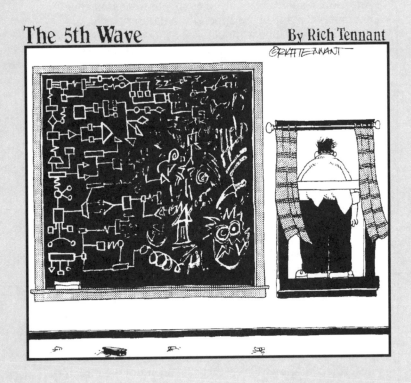

The 5th Wave   By Rich Tennant

In this part . . .

This is the part of every book where you find things that just didn't fit into the flow of the chapters. This part includes the fun and exciting appendixes.

Appendix A shows you how to figure out what stuff your computer is made of. An appendix that describes how to install Red Hat Linux without using a mouse follows it. The two make a good pair, because sometimes it is necessary to obtain information about your hardware in order to make the installation easier, or even just to make it work at all. The installation chapter describes a method that does not require a graphics card to work. The text-based method works on more machines — read older machines — than the standard graphical one described in Chapter 3. It's included here as a fall-back mechanism in case the one described in Chapter 3 doesn't work for you.

The venerable, but still highly useful, vi editor is described in Appendix C. vi is a text-based (non-graphical) text editor. It has been around for decades and is widely used by system administrators, around the world, to get their work done. It is useful to know at least a little about vi because it is included on nearly every Linux computer.

Appendix D provides information on Linux man pages. Man pages are the most basic way of distributing information in Linux (and UNIX). They are simple to use, too!

Finally, the contents of the companion CD-ROM's are described in Appendix E. The basic layout of the directory tree is described in that section.

Appendix A

Discovering Your Hardware

. . . .

In This Appendix

▶ Figuring out which resources Red Hat Linux requires

▶ Identifying your hardware and its function

. . . .

This appendix helps you determine what kind of hardware you have on your system. If you have problems installing Red Hat Linux in Chapter 3, or just want to do some extra preparation, then this appendix can help you. By determining what hardware subsystems you have on your computer, you are better able to install Linux.

Generally, Linux runs on any Intel processor that is a 386 or newer, as well as on various Digital Alpha, Sun SPARC, Motorola, MIPS, PowerPC, and HP/PA platforms.

Knowing if Your Hardware Can Handle Red Hat Linux

Linux supports *symmetric multiprocessing (SMP)*, which means you can have more than one CPU per computer. In fact, Linux supports several processors per system. If your system has more than one CPU, Linux can utilize those CPUs also, either by speeding up a specific program written to take advantage of multiple CPUs or by allowing more programs to execute at one time. (If you have an SMP system, would you care to trade with us?)

The Intel processor should have the following amount of RAM (main memory):

✔ Without graphics, Linux runs (er, walks) with 4MB.

✔ With graphics, Linux runs at a minimum with 8MB; with 16MB, the graphics get much faster.

✔ With 32MB, Linux screams and the speed of the application (particularly a graphics-oriented program) increases dramatically.

✔ Some Linux developers have 128MB in the systems because they tend to run many programs at a time, and each program takes up a certain amount of RAM when running.

Some early CD-ROM drives are not IDE; they attach directly to sound cards and other devices. Red Hat Linux can try to detect and use these. If you don't have an IDE/ATAPI or SCSI CD-ROM drive, you need to know the make and model number of your CD-ROM drive and what type of controller (perhaps a specific sound card) the CD-ROM drive is attached to. To do this, you have to open up your system and look for the make and model number of the CD-ROM on the physical drive.

You can install Linux on a notebook (laptop computer) by using the notebook's built-in CD-ROM drive (if it has one), or a CD-ROM drive attached to the note-book's docking station, or a SCSI CD-ROM drive attached to a PCMCIA SCSI con-troller. If you don't have any of these, you can try to get a PCMCIA Ethernet controller and do a network installation, given that another Linux system on the network has a CD-ROM drive installed. If that is the course you take, then con-sult Red Hat's installation documentation at `www.redhat.com/support`.

You also need a keyboard, a mouse, and a video card. Linux supports a wide range of video cards. Even if your card is not supported directly, Linux may support it as a generic VGA, XGA, SVGA, or other graphical hardware, stan-dard video card. Most video cards that have been available for a while are supported.

Finding Out What You Have

One of the most important preliminary steps for a successful installation of Linux is finding out the type of hardware you have. You can find most of this information in the manuals that came with your computer. The manuals won't be much help, however, if:

✔ You threw the manuals out

✔ You lost the manuals

✔ You bought your computer secondhand from someone who threw away or lost the documentation

✔ You bought your PC with Windows already installed

The last reason is the most insidious because it means the people you bought the PC from did not bother to buy the documentation for each part of the PC when they assembled it for you. That would have cost them more money.

Instead, it used OEM parts (read that "sans documentation and colorful box"), and bought only one copy of the documentation for their use. With Windows already installed, the company reasoned that an end user wouldn't need any documentation about the system.

Contact the place where you bought your system. Perhaps you can obtain a copy of the documentation from the dealer.

If that doesn't work, open up your system and look at the components. For instance, a source of information about your hard drive is the label on top of the disk drive. If you don't feel comfortable opening up your system, you may want to take it back to where you bought it — assuming you didn't buy it by mail order — and perhaps the dealer can open it up and tell you what you have.

You can also look to the World Wide Web for information. Many vendors use their Web site to provide technical data about their devices. For that, you need to know your equipment's manufacturer, make, and model number.

Another source of information is Windows itself. Step-by-step instructions in the following sections show you exactly how to use these operating systems to get all the information you need.

If you don't have any literature about your system, and you don't have Windows on your system (perhaps you like to run FAT-free), and no dealer is within hundreds of miles, don't give up hope. Red Hat Linux is good at sniffing out and identifying hardware during the installation.

Talking to Your Computer (And Knowing What You Should Ask)

Knowing how your computer is constructed can help you when you install Red Hat Linux. Your computer is built from several primary groups of equipment. The following list shows what the groups are:

- **Hard drive controllers.** How many do you have, and what are their types (IDE, SCSI)? Which hard drives are connected to which controllers? If a SCSI controller is installed in your machine, what's its make and model number?

- **Hard drives.** How many hard drives do you have? For each drive, what is its size and order (which one is first, second, and so on)?

- **CD-ROM.** What is the interface type? Is it an IDE drive, a SCSI drive, or some other type? For CD-ROM drives other than IDE (ATAPI) or SCSI, what is the make and model number?

✔ **RAM.** How much RAM is installed on the computer?

✔ **Mouse.** What type of mouse do you have — a bus mouse, a PS/2 mouse, or a serial mouse? How many buttons does it have? If you have a serial mouse, which COM port is it attached to and what protocol does it use (such as Microsoft or Logitech)?

✔ **Monitor.** What is the make and model of the monitor? What are its vertical and horizontal refresh rates? You need this information only if you will be using the graphical portion of Linux, called X Window System.

✔ **Video card.** What is the make and model number of the video card or video chip set and the amount of video RAM?

✔ **Network interface card (NIC).** If you have a network connection, what is the make and model number of the network interface card?

✔ **Network information**. If you have a network connection, what is your IP address, netmask, gateway IP address, name server IP addresses, and host and domain names? If you need help, contact your network administrator or Internet service provider (ISP).

To install Red Hat Linux, you need to answer the questions in the preceding list. Now that you know what you should be looking for, the next section delves a bit more into how to locate and capture that information.

Hard drive controllers

The two main types of hard drives are IDE and SCSI, and each type has its own controller. IDE is more common in PCs, and newer PCs usually have two IDE controllers rather than one. For each IDE controller, your system can have only two hard drives: a master and a slave. Therefore, a PC with two IDE controllers can have up to four hard drives. You should know which hard drive is which. Also, if you have a Windows system that you want to preserve, you should know which hard drive it resides on. The following is the normal configuration on a Windows system:

✔ The first controller's master drive is called C.

✔ The next hard drive is called D and is the slave drive on the first controller.

✔ The next hard drive is E and is the master drive on the second controller.

✔ The last hard drive is F and is the slave drive on the second controller.

Normally, Windows is located on your C drive, and data is on your other drives. This lettering scheme is just one possibility; your hard drives may be set up differently and may even include CD-ROMs as drives on your IDE controllers.

Some high-end PCs have a SCSI controller on the motherboard or on a separate SCSI controller board, either in addition to or instead of the IDE controllers. Older SCSI controllers can have up to eight devices on them, numbered 0–7, including the controller. Newer SCSI controllers (known as *wide controllers*) can have up to 16 devices, including the controller itself.

If all you have is a SCSI hard drive, usually drive 0 or drive 1 is your C drive, and others follow in order.

If you have a mixture of IDE and SCSI controllers, your C hard drive could be on any of them. The sections later in this chapter — "Getting Information from Windows 95/98" and "Getting Information from MS-DOS" — show you how to identify how many hard drives you have, what type they are, and the controllers to which they are attached.

Introducing hard drives

You need to decide whether you want to put Linux on a separate hard drive from MS-DOS and Windows or whether you want the two operating systems to share one hard drive.

Most people think of Windows (either Windows 3.1, Windows 95, or Windows 98) as an operating system. All Windows systems, however, have an underlying system called MS-DOS that manages the hard drives and many hardware components of your PC. From here on, unless we mention a particular system, consider MS-DOS and Windows as the same thing.

We strongly recommend that you put Linux on a separate hard drive. First, you can now find 2GB hard drives for less than $100 (U.S.). Second, the task of shrinking MS-DOS and Windows small enough to allow Linux to reside in its full glory on an existing hard drive is difficult at best and impossible at worst. And although splitting the Red Hat Linux distribution across hard drives is possible, doing so will make updating the distribution difficult.

If you do purchase another hard drive, install it as the second hard drive on the first IDE controller or as drive 1 on your SCSI controller (assuming that your existing Windows hard drive is either the first hard drive on your IDE controller or ID 0 on your SCSI controller). Adding hard drives is a hardware thing; the store where you buy the hard drive should be able to add it to your system for you. And while the system is there, you can ask the store folks to tell you the details on the other hardware in your system.

While installing Red Hat Linux on your hard drive, you may be asked to supply the number of drive heads (or tracks), the number of cylinders, and the number of sectors per track. Most modern hard drives provide this information on a paper label on the outside of the drive. Some modern hard drives are set up for Windows, and Linux can access the number of drive heads, cylinders, and sectors.

Old systems and new hard drives

Hard drives are made up of cylinders of information, which in turn are made up of tracks of information, which in turn are made up of blocks of information. Newer hard drives have more cylinders than older computer systems can handle easily. Therefore, a method called *logical block addressing,* or LBA, was created so that older computer systems can work with newer hard drives, which have more than 1,023 cylinders.

The BIOS setup under hard drives typically specifies whether your computer system is capable of LBA. Your hard drive may already be accessed as an LBA hard drive. Some BIOS systems do this automatically the first time a hard drive with a large number of cylinders is accessed. Note, however, that changing your hard drive to an LBA specification, if it is not LBA already, will make the data on the hard drive inaccessible. Therefore, before changing your hard drive to LBA, you should back it up if it contains any data. (You may decide that adding another hard drive is not such a bad idea as an expansion strategy.)

Different hardware systems have different ways to enter the BIOS setup. Usually, you can enter the BIOS setup when you turn on the power and start to boot; when you press the Reset button on the front of the system and start to reboot; or when you go through the normal shutdown of your Windows system, and ask to reboot. As your computer starts, it displays a message telling you what key to press in order to enter the BIOS menu. The key is generally the Delete or F1 key, but can also be F2 or F10.

If you have your computer apart looking for other information (a pox on manufacturers who don't supply such useful information), you may as well write down all the hard drive information you can find. You should look for the number of heads, cylinders, and sectors. This information is used to tell the operating system where to put data with respect to the beginning of the hard drive. If you have trouble, check out the "Getting Information from Windows 95/98" and "Getting Information from MS-DOS" sections. SCSI hard drive users don't have to supply this information because the SCSI controller and device drivers calculate it on-the-fly. SCSI hard drive owners should, however, know the size of their hard drives, which is printed on the hard drive or is available through the sections just mentioned.

Getting Information from Windows 95/98

If you have Windows 95 or Windows 98, you can use the msd program in MS-DOS mode as described in the next section to find out about the hardware in your system. Much more information is available, however, through the Control Panel in Windows 95/98.

With pencil and paper handy, it's time to get to the Control Panel and all that information. Follow along with these steps:

1. **Click the Start button and choose Settings⇨Control Panel.**

   We use a shorthand method for showing menus. When you see a line such as the following:

   Click the Start button and choose Settings⇨Control Panel

   it means "Click the Start button, then click the Settings menu item, and then click the Control Panel item."

2. **Double-click the System icon, and then click the Device Manager tab.**

3. **At the top of the screen, click to select the View Devices by Connection option.**

   This shows all components and how they relate to each other.

   If you have a printer attached to your system, at this point you can click the Print button. Then, in the Print dialog box that appears, select the All Devices and System Summary option. Click OK. This procedure prints a full report about your system. You may not have all the information you need, such as which hard drive goes with which controller, but you will save yourself a lot of writing.

4. **In the list, on the Device Manager tab, click Computer.**

5. **Click the Properties button.**

   The Computer Properties dialog box appears.

6. **Select the Interrupt Request (IRQ) option and write down the displayed information.**

   The Setting column, at left, lists interrupt requests. The hardware using a particular IRQ is listed in the right column. Note that no two devices can use the same IRQ.

7. **Select the Direct Memory Access (DMA) option and write down the displayed information.**

8. **Select the Input/Output (I/O) option and write down the pertinent information.**

   Look for and write down entries regarding a sound card (if you have one) and a parallel port (LPT).

9. **Click Cancel.**

   You return to the Device Manager tab of the System Properties dialog box.

Now you need to find out about the other devices in your system. This process takes some time, so you may want to pause here and grab something to drink, fix something to eat, and put on some tunes before following these steps:

1. **On the Device Manager tab of the System Properties dialog box, select the View Devices by Type option.**

   In the list, notice how a plus or minus sign precedes some icons. A plus sign indicates that the entry is collapsed. A minus sign indicates the entry is expanded to show all subentries.

2. **In the list, make sure that all items are expanded.**

   Expanded simply means that a minus sign precedes the icon. If a plus sign is there instead, click it and it changes to a minus sign. As you expand some entries, you may see more plus signs. Click each plus sign to expand it. You may need to use the scroll bar to the right of the window to bring additional items into view.

3. **Look through the list for Standard IDE/ESDI Hard Disk Controller or SCSI Host Adapter.**

   Write down the complete label, which tells you what type of drive controller you are currently investigating.

4. **Look at the first subentry under that hard drive controller, if any. Write down the type of drive. Now double-click that drive entry.**

   The General tab of the Properties dialog box for that device appears.

   If the controller has no entries, do not despair. Some systems have extra hard drive controllers (particularly if you are using SCSI hard drives) that are not connected to any hard drives. Also, be aware that the first controller may have some other type of device connected to it, such as a tape drive or a CD-ROM. If no drives are attached to this controller, just go on to the next controller.

5. **Click the Settings tab, write down the drive type, and then click Cancel.**

   The screen returns to the Device Manager tab of the System Properties dialog box.

6. **Write down the highlighted information, which is the type of hard drive controller.**

7. **For each disk subentry for that controller, repeat Steps 4 to 6.**

8. **Follow the same general steps for any other hard drive controller entries.**

9. **For the Display adapters entry, simply write down each subentry.**

   Don't bother clicking Properties because it won't supply you with any information that is useful for installing Linux.

10. **For the Keyboard entry, write down each subentry.**

11. **Likewise for the Monitor entry.**

12. **Like-likewise, for the Mouse entry.**

13. **Like-like-likewise, for the Ports (Com & LPT) entry.**

14. **Finally, for the Sound, Video, and Game Controllers entry, copy information on both the General tab and the Resources tab.**

    Double-click the first subentry, and the General tab appears (as usual). Write down the information. Then, instead of clicking Cancel, click Resources at the top of the screen to display the Resources tab. Write down the information, and then click Cancel.

15. **Back at the Device Manager tab, click Cancel.**

    The screen returns to the Control Panel.

Whew. That was a lot of copying, but you aren't finished yet. Follow these steps for fascinating facts about your monitor:

1. **Make sure that the Control Panel is displayed.**

   If it isn't, click the Start button and choose Settings⇨Control Panel.

2. **Double-click the Display icon.**

   The Display Properties dialog box appears.

3. **Click the Settings tab.**

   The screen displays your monitor's settings.

4. **Copy the information under Color Palette and Desktop Area.**

   The Color Palette information is 16 color, 256 color, High Color (16 bit), or True Color (24 bit). The Desktop Area information is 640 by 480 pixels, 800 by 600 pixels, 1,024 by 768 pixels, or some higher numbers.

5. **Click Cancel.**

   You are returned to the Control Panel.

And now, it's time to check the time:

1. **From the Control Panel, click the Date/Time icon.**

   The Date/Time Properties dialog box appears.

2. **Click the Time Zone tab, if necessary, so that it appears on top of the Date & Time tab.**

3. **Copy the text at the top of the screen.**

   The text begins with *GMT,* which stands for Greenwich Mean Time, which is the world standard. The number after GMT indicates the difference between your time and the GMT. Be sure to copy the words that indicate your time zone, such as Eastern Time (U.S. and Canada).

    4. Click Cancel.

Tired of this yet? You're almost finished. Next you discover delightful details about your printer:

1. **From the Control Panel, double-click the Printers icon.**

2. **Double-click to select the first non-networked Printer icon (one without a wire underneath it).**

   Another window appears. This new window has the same name as the printer you double-clicked. Don't click the icon labeled Add Printer.

3. **In the menu bar at the top of the window, choose Printer⇨Properties and then click the Details tab.**

4. **Copy the make and model and the communications port the printer is attached to.**

   The make and model appears at the top of the screen, next to the printer icon. The communications port is listed after `Print to the Following Port`.

5. **Click Cancel.**

6. **Double-click the next Printer icon, and repeat Steps 3 through 5.**

7. **Close any open windows by clicking the Close button.**

   The Close button is the one with the X, in the upper-right corner of a window.

The following, we promise, is the last set of steps. Here's how you get the hard facts about your hard drives:

1. **Double-click the My Computer icon on the Windows 95/98 desktop.**

2. **Select the first hard drive by clicking its icon. Copy down the capacity and the free space left.**

3. **Repeat Step 2 for all other hard drives.**

This information will be useful later as you make decisions about how much space to leave for Windows 95 or Windows 98 (if any) and how much space you have for Linux on each hard drive.

Getting Information from MS-DOS

If you're running MS-DOS or Windows 3.1 — egads! — you have a program on your system called Microsoft Diagnostics, or msd. This program will tell you information about the hardware on your system, which you can then use to determine how to set up Linux.

If you have a printer attached to your system, you're in luck. You can avoid writer's cramp by following these steps:

1. **Make sure your system is in DOS or MS-DOS mode.**

   If you have just booted, you may be in MS-DOS mode. The screen will mostly be black with a prompt like this `c:\>`.

   If you have booted and are in Microsoft Windows 3.1, press Alt+F+X, which exits Windows and returns you to DOS. Then you will see the `c:\>` prompt.

2. **Type** msd **to start the program.**

   The main screen appears, with categories such as computer and memory.

3. **Press Alt+F+P.**

4. **Press the spacebar and choose Report All.**

5. **Press the Tab key until the cursor is in the Print To section.**

6. **Use the up- and down-arrow keys on the keyboard to select the port your printer is attached to or to create a file to hold the information.**

7. **Press Tab until the cursor is on the OK button.**

8. **Press the Enter key.**

9. **Fill in the Customer Information, if you want.**

10. **Press the Tab key until the cursor is on the OK button.**

11. **Press the Enter key to print the report or create the file.**

   If you're creating a file, you may want to press the Tab key to move to the text box that contains the name of the file that will be holding the report, and change the file extension to txt, so that the file will be easier to print later from Windows.

Although you may not get all the information you need from this printout, you will get a great deal of it, and it will probably be more accurate than information you write by hand.

If you don't have a printer, get some paper and a pen and prepare to copy some information:

1. **Make sure your system is in DOS or MS-DOS mode.**

   See Step 1 in the preceding set of steps for more information.

2. **Type** msd **to start the program.**

   The main screen appears, with categories such as computer and memory.

3. **Press P (for processor) and copy the information on the screen.**

   The screen displays the type of processor in your system (usually a 386, 486, or some other type of Intel chip).

4. **Press Enter to return to the main screen.**

5. **Press V (for video screen) and copy the displayed information.**

   You see your system's video adapter type (usually VGA, XGA, or SVGA). Also look for the display type (such as VGA Color or SVGA Color), manufacturer, and video BIOS version. Pay particular attention to the video BIOS version because it may also list the computer chip set used to make the video controller, which in turn will be used to set up the graphical part of Linux.

6. **Press Enter to return to the main screen.**

7. **Press N (for network) and copy the displayed information.**

   If your system has no networking capability or none that msd knows about, you may see a message that says no network.

8. **Press Enter.**

9. **Press U (for mouse) and copy the displayed information.**

   Look for entries for mouse hardware, the driver manufacturer, the DOS driver type, and the number of mouse buttons. Well, you don't really need to refer to the screen to figure out that last one.

10. **Press Enter.**

11. **Press D (for disk drives) and copy the pertinent information.**

    Now it gets interesting. Copy your floppy drive's capacity and number of cylinders. (For a floppy drive, these values are usually 1.44MB and 80 cylinders, respectively.) Then look for your hard drives, usually designated as C, D, E, and so on. Each one should have a Total Size entry and a number such as 400M, which stands for 400 megabytes. You should also see an entry such as CMOS Fixed Disk Parameters, followed by something like 731 Cylinders, 13 heads, 26 sectors/track. This information is useful in setting up your disks for Linux.

12. **Press Enter.**

13. **Press L (for parallel ports) and write down the pertinent information.**

    The screen displays entries such as LPT1 and LPT2. Linux usually finds out about these all by itself. In case it doesn't, write down the port address, which is usually a number such as 0378H.

14. **Press Enter.**

15. **Press C (for the COM ports) and write down the pertinent information.**

    The COM ports are your serial ports, which are typically used for a modem, a serial printer, and other interesting gadgets. Copy the port address, baud rate, parity, data bits, stop bits, and UART chip used. Usually, you don't need any of this information for Linux, but it's useful to have a complete record of your system.

16. **Press Enter.**

17. **Press Q (for IRQ list) and copy the information.**

    The different hardware pieces use IRQ, which stands for *interrupt request,* to signal the main CPU that they have some data that has to be processed.

    No two devices can have the same IRQ. Copying the information in these columns for all 16 IRQs (0–15) is important for later sanity.

18. **Press Enter to go back to the main screen, and then press F3 to end the msd program.**

Leaving a Trail of Bread Crumbs

This next step is very important: Back up your system! It's beyond the scope of this book to describe how to back up Windows computers. You should consult the Microsoft Web site at www.microsoft.com to investigate what back-up utilities are available to you.

Appendix B

Installing Red Hat Linux in Text Mode (The Ugly Way)

• •

*R*ed Hat Linux gives you two installation interface choices: a graphical and a menu-based one. The graphical system simplifies the process by grouping similar configuration choices together. The menu-based one takes you step-by-step through the entire installation. The menu-based installation system works on more computers than the graphical one. The graphical system doesn't work on all video cards. Therefore, we describe the menu-based one here.

Stage 1: Starting the Installation

To begin the menu-based installation, follow these steps:

1. **Insert the *Red Hat Linux 7 For Dummies* CD1 into your CD-ROM drive (and your boot floppy disk if you can't boot from CD) and boot or reboot your computer.**

   In Chapter 2 we show you how to test and see if you can boot from CD-ROM and, if you can't, how to create a boot floppy disk with Windows, MS-DOS, or Linux.

   The Welcome to Red Hat Linux screen appears and the boot: prompt appears at the bottom of the screen.

   During the installation, you and Red Hat Linux talk to each other by using — what else — dialog boxes. To maneuver between highlighted options in a dialog box and make your choices, use the following keys (note that *cursor* means the cursor or the highlight): Table B-1 gives you the lowdown on how to maneuver through those text boxes like a pro.

Table B-1	Installation Keyboard Shortcuts
Key	*What It Does*
Tab	Moves the cursor to the next section in the screen
Alt+Tab	Moves the cursor to the previous section in the screen
Left arrow	Moves the cursor backward through a list of options
Right arrow	Moves the cursor forward through a list of options
Up arrow	Moves the cursor up through a list of options
Down arrow	Moves the cursor down through a list of options
Spacebar	Selects an item from a list of options
Enter	Selects the highlighted item
F12	Accepts the values you chose and displays the next screen

2. **Type in** text **at the boot prompt and press Enter (the graphical installation process will begin after 5 seconds if you don't enter anything).**

   The Linux kernel loads and shows you a couple of pages of hardware and system information, indicating whether your hardware is being detected by the Linux kernel. From here on you can use the keyboard shortcuts described in Table B-1 to manuever through the dialog boxes.

   If the hardware is not being detected, you can get more installation information from Red Hat's online installation manual — in HTML format — located on CD1 in the `/mnt/cdrom/doc/rhmanual/manual` directory. You can mount CD1 on another Linux or Windows system and view the document with Netscape. Most of the time, thankfully, and particularly with newer systems, Linux detects all your computer's basic hardware.

   If you want to stop the installation process, simply eject the boot disk, remove the CD from the drive, and reboot or shut down your machine.

3. **In the Language Selection dialog box, select the language that you speak and select OK.**

   You can choose from several languages, but by all means, pick one that you can read.

4. **In the Keyboard Selection dialog box, select the keyboard that you want to use and select OK.**

   Red Hat Linux displays an introducory Welcome to Red Hat Linux! screen. You're now finished with the preliminary configuration process.

Red Hat provides a complete and detailed installation guide with the CDs that come with this book (CD3), which is included on the Red Hat Linux Publisher's Edition CD-ROM that comes with this book. You obviously can't use the computer that you're installing Red Hat Linux on until you install Red Hat Linux. But after you install Red Hat Linux, you probably don't need the installation guide. However, if you have access to another computer — Linux or Windows — you can mount the Red Hat Linux CD-ROM on that computer and look at the manual with Netscape or another browser. If you have another Linux computer, then open the `/mnt/cdrom/doc/rhmanual/manual/index.htm` file. On a Windows computer, you will want to look at `D:\doc\rhmanu\manual\index.htm`, assuming that your CD-ROM drive is the D: drive.

5. In the Installation Type dialog box, select OK.

The Workstation option is selected by default in the Installation Type window. Red Hat provides several installation methods, two standard workstation classes, and one server class. You can also use a custom method as well as upgrading an existing Red Hat Linux installation, but this book uses the Workstation installation because it includes just about everything the average user needs and is one heck of a lot easier to boot.

Linux asks next if you want to let the Red Hat Linux installation system automatically partition your disk or if you will do so manually.

6. In the Automatic Partitioning dialog box, select OK.

The default action (Continue) is to automatically partition your disk. The process starts immediately after selecting OK.

This book uses the automatic method because it provides the most straightforward installation process for you with by far the least hassle. The manual method can be quite difficult to perform, and unless you have a compelling reason to do so, there isn't much point.

The automatic partitioning process removes all the data from your hard drive.

Eventually the Network Configuration dialog box appears. The next section shows you how to connect your network from this dialog box.

7. If you want your machine to be a stand-alone workstation, select No, press the Enter key, and go on to the next section; if your system is connected to a network, select Yes and press the Enter key.

As you fill in the dialog boxes, you may find that Red Hat Linux guesses what information is needed and fills in some sections automatically. If Linux has guessed incorrectly, simply change the information.

Stage 2: Configuring Your Network

If you have an Ethernet adapter and are connected to a Local Area Network (LAN), and you chose to configure your Red Hat Linux computer network connection, this section is for you. If you skipped the network nonsense, you can skip this section.

The following steps describe how to configure your Red Hat Linux computer network connection:

1. **In the Hostname Configuration dialog box, type the name of your Linux computer.**

   For example, type the name **chivas** at the prompt, select the OK button, and press Enter.

    Press the Tab key to get to the OK button and press Enter.

2. **In the Load Module dialog box, select the type of Ethernet adapter that you have.**

   You are given a list of Ethernet adapters to choose from. You must select the manufacturer and model of your adapter. Note that Ethernet adapters are often referred to as network interface connectors (NIC).

3. **Configure your Ethernet adapter.**

   Red Hat can attempt to find the configuration information about your adapter. If you select the Autoprobe option and your Ethernet adapter is less than a few years old, then Red Hat Linux most likely will detect the information. Otherwise, use the Specify Options and enter the information yourself.

4. **Choose whether to enter your IP address manually or to have a BOOTP or a DHCP server hand you a dynamic IP.**

   The latter two options — BOOTP and DHCP — are not frequently used in home or small networks. This book uses, and you should select, the Static IP address option.

5. **Enter your IP Address, Netmask, Default Gateway (IP), and Primary Nameserver.**

   The following list gives a brief description of the four parameters. But describing the Internet Protocol (IP) is beyond the scope of this book. Please consult the various networking HOWTOs on CD1.

   • **IP address.** This is the numeric network address of your Linux computer and is what your computer is known as on your local network and — in many cases — the Internet. If you haven't registered your private network's (also known as local networks or LANs) address space with the InterNic (the organization that is in charge of distributing IP addresses), then you can use the public address space that goes from 192.168.1.1 to 192.168.254.254.

- **Netmask.** Private networks based on the Internet Protocol (IP) are divided into subnetworks. The netmask determines how the network is divided. For addresses such as the one in the preceding bullet (192.168.1.1, and so on), the most common netmask is 255.255.255.0.

- **Default gateway (IP).** This is the numeric IP address of the computer that connects your private network to the Internet (or another private network). Red Hat guesses the address of 192.168. 1.254, for example, if you choose an address of 192.168.1.{1-254} for the IP address. You can accept this address, but leaving it blank is a better option, unless that address is your actual gateway. Chapter 15 describes how to configure your Linux computer to connect to the Internet via a telephone connection. If you do that, then setting a default route now can interfere with your connection.

- **Primary namesever.** The Internet Protocol uses a system called Domain Name Service (DNS) to convert names such as `www.redhat.com` into numeric IPs. A computer that acts as a DNS is called a nameserver. Red Hat Linux again makes a guess based on the IP address and netmask that you use. We suggest, however, leaving this box blank, unless you are on a private network with a nameserver or will be connected to the Internet (your ISP will supply a DNS). When you designate a nonexistent nameserver, then many networking programs work very slowly as they wait in vain for the absent server.

6. **When you finish with this dialog box, select the OK button and press Enter.**

   The Configure Network dialog box appears.

7. **Enter the information for your computer.**

   The Configure Network dialog box wants information about the following items:

   - **Domain name.** A domain name is, as you may guess, the name that your network is known as. It's like a nickname. For instance, `redhat.com` is the domain name of the Red Hat people.

   - **Host name.** This is the name of your computer with the domain name added. For instance, if your domain name is `paunchy.net`, then your host name can be `chivas.paunchy.net`.

   - **Secondary and Tertiary nameservers (IPs).** These are the IP addresses of the second and third DNS servers that your computer will use. They are generally the addresses of your ISP nameservers.

8. **When you finish filling in this dialog box, select the OK button and press Enter.**

9. **In the Root Password dialog box, type a password to use for logging in to your Linux system for the first time, then type your password again and select OK.**

The password is for the *root user,* also known as the *superuser,* who has access to the entire system.

10. **In the Add User dialog box, type the account name and password that you want to use for yourself.**

For instance, if you're Joe Sixpack, then you can enter a Linux user name like *j6pack* in the User ID box. You can optionally enter your full name in the (guess what?) Full Name box. Finally, you must enter your password twice just like for root. Using a good password as you did for root is important. You don't want Joe Blow to be able to look at your valuable information.

11. **In the User Account Setup dialog box, enter any or all of the people who you want to be able to log in to your Linux computer.**

Your new user name is displayed. This screen allows you to add, delete, and edit new or old users. Don't worry about getting everyone added at this point because you can do so at any time after you've installed Linux.

Stage 3: The Point of No Return

Now you have chosen what software to install and how to configure your soon-to-be Red Hat Linux computer. You are now at the point where your hard drive needs to be formatted and the Red Hat Linux software installed on your computer. To put it as dramatically as possible, you are at the point of no return.

1. **The Installation to Begin dialog box opens (picking up from the end of the last section).**

2. **If you want to install Red Hat Linux on your computer now, select OK.**

Your hard drive partitions — which are selected automatically by the installation process when the Workstation option is used — are formatted and the Red Hat Linux software is installed.

If you do not want to continue, then select Back. You return to the last step of the previous section. You can continue going back one step at a time.

After the installation has finished (it can take at least 15 minutes or so, depending on your computer), the Create a Bootdisk dialog box opens.

3. **Insert a blank DOS-formatted floppy disk and select OK.**

Creating a boot disk is a good idea, just in case something happens to the boot partition on your disk. Microsoft products, for example, have a bad habit of overwriting the Master Boot Record (MBR) — and therefore your Linux booting system — when they are installed or even updated. If you think that nothing will ever happen to your MBR, select No, press Enter, and then listen while we tell you about a bridge we have for sale in New York City. . . .

The Red Hat installation process is ready to start writing software to your hard drive.

Configuring X

Phew. You're almost to the finish line. Really.

One of the last things that you need to do is install X Server so that you can use the X Window System graphical user interface (GUI) to interact with Linux. Configuring an X Server means you specify the video card and monitor for your system, including how much video memory it has, what speed it runs at, and a series of other options. Sometimes — particularly with newer systems and newer graphics cards — most of this information is provided automatically by the system.

1. **After configuring your network (or not configuring it, either way), the Red Hat Linux installation system attempts to detect your video card.**

   If Linux finds your card, press the Enter key and skip to Step 3. If the system can not detect your video card it displays the select a video card window containing a long list of video cards, and you can continue on to Step 2.

2. **Use the arrow keys to move through the list and select your video card, then press the Tab key to move to the OK button, and press Enter.**

   If you don't see your video card but you see a previous model by the same manufacturer, then select that. If you don't see a video card that matches your equipment or an older model, then you have the following choices:

   • **Unlisted Card:** This is the very last option in the menu. You can select to use a generic driver. One negative aspect to this option is that if you select a generic driver, then your graphical display runs slower. The positive aspect is that your have a graphical display that works.

   • **Generic VGA:** If you choose this option, then the points made above apply here too. The only difference is that Generic VGA can not supply as high a resolution as some of the options available under the Unlisted Card option.

If none of these options work, then we strongly suggest that you consider purchasing a modern video card if you want to see Red Hat Linux in its GUI glory!

After you select the video card, Red Hat installs the RPM video driver package from the CD. The Monitor Setup dialog box then appears with a list of monitors to select from.

3. Select a monitor that fits your own.

Older monitors can't handle resolution rates and scan frequencies higher than what they were designed for. A monitor designed for a 640 x 480 resolution (and a low scan frequency) can't display a 2,048 x 1,024 resolution (and a high scan frequency). More importantly, if you try to make the monitor display that high of a frequency, it may burst into flames. (Some don't believe this until they see a monitor start smoking.) Modern monitors, called multiscanning, can automatically match themselves to a series of scan frequencies and resolutions. Some of these monitors are even smart enough to turn themselves off if the frequencies become too high, instead of bursting into flames. Finding the documentation and matching your vertical and horizontal frequencies properly is the best way to go (particularly with older monitors). Lacking this information, try a lower resolution (VGA or SVGA) first, just to get X running.

4. In the Screen Configuration dialog box, specify whether you want to probe to find out the configuration of your video card.

To probe or not to probe? Probing tries to determine the configuration of your video card. If the probe is successful, then you don't have to make any guesses about your hardware.

Some computers can *hang up* — that is, stop responding to your keyboard — as the result of probing. If that happens, you must restart the installation process.

If you decide not to probe, then the next screen asks you to specify the amount of video memory that you have.

5. Specify the amount of memory on your video card. After you select the memory amount, press the Tab key to select OK and then press Enter.

Note that this memory is different than the amount of main memory. Most modern cards have 1, 2, 8MB or more of video memory. Use your arrow keys to move down the list.

If you don't know how much video memory your card has, try 1MB (the 1 Meg option). Although this setting limits the resolution of your screen, you will probably be able to get X going. Later, you can experiment with the Xconfigurator program (described in Chapter 19) to figure out the best values for how much video memory you have.

6. **Specify your video clockchip.**

   This specification is a vestige of older systems and older video boards. We recommend that you select the No Clockchip Setting option. After you make your selection, use the Tab key to select the OK button and then press Enter.

   Note that this dialog box doesn't appear if the probe was successful.

7. **Select the video mode that you want to use.**

   You are asked to select the combination of screen resolution and the number of colors. You need to make the choice because the memory in your video card must be used for both purposes. The fewer color bits that you use mean the fewer shades of color that your display will use. The higher resolutions pack more detail onto your screen.

   Make a reasonable choice. If you're already running Windows on your system, you can look at the Display dialog box in the Control Panel to see how it's set up and then use that configuration as your starting point for Linux.

8. **In the Starting X dialog box, select OK.**

   Red Hat now tests your new X configuration.

   If you configured X correctly, this message appears: Can you see this message?. You have 10 seconds to either select Yes or press the Enter key.

9. **If you want to start X automatically at boot time, choose Yes; otherwise, choose No.**

   You have the option of starting X every time you boot or reboot your computer. This book assumes that you choose that option, and X is the default environment used in all further discussions.

   If you choose No, then your system will start up in character-cell or text mode. You can always manually start X with the startx command or modify the /etc/inittab to automatically start X. The line id:3: initdefault should be changed to id:5:initdefault in the inittab file to do that.

   After you make your choice, an informational screen appears, telling you where the configuration file can be found. It also points you to the X README.Config file for more information.

   If you have a problem with your X configuration, then you are regretfully informed about the situation. You have the option of quitting or going back and starting over. If you're game, go back and try, try again.

If, for some reason, you can't get X working at this point, you can always try finishing the configuration of X later by running the Xconfigurator program.

Restarting Your System

Ta Da! You're finished with the installation. Not surprisingly, the Done dialog box appears.

Follow these steps to start your system:

1. **All that's left to do is select OK.**

   Before the system reboots, remove the CD and the floppy disk. Otherwise, you'll be faced with going through the entire installation process again. There's no need to groan — you can always re-reboot and remove the pesky critters.

   Your system reboots, and you can start Linux.

2. **When you see the** LILO boot: **prompt, press the Tab key.**

   You see a list of operating system names that you chose to represent your different systems to LILO. Type the name that represents Linux and then press Enter. Watch the next glorious event: Your Linux system boots! Pass out the champagne.

3. **After the startup messages stop and the** login: **prompt appears, type** root **and then press Enter. Then enter the root password.**

   You are now logged in as superuser, also known as root. Chapter 4 can help you get up to speed with your new Linux system.

If you did not give your computer a name and domain name during the network configuration process, then it's now referred to as localhost. localdomain. Otherwise, the welcome screen refers to whatever name you gave it, for example:

```
Welcome to chivas.paunchy.net.
```

Appendix C

vi Me

● ●

*E*veryone who manages a Linux computer needs a good editor. Whether you're an administrator for a star-struck dot-com or a single, lonely Red Hat Linux computer, you need to edit simple text files. The ubiquitous vi editor fills the bill. vi is lean, fast, and an effective editor that's found on all Linux distributions.

Comprehending Text Editors

A text editor is an essential tool for Linux. It enables you to create and modify an array of text files, including the following:

- ✔ User files, such as the login file
- ✔ System configuration files, such as /etc/fstab, /etc/inittab, and /etc/lilo.conf
- ✔ C and C++ programs
- ✔ Shell programs
- ✔ Mail messages

Red Hat Linux comes with not one but two text editors: ed and vi. The ed editor is a line-oriented text editor. It was one of the first editors for Unix systems and traditionally is included with every Unix and Linux system. It's also a small editor, so small distributions of Unix and Linux can include it. You can always count on ed being there.

The second editor that comes with Linux is vi; it's included with almost every Linux distribution (some specialized distributions such as Trinux don't necessarily include it). This full-screen editor also supports the command set of a line-oriented editor named ex. The third major text editor for Linux is emacs; some people prefer to use this editor for most of their work.

In Red Hat Linux, `ex` and `vi` are emulated by another text editor named `vim`. The commands for `vi` work just fine with `vim`. In addition, `vim` has more capability than `vi`. For instance, `vim` makes editing easier by allowing you to switch from command to insert mode and still move around the file with the cursor keys. On the other hand, `vi` forces you to continually toggle between the two modes in order to insert text and move around the file. Therefore, `vi` isn't included as a separate program with Linux systems. When you type **vi**, you're really using `vim`, but this fact is invisible to you.

Getting Friendly with vi

The `vi` editor on your Red Hat Linux system is really the `vim` editor. With a little vim and vigor, you can invoke it by using `vi`, because a symbolic link exists between `vi` and `vim`.

Like the `ed` editor, the `vi` editor has two modes of operation and the same type of single-letter commands. To start `vi`, you type **vi** at the command line. The screen clears, and the left-most column displays tildes (~). You are looking at an empty, unnamed buffer in memory, into which you can enter text until you save the text to a named file.

You can start the `vi` editor in a number of ways, with different options, but the most common way is to start `vi` is with only a filename as the argument, like this:

```
vi /etc/hosts
```

where `/etc/hosts` is the name of either an existing file that you want to edit or a new file that you want to create.

The `vi` editor has three modes of operation:

- ✔ Visual command mode
- ✔ Colon command mode
- ✔ Text mode

When you invoke `vi` with a filename, the editor screen appears. At the bottom-left corner is the following line:

```
"filename" [New File]
```

This status line tells you what the editor is doing. In this case, the editor has opened a buffer, and the save and quit option saves the contents of the buffer to the `filename` file. If you did indeed invoke `vi` with the following command:

```
vi /etc/hosts
```

the bottom-left corner would display the following line:

```
"/etc/hosts" [readonly]
```

When you first invoke vi, you are in visual command mode, which is the default. You can use four special commands to either locate text or transition to more complex commands:

/	Forward search
?	Backward search
n	Continue the search in whichever direction you were currently going
:	ex command (ex is the line editor included in vi)

In command mode, the characters you type are used as commands, not as input into the file. To use commands, type the character on the command line. For the first two search commands (/ and ?), the cursor moves to the bottom of the screen, where you then type the string that you're searching for. After you press Enter, the search begins. If you want to search for an additional string, you can just press the lowercase n key to reexecute the search; to search backwards, press the uppercase N key.

When you type the : command, the cursor moves to the bottom of the screen and waits for you to enter a command or a command string. You must press the Enter key to execute the command.

Given that characters you type are interpreted as commands in command mode, how do you get from command mode to text mode? Simple. Enter a command to do something in text mode, and vi takes you there. Here are some commands that you can use to switch from command mode to text mode:

i	Insert text before the cursor
a	Insert text after the cursor
I	Insert text at the beginning of the current line
A	Insert text at the end of the current line

As soon as you type any of these commands, Linux puts you in text input mode. Do not press Enter after entering the command. Any text you type after you invoke the command is placed in a buffer and echoed to the screen.

You may be asking yourself (because the directions are skimpy or you have no one else to ask), "How do I get out of text mode and back to command mode?" Again the answer is simple. If you want out, just press the Escape (Esc) key, and you're immediately whisked back to command mode. That's pretty easy, isn't it?

If you don't know whether you're in command mode, just press Esc a few times.

Moving around in a file

After you know how to open a file in vi, you're ready to find out how to move around in it. The commands in Table C-1 move the cursor around. First, make sure that you're in command mode; otherwise, Linux places these keys in your file just like any other data.

Table C-1	Moving Around in vi
Command	*What It Does*
j	Move one line down
k	Move one line up
h	Move one character to the left
l	Move one character to the right
Ctrl+f	Scroll down a full screen
Ctrl+b	Scroll up a full screen

If you want to go to a specific line number, you use a colon command. Type a colon (:), and it appears at the bottom of the screen. Next, type the line number where you want to be. Here's an example:

```
:12
```

When you press Enter, the cursor moves to the beginning of line 12.

Deleting and moving text in vi

This section describes how to delete and move text in vi. The vi editor has several commands for deleting. You can delete characters, words, or lines. The command for deleting a word is dw; this command deletes the word to the right of the cursor. You can delete more words at once by prefacing the dw command with the number of words you want deleted from the cursor position. For example, the command 6dw deletes the next six words following the cursor. Table C-2 lists additional deletion commands.

Table C-2	Deleting in vi
Command	**What It Does**
D	Deletes up to the end of the current line
dd	Deletes the current line
x	Deletes the character under the cursor (4x, 5x, and so on)

A handy command to remember is u, which is the undo command. You can immediately undo edits with this command, in the unlikely event that you make a mistake.

The business of moving text around in the file usually requires the following general steps:

1. **Position the cursor at the beginning of the first line you want to move or copy.**

2. **Type** ma, **marking that position with the letter** *a.*

3. **Position the cursor at the beginning of the last line that you want to move or copy.**

4. **Type** mb, **marking that position with the letter** *b.*

5. **Position the cursor at the line where you want to insert the text.**

6. **Type** `a, bm. **if you want to move the text, or** `a,bt. **if you want to copy the text.**

   Note that the single quotation marks and period are required.

Controlling your editing environment

You can control your editing environment in vi by setting options with the :set command. Table C-3 lists some common :set command options.

Table C-3	Everyday :set Options
Command	**What It Does**
all	Displays a list of all :set commands and their status
errorbells	Sounds the terminal bell when errors occur
ignorecase	Makes searches case insensitive

(continued)

Table C-3 *(continued)*

Command	What It Does
number	Displays line numbers in the leftmost column on the screen
showmode	Displays an indicator at the bottom-right of the screen, indicating which mode you are in: input mode, change mode, replace mode, and so on

Note: You can turn off `:set` command options by prefixing the command with `no`, as in

```
:set nonumber
```

This turns line numbering off.

Checking out common vi commands

Table C-4 summarizes common vi commands. We describe some of these commands elsewhere in the book; others are new.

Table C-4	**Everyday vi Commands**
Command	*What It Does*
a	Inserts text after the cursor
A	Inserts text at the end of the current line
I	Inserts text at the beginning of the current line
i	Inserts text before the cursor
o	Opens a line below the current line
O	Opens a line above the current line
C	Changes up to the end of the current line
cc	Changes the current line
cw	Changes the word
J	Joins the current line with the next one
r*x*	Replaces the character under the cursor with *x* (*x* is any character)

Command	What It Does
~	Changes the character under the cursor to the opposite case
$	Moves to the end of the current line
^	Moves to the beginning of the current line
mx	Marks the current location with the letter x
Ctrl+l	Redraws the screen
:e filename	Edits the file
:N	Moves to line N (N is a number)
:q	Quits the editor
:q!	Quits the editor without saving any changes
:r filename	Reads the file and inserts after the current line
:w filename	Writes the buffer to a file
:wq	Saves changes and exits the editor
/string	Searches forward for string
?string	Searches backward for string
n	Finds the next string
u	Undoes the last command
Esc	Ends input mode and enters visual command mode

Don't worry about the sheer large number of options and commands. We've used vi now for 20 years and have never learned — or used — more than 20 percent of them. vi is our workhorse for system administration, and it works quite well with one hand tied behind your back!

Appendix D

Diggin' Them Linux man Pages

. . . .

In This Appendix

▶ Starting the man command

▶ Reading the man pages

▶ Finding commands

. . . .

*U*nix and Linux systems are largely made up of small, terse commands executed on the command line. Typically, each command is associated with at least one man page. The Linux man pages have nothing to do with gender: The *man* stands for *manual*.

At one time, the man pages were the only documentation that came with Unix systems. Somewhere, we still have the thin book we received as first-time Unix users and system administrators. All that it contained was the man pages, and from that, we were supposed to install a Unix system. Many years later, we still look at the man pages first to get a quick idea of what a command should do, and what arguments to use on the command line or what values to set.

This appendix shows you how to use the man(1) command, how to read and understand the man pages, and how to locate other man pages that may help you understand the Linux command you're investigating.

A MAN!!! Getting Going with the man Command

Okay, if you didn't get the pun in the heading, you need to watch more cartoons.

To get started using the man pages, follow these steps:

1. **With Linux up and running, log in as a user (either a general user or root).**

2. **Type the** `man` **command.**

   The system asks what manual page you want. The syntax of the `man` command (like many other commands) requires at least one argument.

3. **Supply an argument by typing** `man man`.

   The first `man` is the command name, and the second `man` tells Linux that you want information on the manual program itself. The system may tell you to wait a moment while it formats the page to your screen, and then it displays the reference page for the `man` command.

4. **If a colon (:) appears at the bottom of the screen, press the spacebar to see the next page, or use the arrow keys to maneuver around the pages.**

5. **To quit the program, press the** q **key.**

Checking Out How the man Pages Are Organized

You can usually find the man pages in several directories throughout the system:

- ✔ /usr/man
- ✔ /usr/local/man
- ✔ /usr/X11/man
- ✔ /usr/lib/perl5/man

Each directory is broken up into subdirectories representing sections of the manual, as follows:

- ✔ **man1:** User commands
- ✔ **man2:** System calls
- ✔ **man3:** Library functions
- ✔ **man4:** Special files
- ✔ **man5:** File formats
- ✔ **man6:** Games (look at everyone going to that section!)
- ✔ **man7:** Miscellany
- ✔ **man8:** System administration commands
- ✔ **mann:** nroff, troff, and groff (and now tk) macros

Note that most directories have more than one section.

Two sections may have entries for a command of the same name. For example, section 1 has an open command, and section 2 has an open system call. To make sure that you're reading about the right one, you can specify the command on the man command line. For example:

```
[paul@veracruz paul]$ man 2 open
```

Most sections of the man database (because that is basically what it is) have two parts:

- An intro page represented by a file called intro.n, where the *n* is a number that corresponds to the section number.
- All commands, calls, library names, and filenames, represented by files with the name command.n, where *n* is the section number name.

  If you use cd to change to the /usr/man/man1 directory and issue the ls command, you see files such as cat.1 and grep.1. Oddly, you don't find a file called cd.1, because the cd command is built into the different shells, and its documentation is covered in the bash.1 file, or the csh.1 file.

If you're using bash as a shell, you can get information about the rest of the built-ins as follows:

```
[paul@veracruz paul]$ help
```

The intro page briefly describes that section of the manual and indicates whether you need to know anything special about that section. Printing an intro page is simple. For example:

```
[paul@veracruz paul]$ man 2 intro
```

or

```
[paul@veracruz paul]$ man 3 intro
```

Checking Out Topics in the man Pages

Each man page is made up of several sections. Here, we list the sections that we think are most important in your quest to figure out how to read man pages. Note that some man pages don't contain all these sections, and other pages contain more sections than those outlined here.

Name

The name is usually the command name, followed by a hyphen, followed by a one-line description of the command's functionality; this is usually what you see if you execute a `man -k` command or an `apropos` command. Either of these commands, when followed by a word, lists the name field from every manual page that contains that word. Type the following:

```
[paul@veracruz paul]$ apropos cat
```

TIP

Your `apropos` command may produce few or no commands. Perhaps no one has generated the database made up of command names and descriptions. To do this, either you or your system's administrator has to become superuser or root and then execute the following command line:

```
/usr/sbin/makewhatis
```

Synopsis

The synopsis is a shorthand way to describe what the command is looking for in terms of an argument list. For example:

```
lpq [-l] [-Pprinter] [job # ...] [user ...]
```

is the synopsis for the `lpq` command (whose job is to show what is in the print queue). The command name (`lpq`) is first, followed by a series of bracketed arguments. If an argument is enclosed in square brackets, the argument is optional, meaning the `lpq` command needs no arguments. If you type

```
[paul@veracruz paul]$ lpq
```

you probably get a `no entries` message — which means nothing is waiting to be printed — or a list of people's jobs waiting to be printed on the default printer.

If you want to see what's waiting to be printed on another printer, you use the optional argument -p followed by the name of the printer. For example:

```
[paul@veracruz paul]$ lpq -Pzklpsa
```

Now if you type this command, you probably get a message like `lpq: zklpsa: unknown printer`, indicating that your system does not know about a printer named `zklpsa`. If you get something else, please let us know because that may explain where our print jobs are going . . . no, no, just kidding.

If, however, you have a printer called hp5l, then you can enter the following command to find out its status:

```
[paul@veracruz paul]$ lpq -Php5l
```

In any case, the purpose of this section is not to show you all the functionality of the `lpq` command. Rather, the synopsis section shows in a shorthand way how you should use the command, including which arguments are optional.

Another confusing thing you may see is the . . . notation. Looking back at the `lpq` command synopsis, you see it twice, once following the `job #` argument, and once following the `user` argument. This notation tells you that you can list as many job numbers on the line as you want, separated by spaces, and as many user names as you want, separated by spaces.

Sometimes you see a command argument that begins with one hyphen (-) or two (--). These notations are technically known as *options,* whereas `job #` and `user` of the `lpq` command are *arguments.* Options tell the command how to manipulate arguments. You may see an option line that looks like this:

```
cat   [-benstuvAET]
```

or even

```
ls [-abcdfgiklmnpqrstuxABCFGLNQRSUX1]
```

Don't be overwhelmed. If you deal with the options one at a time, you'll be able to understand how the command works. Take heart in the fact that most of the time, most people use only one or two options.

If you issue the `man ls` command, you will see that `ls` has many more options. That's why `ls` has been described as "a command that went bad with good intentions."

Description

The description section is a brief introduction to the command's functionality, which is then expanded on by what the options specify the command to do. A good example of a description is the manual page for `man` itself.

Options

The options section tells how the command treats data in the arguments. Each option modifies the command's actions, drastically or subtly. The options can also pass information to the command about where to find files. The three types of options are:

- ✔ No argument
- ✔ Attached argument
- ✔ Positional argument

No argument means the option has a hyphen, followed by one or more single-character options. For example:

```
[paul@veracruz paul]$ ps -ax
```

The a and the x do not have any other values that they have to look at. But in the following command:

```
[paul@veracruz paul]$ lpq -Pzklpsa
```

the -P option needs you to supply an argument, in this example, zklpsa.

Environmental variables

Sometimes, to cut down on the information you have to give the command, you can set an *environmental variable*. Each shell (or command interpreter) has an *environment* that it works in. This environment (when it is created) consists of certain files that are open, some memory, and almost always some environmental variables.

Using the bash shell, type the following (if you're not sure that you're using the bash shell, type bash at the command prompt and then continue with the example):

```
[paul@veracruz paul]$ printenv
```

You see something like this:

```
USERNAME=
COLORTERM=gnome-terminal
HISTSIZE=1000
HOSTNAME=veracruz.paunchy.net
LOGNAME=paul
HISTFILESIZE=1000
INIT_VERSION=sysvinit-2.74
MAIL=/var/spool/mail/paul
LD_LIBRARY_PATH=/usr/local/applixware/axdata/axshlib/lib
TERM=xterm
HOSTTYPE=i386
```

```
PATH=/usr/bin:/usr/bin:/usr/local/bin:/usr/X11R6/bin:/bin:
 /usr/X11R6/bin:/usr/local/netscape:
 /home/paul/bin:/usr/X11R6/bin:
 /usr/local/netscape:/home/paul/bin
CONSOLE=/dev/console
KDEDIR=/usr
HOME=/home/paul
INPUTRC=/etc/inputrc
PREVLEVEL=N
RUNLEVEL=5
SHELL=/bin/bash
XAUTHORITY=/home/paul/.Xauthority
USER=paul
PGDATA=/var/lib/pgsql
BASH_ENV=/home/paul/.bashrc
BOOT_IMAGE=linux
DISPLAY=:0
SESSION_MANAGER=local/atlas.paunchy.net:/tmp/.ICE-
            unix/7376,tcp/atlas.paunchy.net:1371
OSTYPE=Linux
WINDOWID=62914566
GDMSESSION=Default
LD_PRELOAD=/usr/local/lib/open.so
SHLVL=3
_=/usr/bin/printenv
```

This list includes lots of environmental variables, but we don't have the space to describe them all. So, here are the most important ones:

- ✔ **PATH** tells the shell all the places to look for commands.
- ✔ **HOME** tells cd where to go when you don't supply any arguments.
- ✔ **OSTYPE** tells the shell and programs what operating system they're on.

Different shells have different ways to set these variables (and create and set others) to tell the commands what to do.

Note that a variable not being set to some value (null) is different than a variable that doesn't exist (unset), and these differences vary from command to command. For example, in the preceding listing, the first variable, USERNAME, is set to NULL. The fact that it's there at all is significant. The fact that it is set to NULL instead of some other value is also significant to various programs.

Diagnostics

Error messages or exit codes indicate that something has gone wrong in the program or the shell. Normally, Unix error messages are terse. Sometimes things may seem to be wrong when they really are okay. For example, most new Unix users think that when they issue an ls command in an empty directory, they should get an error message such as directory empty or file not found. The problem? The command ls by itself can display the filenames in any order (as opposed to ls *, which displays the files in alphabetical order). Therefore, if you have a directory with three files in it named *file, not,* and *found* — which happen to print in that order — you can't determine whether the directory is empty or not. Granted, this is a contrived example. But the developers of Unix thought that less was better than more (we're not talking about the command names less and more), and that silence is golden (which means something if you've ever heard those old, noisy, hard-copy terminals).

Most programs display an *exit code,* which you normally don't see unless it's a non-zero code, which means the program ended unsuccessfully. If you're a programmer, you can test for this, and if you do programming or shell-script writing, we encourage you to set and test exit codes.

Bugs/deficiencies

Yes, all programs have bugs, and most Linux people are good about correcting them. But some bugs are so arcane that they affect only one in a million people, and to try and correct them would mean redesigning the entire program. Therefore, this type of bug is regarded as a deficiency or a limitation and is listed in the man page.

Compatibility issues

When a new version of a command or a program comes out, it may work slightly differently than the old command or program. This can modification can cause a *compatibility issue* with shell scripts that have been written to use the old command or program. If the author of the command or program thinks a problem may occur, it should be documented here.

Caveats

Caveats are warnings that the programmer wants to give to the user of the command or program. Caveats may include things to think about before executing the command or program, security issues, or how much file system space the program uses on large applications.

Disclaimers

Disclaimers are usually legal statements included at the insistence of the author's employer or the employer's lawyers, telling you that if you use this program and it harms someone, don't come back to them. All programs in all operating systems have disclaimers someplace.

Authors

The authors are simply the people who wrote the command or program that the manual page is describing. Often, this section also explains how to report bugs or discuss new features you may want to see.

Acknowledgments

The acknowledgments section, which is much more pleasant than the disclaimers section, recognizes the previous work put into a program that the author has built on. Allowing and encouraging people to build on the work of others is the essence of Linux and the GNU Public License.

Debugging options

Some programs, such as sendmail, have the capability to diagnose problems. If the manual page has a debugging options section, you can find information on setting and using these options to debug the program.

Configuration files

Along with options and environmental variables, another way to determine what program the manual page is describing how to operate is through *configuration files,* sometimes known as *startup files.* These files may be in your home directory, a systemwide directory, or a sitewide directory. Often, Linux looks for them in a certain order: Sitewide files have the strongest influence, and systemwide files and local user (your startup) files have the second and third strongest influence, respectively. The systems administrator can use those files to set policies across companies and systems, while allowing you to tailor the program to your needs.

Two examples of startup files are the .bashrc file, which is probably in your home directory, and the /etc/bashrc file in the /etc directory. Note that the file in your home directory starts with a period. This type of file is called a *hidden,* or *dot,* file. You don't normally see hidden files when you list your directory, unless you issue the ls -a or ls .* command.

Copyrights

Many people mistakenly believe that Linux code or other freeware code is not copyrighted. This is typically not true. The authors of the code often take great care to copyright their code because they want to receive credit for their work.

Copying permissions/distribution policy

The copyright holder gives away most Linux code through the GNU Public License, or what is commonly called *copyleft.* The copyleft stipulates that those holding a copy of the code can use it for whatever purpose they want, as long as they make the code freely available to anyone who wants it. If they change the code, they must make the changed code (including the source code) freely available to those who want it.

Sometimes, other copying and distribution policies are associated with the command or program that the manual page is describing. These policies can include the following types of permissions, where you may:

- ✔ Use but not redistribute the code
- ✔ Use the code, but no source code is available
- ✔ Use and distribute the code as shareware, by paying a fee for continued use
- ✔ Have limited use, such as educational or personal (but not commercial) use
- ✔ Use the code on one machine only

If you bought the operating system, or a *layered product distribution* (a distribution that includes both the operating system and a commercial application), or both from a CD-ROM vendor, then the overall distribution policy on the CD-ROM is usually the most strict (that is, you're limited to installing it on one machine because of its licensed software). You don't have to worry as long as you follow its overall licensing.

POSIX compatibility/standards conformance

In the dark days of computer science, each vendor went off to develop its own operating system, with its own set of commands and programming interfaces. This way of thinking created a Tower of Babel (not to be confused with the Tower of Hanoi, which is a puzzle game) among computer users and programmers. When Unix systems first appeared, however, they were portable across different types of hardware, and you could have the same operating system, commands, and programming interfaces whether you were programming a Digital Equipment Corporation system, a Sun Microsystems computer, an IBM computer, or others. Unfortunately, this approach lasted about ten minutes in the scope of Unix's life, because as Unix escaped from Bell Labs, it went to the University of California, Berkeley, and *poof:* Two different Unix systems were now in existence!

A little later, vendors started introducing their versions of Unix, some using System V as a basis, others using BSD (as the Berkeley version was called). Some vendors, such as Sun Microsystems, started out with BSD and then switched to System V (to the chagrin of its users).

In 1988, the IEEE developed the POSIX standard for operating systems. The IEEE is a great organization, and probably the best thing that it did was to build on Unix rather than start over from scratch. It took the interfaces from the existing System V and Berkeley versions of Unix.

If an operating system is POSIX- compatible and a program is written to POSIX standards, the program should run on the operating system with no problems, and users should be able to use that operating system with little or no retraining from the last POSIX operating system they learned.

Other places to look for help

You can find help in several other places on the system. One place is the /usr/doc directory, which contains the documentation that comes with the individual software packages. For instance, the nmap network security package described in Chapter 5 installs documentation about what it does and how to use it in the /usr/doc/nmap directory.

Note: Some system administrators conserve disk space by not loading /usr/doc on their systems. With the abundance of inexpensive disks, this is usually penny wise, pound foolish. Documentation, such as that found in /usr/doc, can be put on one system and then made available to everyone through the magic of the Network File System (NFS). Tell your system administrator to do that. If you are your own system administrator, go into a closet and give yourself a lecture!

Although much work still has to be accomplished both in defining what POSIX is and in vendors implementing POSIX, POSIX compliance and certification are worthy goals.

Other standards should be implemented and met by manufacturers, distribution makers, and developers (not necessarily in that order) — standards for network communication, for the way data is put on the CD-ROM, and so on. Both formal standards and informal defacto standards exist, both of which help your system work better with the next system.

Linux was built with POSIX compatibility as a goal, and it follows many of the other standards. This makes it easy to port code from one set of POSIX-compatible interfaces to another and from one POSIX-compatible operating system to another. It also allows Linux to interoperate with other operating systems. Many Linux people are active in standards bodies, and the movement toward standards is generally supported in the Linux community.

Files

In addition to the startup or configuration files mentioned previously, sometimes the command or program that the manual page is describing uses other files in the system and temporary files for holding intermediate work. Such files are listed in this section of the man page. If a command does not work, perhaps one of these files is missing, has the wrong file permissions (or the directories they are in have the wrong permissions), is owned by the wrong person, or has corrupt data.

Future work

The future work section lists the author's plans for the command or program that the manual page is describing, often in an attempt to generate interest and help from other people.

See also/related software

The see also/related software section lists programs associated with the command or program that the manual page is describing. Often, several programs make up a system of programs to do a particular task. Some programs have similar capabilities, but are not quite the same. Some programs are the antithesis of the program you're looking at (for example, cut and paste). The *see also* often gives you an overall picture of what the program is supposed to do or leads you to the right program for the job.

Finding the Right man Page

If you don't know what command you're looking for, use the apropos command followed by the word you're interested in. The apropos command searches all the man pages looking for that word, and lists the man command names along with one-line descriptions of all the commands that contain that word. You should probably pipe the output of the apropos command into the more command:

```
[paul@veracruz paul]$ apropos print | more
```

Note that apropos matches on partial words (called *strings*), which is why we suggested print instead of printer. The shorter your *keyword*, the more matches the command finds.

Second, after you have the pages you want to look at, execute the man command for each one. From the one-line description, you can probably decide which commands fit your needs.

Third, look at the description field, which gives you a better idea of what the command can do. If you're still not sure about the command's basic functionality, look at the see also section, to see whether any other commands fit the bill.

After that, skip the synopsis section — it's usually a reminder of how to type the command — and go directly to the options section. Read through the options section, trying to apply the options to the basic description of the command.

After you've read several man pages, you'll notice that the same options appear for similar commands.

This is all pretty much passive work. To find out what a command really does, you should try it out. Create a small test file by using an editor, or use an existing file, such as the /etc/passwd file, as input. (It's better not to practice while logged in as root as you could accidentally damage a file or directory.)

From time to time, we read all the man pages in the system, concentrating on the command descriptions. We do this because we want to become familiar with new commands. Also, our memories aren't what they used to be. But to be fair to our failing memories, the system does have close to 1,200 general-user commands and about 260 system administration commands.

Appendix E

About the CD-ROMs

• •

*T*he CD-ROMs that comes with this book contain the full GNU Public License distribution of Red Hat Linux 7.0, as well as Netscape Communicator 4.75.

System Requirements

Make sure that your computer meets the minimum system requirements listed here. If your computer doesn't match up to most of these requirements, you may have problems using the contents of the CDs:

- ✔ A PC with a 486 or faster processor.
- ✔ At least 8MB of total RAM installed on your computer. For the best performance, we recommend that people who want to use X Window System have at least 16MB and preferably 32MB of main memory.
- ✔ At least 800MB of hard drive space available to install all the software from the CDs. You'll need less space if you don't install every program. For example, if you want to install only the smallest subset of the base system and X Window System, you can do that in about 180 bytes.
- ✔ A CD-ROM drive.
- ✔ A 3¼-inch floppy disk drive and a blank 3¼-inch disk.
- ✔ A monitor capable of displaying at least 256 colors or grayscale.
- ✔ An IDE or a SCSI hard drive.
- ✔ A keyboard and a mouse.
- ✔ A modem with a speed of at least 14,400 bps if you want to go online.

Using the CD

You receive a complete Red Hat Linux distribution on the companion CDs. The instructions for installing the Red Hat Linux operating system from CD are detailed in Part I. After you install the software, return the CDs to their plastic jacket, or other appropriate place, for safekeeping.

What You'll Find

You can obtain the Red Hat Linux installation manual by sending in your CD-ROM coupon to Hungry Minds. You can also download the document from Red Hat's Web site: `www.redhat.com/support`.

The CD does not contain the freely distributable parts (or source code) of Red Hat Linux Version 7.0, but if you want access to the source code you can send in the coupon at the back of this book for a CD. You may view a lot of the documentation on this CD through an HTML viewer such as Netscape, which is also included on the CD, or you may print it. You can also view most of this documentation from other operating systems such as DOS, Windows, or Unix.

We recommend that you look at the "The Official Red Hat Linux Installation Guide," which is in the following directory (accessed from a DOS or Windows machine):

```
D:\doc\rhmanual\manual\index.htm
```

Or from Red Hat Linux:

```
/mnt/cdrom/doc/rhmanual/manual/index.html
```

The guide is included in HTML format, so you can view it with a Web browser.

Because the CD-ROM has a full implementation of Linux, to list all the accompanying tools and utilities would take too much room. Briefly, the CD includes most of the software you need to access the Internet; write programs in several computer languages; create and manipulate images; create, manipulate, and play back sounds (if you have a sound board); play certain games; and work with electrical design. And of course, all the source code is included.

If You Have Problems (Of the CD Kind)

We tried our best to test various computers with the minimum system requirements. Alas, your computer may differ, and Linux may not install or work as stated.

The two likeliest problems are that you don't have enough RAM for the programs you want to use, or you have some hardware that Linux doesn't support. Luckily, the latter problem occurs less frequently each day as more hardware is supported under Linux.

You may also have SCSI hard drives that use a controller not supported by Linux or a controller that is simply too new for the Linux development team to have given it the proper support at the time these CDs were pressed.

If you have trouble with corrupt files on the CDs, please call the Hungry Minds Customer Care phone number: 800-762-2974 (outside the United States: 317-572-3993). Customer service won't be able to help with complications relating to the program or how it works. Please see the Installation Instructions at the end of this book.

Index

Dummies Books™
Bestsellers on Every Topic!

 ## GENERAL INTEREST TITLES

BUSINESS & PERSONAL FINANCE

Accounting For Dummies®	John A. Tracy, CPA	0-7645-5014-4	$19.99 US/$27.99 CAN
Business Plans For Dummies®	Paul Tiffany, Ph.D. & Steven D. Peterson, Ph.D.	1-56884-868-4	$19.99 US/$27.99 CAN
Business Writing For Dummies®	Sheryl Lindsell-Roberts	0-7645-5134-5	$16.99 US/$27.99 CAN
Consulting For Dummies®	Bob Nelson & Peter Economy	0-7645-5034-9	$19.99 US/$27.99 CAN
Customer Service For Dummies®, 2nd Edition	Karen Leland & Keith Bailey	0-7645-5209-0	$19.99 US/$27.99 CAN
Franchising For Dummies®	Dave Thomas & Michael Seid	0-7645-5160-4	$19.99 US/$27.99 CAN
Getting Results For Dummies®	Mark H. McCormack	0-7645-5205-8	$19.99 US/$27.99 CAN
Home Buying For Dummies®	Eric Tyson, MBA & Ray Brown	1-56884-385-2	$16.99 US/$24.99 CAN
House Selling For Dummies®	Eric Tyson, MBA & Ray Brown	0-7645-5038-1	$16.99 US/$24.99 CAN
Human Resources Kit For Dummies®	Max Messmer	0-7645-5131-0	$19.99 US/$27.99 CAN
Investing For Dummies®, 2nd Edition	Eric Tyson, MBA	0-7645-5162-0	$19.99 US/$27.99 CAN
Law For Dummies®	John Ventura	1-56884-860-9	$19.99 US/$27.99 CAN
Leadership For Dummies®	Marshall Loeb & Steven Kindel	0-7645-5176-0	$19.99 US/$27.99 CAN
Managing For Dummies®	Bob Nelson & Peter Economy	1-56884-858-7	$19.99 US/$27.99 CAN
Marketing For Dummies®	Alexander Hiam	1-56884-699-1	$19.99 US/$27.99 CAN
Mutual Funds For Dummies®, 2nd Edition	Eric Tyson, MBA	0-7645-5112-4	$19.99 US/$27.99 CAN
Negotiating For Dummies®	Michael C. Donaldson & Mimi Donaldson	1-56884-867-6	$19.99 US/$27.99 CAN
Personal Finance For Dummies®, 3rd Edition	Eric Tyson, MBA	0-7645-5231-7	$19.99 US/$27.99 CAN
Personal Finance For Dummies® For Canadians, 2nd Edition	Eric Tyson, MBA & Tony Martin	0-7645-5123-X	$19.99 US/$27.99 CAN
Public Speaking For Dummies®	Malcolm Kushner	0-7645-5159-0	$16.99 US/$24.99 CAN
Sales Closing For Dummies®	Tom Hopkins	0-7645-5063-2	$14.99 US/$21.99 CAN
Sales Prospecting For Dummies®	Tom Hopkins	0-7645-5066-7	$14.99 US/$21.99 CAN
Selling For Dummies®	Tom Hopkins	1-56884-389-5	$16.99 US/$24.99 CAN
Small Business For Dummies®	Eric Tyson, MBA & Jim Schell	0-7645-5094-2	$19.99 US/$27.99 CAN
Small Business Kit For Dummies®	Richard D. Harroch	0-7645-5093-4	$24.99 US/$34.99 CAN
Taxes 2001 For Dummies®	Eric Tyson & David J. Silverman	0-7645-5306-2	$15.99 US/$23.99 CAN
Time Management For Dummies®, 2nd Edition	Jeffrey J. Mayer	0-7645-5145-0	$19.99 US/$27.99 CAN
Writing Business Letters For Dummies®	Sheryl Lindsell-Roberts	0-7645-5207-4	$16.99 US/$24.99 CAN

TECHNOLOGY TITLES

INTERNET/ONLINE

America Online® For Dummies®, 6th Edition	John Kaufeld	0-7645-0670-6	$19.99 US/$27.99 CAN
Banking Online Dummies®	Paul Murphy	0-7645-0458-4	$24.99 US/$34.99 CAN
eBay™ For Dummies®, 2nd Edition	Marcia Collier, Roland Woerner, & Stephanie Becker	0-7645-0761-3	$19.99 US/$27.99 CAN
E-Mail For Dummies®, 2nd Edition	John R. Levine, Carol Baroudi, & Arnold Reinhold	0-7645-0131-3	$24.99 US/$34.99 CAN
Genealogy Online For Dummies®, 2nd Edition	Matthew L. Helm & April Leah Helm	0-7645-0543-2	$24.99 US/$34.99 CAN
Internet Directory For Dummies®, 3rd Edition	Brad Hill	0-7645-0558-2	$24.99 US/$34.99 CAN
Internet Auctions For Dummies®	Greg Holden	0-7645-0578-9	$24.99 US/$34.99 CAN
Internet Explorer 5.5 For Windows® For Dummies®	Doug Lowe	0-7645-0738-9	$19.99 US/$28.99 CAN
Researching Online For Dummies®, 2nd Edition	Mary Ellen Bates & Reva Basch	0-7645-0546-7	$24.99 US/$34.99 CAN
Job Searching Online For Dummies®	Pam Dixon	0-7645-0673-0	$24.99 US/$34.99 CAN
Investing Online For Dummies®, 3rd Edition	Kathleen Sindell, Ph.D.	0-7645-0725-7	$24.99 US/$34.99 CAN
Travel Planning Online For Dummies®, 2nd Edition	Noah Vadnai	0-7645-0438-X	$24.99 US/$34.99 CAN
Internet Searching For Dummies®	Brad Hill	0-7645-0478-9	$24.99 US/$34.99 CAN
Yahoo!® For Dummies®, 2nd Edition	Brad Hill	0-7645-0762-1	$19.99 US/$27.99 CAN
The Internet For Dummies®, 7th Edition	John R. Levine, Carol Baroudi, & Arnold Reinhold	0-7645-0674-9	$19.99 US/$27.99 CAN

OPERATING SYSTEMS

DOS For Dummies®, 3rd Edition	Dan Gookin	0-7645-0361-8	$19.99 US/$27.99 CAN
GNOME For Linux® For Dummies®	David B. Busch	0-7645-0650-1	$24.99 US/$37.99 CAN
LINUX® For Dummies®, 2nd Edition	John Hall, Craig Witherspoon, & Coletta Witherspoon	0-7645-0421-5	$24.99 US/$34.99 CAN
Mac® OS 9 For Dummies®	Bob LeVitus	0-7645-0652-8	$19.99 US/$28.99 CAN
Red Hat® Linux® For Dummies®	Jon "maddog" Hall	0-7645-0663-3	$24.99 US/$37.99 CAN
Small Business Windows® 98 For Dummies®	Stephen Nelson	0-7645-0425-8	$24.99 US/$34.99 CAN
UNIX® For Dummies®, 4th Edition	John R. Levine & Margaret Levine Young	0-7645-0419-3	$19.99 US/$27.99 CAN
Windows® 95 For Dummies®, 2nd Edition	Andy Rathbone	0-7645-0180-1	$19.99 US/$27.99 CAN
Windows® 98 For Dummies®	Andy Rathbone	0-7645-0261-1	$19.99 US/$27.99 CAN
Windows® 2000 For Dummies®	Andy Rathbone	0-7645-0641-2	$19.99 US/$27.99 CAN
Windows® 2000 Server For Dummies®	Ed Tittle	0-7645-0341-3	$24.99 US/$37.99 CAN
Windows® ME Millenium Edition For Dummies®	Andy Rathbone	0-7645-0735-4	$19.99 US/$27.99 CAN

Dummies Books™
Bestsellers on Every Topic!

GENERAL INTEREST TITLES

FOOD & BEVERAGE/ENTERTAINING

Bartending For Dummies®	Ray Foley	0-7645-5051-9	$14.99 US/$21.99 CAN
Cooking For Dummies®, 2nd Edition	Bryan Miller & Marie Rama	0-7645-5250-3	$19.99 US/$27.99 CAN
Entertaining For Dummies®	Suzanne Williamson with Linda Smith	0-7645-5027-6	$19.99 US/$27.99 CAN
Gourmet Cooking For Dummies®	Charlie Trotter	0-7645-5029-2	$19.99 US/$27.99 CAN
Grilling For Dummies®	Marie Rama & John Mariani	0-7645-5076-4	$19.99 US/$27.99 CAN
Italian Cooking For Dummies®	Cesare Casella & Jack Bishop	0-7645-5098-5	$19.99 US/$27.99 CAN
Mexican Cooking For Dummies®	Mary Sue Miliken & Susan Feniger	0-7645-5169-8	$19.99 US/$27.99 CAN
Quick & Healthy Cooking For Dummies®	Lynn Fischer	0-7645-5214-7	$19.99 US/$27.99 CAN
Wine For Dummies®, 2nd Edition	Ed McCarthy & Mary Ewing-Mulligan	0-7645-5114-0	$19.99 US/$27.99 CAN
Chinese Cooking For Dummies®	Martin Yan	0-7645-5247-3	$19.99 US/$27.99 CAN
Etiquette For Dummies®	Sue Fox	0-7645-5170-1	$19.99 US/$27.99 CAN

SPORTS

Baseball For Dummies®, 2nd Edition	Joe Morgan with Richard Lally	0-7645-5234-1	$19.99 US/$27.99 CAN
Golf For Dummies®, 2nd Edition	Gary McCord	0-7645-5146-9	$19.99 US/$27.99 CAN
Fly Fishing For Dummies®	Peter Kaminsky	0-7645-5073-X	$19.99 US/$27.99 CAN
Football For Dummies®	Howie Long with John Czarnecki	0-7645-5054-3	$19.99 US/$27.99 CAN
Hockey For Dummies®	John Davidson with John Steinbreder	0-7645-5045-4	$19.99 US/$27.99 CAN
NASCAR For Dummies®	Mark Martin	0-7645-5219-8	$19.99 US/$27.99 CAN
Tennis For Dummies®	Patrick McEnroe with Peter Bodo	0-7645-5087-X	$19.99 US/$27.99 CAN
Soccer For Dummies®	U.S. Soccer Federation & Michael Lewiss	0-7645-5229-5	$19.99 US/$27.99 CAN

HOME & GARDEN

Annuals For Dummies®	Bill Marken & NGA	0-7645-5056-X	$16.99 US/$24.99 CAN
Container Gardening For Dummies®	Bill Marken & NGA	0-7645-5057-8	$16.99 US/$24.99 CAN
Decks & Patios For Dummies®	Robert J. Beckstrom & NGA	0-7645-5075-6	$16.99 US/$24.99 CAN
Flowering Bulbs For Dummies®	Judy Glattstein & NGA	0-7645-5103-5	$16.99 US/$24.99 CAN
Gardening For Dummies®, 2nd Edition	Michael MacCaskey & NGA	0-7645-5130-2	$16.99 US/$24.99 CAN
Herb Gardening For Dummies®	NGA	0-7645-5200-7	$16.99 US/$24.99 CAN
Home Improvement For Dummies®	Gene & Katie Hamilton & the Editors of HouseNet, Inc.	0-7645-5005-5	$19.99 US/$26.99 CAN
Houseplants For Dummies®	Larry Hodgson & NGA	0-7645-5102-7	$16.99 US/$24.99 CAN
Painting and Wallpapering For Dummies®	Gene Hamilton	0-7645-5150-7	$16.99 US/$24.99 CAN
Perennials For Dummies®	Marcia Tatroe & NGA	0-7645-5030-6	$16.99 US/$24.99 CAN
Roses For Dummies®, 2nd Edition	Lance Walheim	0-7645-5202-3	$16.99 US/$24.99 CAN
Trees and Shrubs For Dummies®	Ann Whitman & NGA	0-7645-5203-1	$16.99 US/$24.99 CAN
Vegetable Gardening For Dummies®	Charlie Nardozzi & NGA	0-7645-5129-9	$16.99 US/$24.99 CAN
Home Cooking For Dummies®	Patricia Hart McMillan & Katharine Kaye McMillan	0-7645-5107-8	$19.99 US/$27.99 CAN

TECHNOLOGY TITLES

WEB DESIGN & PUBLISHING

Active Server Pages For Dummies®, 2nd Edition	Bill Hatfield	0-7645-0603-X	$24.99 US/$37.99 CAN
Cold Fusion 4 For Dummies®	Alexis Gutzman	0-7645-0604-8	$24.99 US/$37.99 CAN
Creating Web Pages For Dummies®, 5th Edition	Bud Smith & Arthur Bebak	0-7645-0733-8	$24.99 US/$34.99 CAN
Dreamweaver™ 3 For Dummies®	Janine Warner & Paul Vachier	0-7645-0669-2	$24.99 US/$34.99 CAN
FrontPage® 2000 For Dummies®	Asha Dornfest	0-7645-0423-1	$24.99 US/$34.99 CAN
HTML 4 For Dummies®, 3rd Edition	Ed Tittel & Natanya Dits	0-7645-0572-6	$24.99 US/$34.99 CAN
Java™ For Dummies®, 3rd Edition	Aaron E. Walsh	0-7645-0417-7	$24.99 US/$34.99 CAN
PageMill™ 2 For Dummies®	Deke McClelland & John San Filippo	0-7645-0028-7	$24.99 US/$34.99 CAN
XML™ For Dummies®	Ed Tittel	0-7645-0692-7	$24.99 US/$37.99 CAN
Javascript For Dummies®, 3rd Edition	Emily Vander Veer	0-7645-0633-1	$24.99 US/$37.99 CAN

DESKTOP PUBLISHING GRAPHICS/MULTIMEDIA

Adobe® In Design™ For Dummies®	Deke McClelland	0-7645-0599-8	$19.99 US/$27.99 CAN
CorelDRAW 9 For Dummies®	Deke McClelland	0-7645-0523-8	$19.99 US/$27.99 CAN
Desktop Publishing and Design For Dummies®	Roger C. Parker	1-56884-234-1	$19.99 US/$27.99 CAN
Digital Photography For Dummies®, 3rd Edition	Julie Adair King	0-7645-0646-3	$24.99 US/$37.99 CAN
Microsoft® Publisher 98 For Dummies®	Jim McCarter	0-7645-0395-2	$19.99 US/$27.99 CAN
Visio 2000 For Dummies®	Debbie Walkowski	0-7645-0635-8	$19.99 US/$27.99 CAN
Microsoft® Publisher 2000 For Dummies®	Jim McCarter	0-7645-0525-4	$19.99 US/$27.99 CAN
Windows® Movie Maker For Dummies®	Keith Underdahl	0-7645-0749-1	$19.99 US/$27.99 CAN

Dummies Books™
Bestsellers on Every Topic!

GENERAL INTEREST TITLES

EDUCATION & TEST PREPARATION

Title	Author	ISBN	Price
The ACT For Dummies®	Suzee Vlk	1-56884-387-9	$14.99 US/$21.99 CAN
College Financial Aid For Dummies®	Dr. Herm Davis & Joyce Lain Kennedy	0-7645-5049-7	$19.99 US/$27.99 CAN
College Planning For Dummies®, 2nd Edition	Pat Ordovensky	0-7645-5048-9	$19.99 US/$27.99 CAN
Everyday Math For Dummies®	Charles Seiter, Ph.D.	1-56884-248-1	$14.99 US/$21.99 CAN
The GMAT® For Dummies®, 3rd Edition	Suzee Vlk	0-7645-5082-9	$16.99 US/$24.99 CAN
The GRE® For Dummies®, 3rd Edition	Suzee Vlk	0-7645-5083-7	$16.99 US/$24.99 CAN
Politics For Dummies®	Ann DeLaney	1-56884-381-X	$19.99 US/$27.99 CAN
The SAT I For Dummies®, 3rd Edition	Suzee Vlk	0-7645-5044-6	$14.99 US/$21.99 CAN

AUTOMOTIVE

Title	Author	ISBN	Price
Auto Repair For Dummies®	Deanna Sclar	0-7645-5089-6	$19.99 US/$27.99 CAN
Buying A Car For Dummies®	Deanna Sclar	0-7645-5091-8	$16.99 US/$24.99 CAN

LIFESTYLE/SELF-HELP

Title	Author	ISBN	Price
Dating For Dummies®	Dr. Joy Browne	0-7645-5072-1	$19.99 US/$27.99 CAN
Making Marriage Work For Dummies®	Steven Simring, M.D. & Sue Klavans Simring, D.S.W	0-7645-5173-6	$19.99 US/$27.99 CAN
Parenting For Dummies®	Sandra H. Gookin	1-56884-383-6	$16.99 US/$24.99 CAN
Success For Dummies®	Zig Ziglar	0-7645-5061-6	$19.99 US/$27.99 CAN
Weddings For Dummies®	Marcy Blum & Laura Fisher Kaiser	0-7645-5055-1	$19.99 US/$27.99 CAN

TECHNOLOGY TITLES

SUITES

Title	Author	ISBN	Price
Microsoft® Office 2000 For Windows® For Dummies®	Wallace Wang & Roger C. Parker	0-7645-0452-5	$19.99 US/$27.99 CAN
Microsoft® Office 2000 For Windows® For Dummies® Quick Reference	Doug Lowe & Bjoern Hartsfvang	0-7645-0453-3	$12.99 US/$17.99 CAN
Microsoft® Office 97 For Windows® For Dummies®	Wallace Wang & Roger C. Parker	0-7645-0050-3	$19.99 US/$27.99 CAN
Microsoft® Office 97 For Windows® For Dummies® Quick Reference	Doug Lowe	0-7645-0062-7	$12.99 US/$17.99 CAN
Microsoft® Office 98 For Macs® For Dummies®	Tom Negrino	0-7645-0229-8	$19.99 US/$27.99 CAN
Microsoft® Office X For Macs For Dummies®	Tom Negrino	0-7645-0702-8	$19.95 US/$27.99 CAN

WORD PROCESSING

Word 2000 For Windows® For Dummies® Quick Reference	Peter Weverka	0-7645-0449-5	$12.99 US/$19.99 CAN
Corel® WordPerfect® 8 For Windows® For Dummies®	Margaret Levine Young, David Kay & Jordan Young	0-7645-0186-0	$19.99 US/$27.99 CAN
Word 2000 For Windows® For Dummies®	Dan Gookin	0-7645-0448-7	$19.99 US/$27.99 CAN
Word For Windows® 95 For Dummies®	Dan Gookin	1-56884-932-X	$19.99 US/$27.99 CAN
Word 97 For Windows® For Dummies®	Dan Gookin	0-7645-0052-X	$19.99 US/$27.99 CAN
WordPerfect® 9 For Windows® For Dummies®	Margaret Levine Young	0-7645-0427-4	$19.99 US/$27.99 CAN
WordPerfect® 7 For Windows® 95 For Dummies®	Margaret Levine Young & David Kay	1-56884-949-4	$19.99 US/$27.99 CAN

SPREADSHEET/FINANCE/PROJECT MANAGEMENT

Excel For Windows® 95 For Dummies®	Greg Harvey	1-56884-930-3	$19.99 US/$27.99 CAN
Excel 2000 For Windows® For Dummies®	Greg Harvey	0-7645-0446-0	$19.99 US/$27.99 CAN
Excel 2000 For Windows® For Dummies® Quick Reference	John Walkenbach	0-7645-0447-9	$12.99 US/$17.99 CAN
Microsoft® Money 99 For Dummies®	Peter Weverka	0-7645-0433-9	$19.99 US/$27.99 CAN
Microsoft® Project 98 For Dummies®	Martin Doucette	0-7645-0321-9	$24.99 US/$34.99 CAN
Microsoft® Project 2000 For Dummies®	Martin Doucette	0-7645-0517-3	$24.99 US/$37.99 CAN
Microsoft® Money 2000 For Dummies®	Peter Weverka	0-7645-0579-3	$19.99 US/$27.99 CAN
MORE Excel 97 For Windows® For Dummies®	Greg Harvey	0-7645-0138-0	$22.99 US/$32.99 CAN
Quicken® 2000 For Dummies®	Stephen L . Nelson	0-7645-0607-2	$19.99 US/$27.99 CAN
Quicken® 2001 For Dummies®	Stephen L . Nelson	0-7645-0759-1	$19.99 US/$27.99 CAN
Quickbooks® 2000 For Dummies®	Stephen L . Nelson	0-7645-0665-x	$19.99 US/$27.99 CAN

Dummies Books™
Bestsellers on Every Topic!

GENERAL INTEREST TITLES

CAREERS

Title	Author	ISBN	Price
Cover Letters For Dummies®, 2nd Edition	Joyce Lain Kennedy	0-7645-5224-4	$12.99 US/$17.99 CAN
Cool Careers For Dummies®	Marty Nemko, Paul Edwards, & Sarah Edwards	0-7645-5095-0	$16.99 US/$24.99 CAN
Job Hunting For Dummies®, 2nd Edition	Max Messmer	0-7645-5163-9	$19.99 US/$26.99 CAN
Job Interviews For Dummies®, 2nd Edition	Joyce Lain Kennedy	0-7645-5225-2	$12.99 US/$17.99 CAN
Resumes For Dummies®, 2nd Edition	Joyce Lain Kennedy	0-7645-5113-2	$12.99 US/$17.99 CAN

FITNESS

Title	Author	ISBN	Price
Fitness Walking For Dummies®	Liz Neporent	0-7645-5192-2	$19.99 US/$27.99 CAN
Fitness For Dummies®, 2nd Edition	Suzanne Schlosberg & Liz Neporent	0-7645-5167-1	$19.99 US/$27.99 CAN
Nutrition For Dummies®, 2nd Edition	Carol Ann Rinzler	0-7645-5180-9	$19.99 US/$27.99 CAN
Running For Dummies®	Florence "Flo-Jo" Griffith Joyner & John Hanc	0-7645-5096-9	$19.99 US/$27.99 CAN

FOREIGN LANGUAGE

Title	Author	ISBN	Price
Spanish For Dummies®	Susana Wald	0-7645-5194-9	$24.99 US/$34.99 CAN
French For Dummies®	Dodi-Kartrin Schmidt & Michelle W. Willams	0-7645-5193-0	$24.99 US/$34.99 CAN

TECHNOLOGY TITLES

DATABASSE

Title	Author	ISBN	Price
Access 2000 For Windows® For Dummies®	John Kaufeld	0-7645-0444-4	$19.99 US/$27.99 CAN
Access 97 For Windows® For Dummies®	John Kaufeld	0-7645-0048-1	$19.99 US/$27.99 CAN
Access 2000 For Windows For Dummies® Quick Reference	Alison Barrons	0-7645-0445-2	$12.99 US/$17.99 CAN
Approach® 97 For Windows® For Dummies®	Deborah S. Ray & Eric J. Ray	0-7645-0001-5	$19.99 US/$27.99 CAN
Crystal Reports 8 For Dummies®	Douglas J. Wolf	0-7645-0642-0	$24.99 US/$34.99 CAN
Data Warehousing For Dummies®	Alan R. Simon	0-7645-0170-4	$24.99 US/$34.99 CAN
FileMaker® Pro 4 For Dummies®	Tom Maremaa	0-7645-0210-7	$19.99 US/$27.99 CAN

NETWORKING/GROUPWARE

Title	Author	ISBN	Price
ATM For Dummies®	Cathy Gadecki & Christine Heckart	0-7645-0065-1	$24.99 US/$34.99 CAN
Client/Server Computing For Dummies®, 3rd Edition	Doug Lowe	0-7645-0476-2	$24.99 US/$34.99 CAN
DSL For Dummies®, 2nd Edition	David Angell	0-7645-0715-X	$24.99 US/$35.99 CAN
Lotus Notes® Release 4 For Dummies®	Stephen Londergan & Pat Freeland	1-56884-934-6	$19.99 US/$27.99 CAN
Microsoft® Outlook® 98 For Windows® For Dummies®	Bill Dyszel	0-7645-0393-6	$19.99 US/$28.99 CAN
Microsoft® Outlook® 2000 For Windows® For Dummies®	Bill Dyszel	0-7645-0471-1	$19.99 US/$27.99 CAN
Migrating to Windows® 2000 For Dummies®	Leonard Sterns	0-7645-0459-2	$24.99 US/$37.99 CAN
Networking For Dummies®, 4th Edition	Doug Lowe	0-7645-0498-3	$19.99 US/$27.99 CAN
Networking Home PCs For Dummies®	Kathy Ivens	0-7645-0491-6	$24.99 US/$35.99 CAN
Upgrading & Fixing Networks For Dummies®, 2nd Edition	Bill Camarda	0-7645-0542-4	$29.99 US/$42.99 CAN
TCP/IP For Dummies®, 4th Edition	Candace Leiden & Marshall Wilensky	0-7645-0726-5	$24.99 US/$35.99 CAN
Windows NT® Networking For Dummies®	Ed Tittel, Mary Madden, & Earl Follis	0-7645-0015-5	$24.99 US/$34.99 CAN

PROGRAMMING

Title	Author	ISBN	Price
Active Server Pages For Dummies®, 2nd Edition	Bill Hatfield	0-7645-0065-1	$24.99 US/$34.99 CAN
Beginning Programming For Dummies®	Wally Wang	0-7645-0596-0	$19.99 US/$29.99 CAN
C++ For Dummies® Quick Reference, 2nd Edition	Namir Shammas	0-7645-0390-1	$14.99 US/$21.99 CAN
Java™ Programming For Dummies®, 3rd Edition	David & Donald Koosis	0-7645-0388-X	$29.99 US/$42.99 CAN
JBuilder™ For Dummies®	Barry A. Burd	0-7645-0567-X	$24.99 US/$34.99 CAN
VBA For Dummies®, 2nd Edition	Steve Cummings	0-7645-0078-3	$24.99 US/$37.99 CAN
Windows® 2000 Programming For Dummies®	Richard Simon	0-7645-0469-X	$24.99 US/$37.99 CAN
XML For Dummies®, 2nd Edition	Ed Tittel	0-7645-0692-7	$24.99 US/$37.99 CAN

Dummies Books™
Bestsellers on Every Topic!

GENERAL INTEREST TITLES

THE ARTS

TArt For Dummies®	Thomas Hoving	0-7645-5104-3	$24.99 US/$34.99 CAN
Blues For Dummies®	Lonnie Brooks, Cub Koda, & Wayne Baker Brooks	0-7645-5080-2	$24.99 US/$34.99 CAN
Classical Music For Dummies®	David Pogue & Scott Speck	0-7645-5009-8	$24.99 US/$34.99 CAN
Guitar For Dummies®	Mark Phillips & Jon Chappell of Cherry Lane Music	0-7645-5106-X	$24.99 US/$34.99 CAN
Jazz For Dummies®	Dirk Sutro	0-7645-5081-0	$24.99 US/$34.99 CAN
Opera For Dummies®	David Pogue & Scott Speck	0-7645-5010-1	$24.99 US/$34.99 CAN
Piano For Dummies®	Blake Neely of Cherry Lane Music	0-7645-5105-1	$24.99 US/$34.99 CAN
Shakespeare For Dummies®	John Doyle & Ray Lischner	0-7645-5135-3	$19.99 US/$27.99 CAN

HEALTH

Allergies and Asthma For Dummies®	William Berger, M.D.	0-7645-5218-X	$19.99 US/$27.99 CAN
Alternative Medicine For Dummies®	James Dillard, M.D., D.C., C.A.C., & Terra Ziporyn, Ph.D.	0-7645-5109-4	$19.99 US/$27.99 CAN
Beauty Secrets For Dummies®	Stephanie Seymour	0-7645-5078-0	$19.99 US/$27.99 CAN
Diabetes For Dummies®	Alan L. Rubin, M.D.	0-7645-5154-X	$19.99 US/$27.99 CAN
Dieting For Dummies®	The American Dietetic Society with Jane Kirby, R.D.	0-7645-5126-4	$19.99 US/$27.99 CAN
Family Health For Dummies®	Charles Inlander & Karla Morales	0-7645-5121-3	$19.99 US/$27.99 CAN
First Aid For Dummies®	Charles B. Inlander & The People's Medical Society	0-7645-5213-9	$19.99 US/$27.99 CAN
Fitness For Dummies®, 2ⁿᵈ Edition	Suzanne Schlosberg & Liz Neporent, M.A.	0-7645-5167-1	$19.99 US/$27.99 CAN
Healing Foods For Dummies®	Molly Siple, M.S. R.D.	0-7645-5198-1	$19.99 US/$27.99 CAN
Healthy Aging For Dummies®	Walter Bortz, M.D.	0-7645-5233-3	$19.99 US/$27.99 CAN
Men's Health For Dummies®	Charles Inlander	0-7645-5120-5	$19.99 US/$27.99 CAN
Nutrition For Dummies®, 2ⁿᵈ Edition	Carol Ann Rinzler	0-7645-5180-9	$19.99 US/$27.99 CAN
Pregnancy For Dummies®	Joanne Stone, M.D., Keith Eddleman, M.D., & Mary Murray	0-7645-5074-8	$19.99 US/$27.99 CAN
Sex For Dummies®	Dr. Ruth K. Westheimer	1-56884-384-4	$16.99 US/$24.99 CAN
Stress Management For Dummies®	Allen Elkin, Ph.D.	0-7645-5144-2	$19.99 US/$27.99 CAN
The Healthy Heart For Dummies®	James M. Ripple, M.D.	0-7645-5166-3	$19.99 US/$27.99 CAN
Weight Training For Dummies®	Liz Neporent, M.A. & Suzanne Schlosberg	0-7645-5036-5	$19.99 US/$27.99 CAN
Women's Health For Dummies®	Pamela Maraldo, Ph.D., R.N., & The People's Medical Society	0-7645-5119-1	$19.99 US/$27.99 CAN

TECHNOLOGY TITLES

MACINTOSH

Macs® For Dummies®, 7ᵗʰ Edition	David Pogue	0-7645-0703-6	$19.99 US/$27.99 CAN
The iBook™ For Dummies®	David Pogue	0-7645-0647-1	$19.99 US/$27.99 CAN
The iMac For Dummies®, 2ⁿᵈ Edition	David Pogue	0-7645-0648-X	$19.99 US/$27.99 CAN
The iMac For Dummies® Quick Reference	Jenifer	0-7645-0648-X	$12.99 US/$19.99 CAN

PC/GENERAL COMPUTING

Building A PC For Dummies®, 2nd Edition	Mark Chambers	0-7645-0571-8	$24.99 US/$34.99 CAN
Buying a Computer For Dummies®	Dan Gookin	0-7645-0632-3	$19.99 US/$27.99 CAN
Illustrated Computer Dictionary For Dummies®, 4ᵗʰ Edition	Dan Gookin & Sandra Hardin Gookin	0-7645-0732-X	$19.99 US/$27.99 CAN
Palm Computing® For Dummies®	Bill Dyszel	0-7645-0581-5	$24.99 US/$34.99 CAN
PCs For Dummies®, 7ᵗʰ Edition	Dan Gookin	0-7645-0594-7	$19.99 US/$27.99 CAN
Small Business Computing For Dummies®	Brian Underdahl	0-7645-0287-5	$24.99 US/$34.99 CAN
Smart Homes For Dummies®	Danny Briere	0-7645-0527-0	$19.99 US/$27.99 CAN
Upgrading & Fixing PCs For Dummies®, 5ᵗʰ Edition	Andy Rathbone	0-7645-0719-2	$19.99 US/$27.99 CAN
Handspring Visor For Dummies®	Joe Hubko	0-7645-0724-9	$19.99 US/$27.99 CAN

Hungry Minds, Inc.
Linux source code mail-in coupon

In an attempt to provide you with CDs packed with greater amounts of accompanying software, we're offering the source code (which usually comes packaged with the Linux operating system) via mail. This offer is valid for a period of 1 year from the date of purchase of this book. After you mail in the coupon below with a dated cash-register receipt and a money order for **$8.95** for orders within the U.S. or **$12.95** for orders outside the U.S., you will receive the corresponding source code on CD-ROM.

Return this coupon, with original receipt and money order (U.S. funds only), to the address listed below. Please make sure that you list Part #0795-8 on your check or money order so that we can ensure that you receive the correct CD. Please allow 4–6 weeks for delivery.

Name _____

Company _____

Address _____

City _____ State _____ Postal Code _____

Country _____

E-mail _____ Telephone _____

Detach and return this coupon to:
Media Development Department
Hungry Minds, Inc.
Part #0795-8 Fulfillment
10475 Crosspoint Blvd.
Indianapolis, IN 46256

Hungry Minds™

Terms: Must include original, dated cash-register receipt; no copies of cash-register receipts or this coupon will be accepted. Void where prohibited, taxed, or restricted by law. Allow 4-6 weeks delivery. Hungry Minds is not responsible for lost, late, illegible, or incomplete orders. For questions, please call (877) 404-9175.

GNU GENERAL PUBLIC LICENSE

Version 2, June 1991
Copyright (C) 1989, 1991 Free Software Foundation, Inc.
59 Temple Place - Suite 330, Boston, MA 02111-1307, USA

Preamble

The licenses for most software are designed to take away your freedom to share and change it. By contrast, the GNU General Public License is intended to guarantee your freedom to share and change free software—to make sure the software is free for all its users. This General Public License applies to most of the Free Software Foundation's software and to any other program whose authors commit to using it. (Some other Free Software Foundation software is covered by the GNU Library General Public License instead.) You can apply it to your programs, too.

When we speak of free software, we are referring to freedom, not price. Our General Public Licenses are designed to make sure that you have the freedom to distribute copies of free software (and charge for this service if you wish), that you receive source code or can get it if you want it, that you can change the software or use pieces of it in new free programs; and that you know you can do these things.

To protect your rights, we need to make restrictions that forbid anyone to deny you these rights or to ask you to surrender the rights. These restrictions translate to certain responsibilities for you if you distribute copies of the software, or if you modify it.

For example, if you distribute copies of such a program, whether gratis or for a fee, you must give the recipients all the rights that you have. You must make sure that they, too, receive or can get the source code. And you must show them these terms so they know their rights.

We protect your rights with two steps: (1) copyright the software, and (2) offer you this license which gives you legal permission to copy, distribute and/or modify the software.

Also, for each author's protection and ours, we want to make certain that everyone understands that there is no warranty for this free software. If the software is modified by someone else and passed on, we want its recipients to know that what they have is not the original, so that any problems introduced by others will not reflect on the original authors' reputations.

Finally, any free program is threatened constantly by software patents. We wish to avoid the danger that redistributors of a free program will individually obtain patent licenses, in effect making the program proprietary. To prevent this, we have made it clear that any patent must be licensed for everyone's free use or not licensed at all.

The precise terms and conditions for copying, distribution and modification follow.

TERMS AND CONDITIONS FOR COPYING, DISTRIBUTION AND MODIFICATION

0. This License applies to any program or other work which contains a notice placed by the copyright holder saying it may be distributed under the terms of this General Public License. The "Program", below, refers to any such program or work, and a "work based on the Program" means either the Program or any derivative work under copyright law: that is to say, a work containing the Program or a portion of it, either verbatim or with modifications and/or translated into another language. (Hereinafter, translation is included without limitation in the term "modification".) Each licensee is addressed as "you".

   Activities other than copying, distribution and modification are not covered by this License; they are outside its scope. The act of running the Program is not restricted, and the output from the Program is covered only if its contents constitute a work based on the Program (independent of having been made by running the Program). Whether that is true depends on what the Program does.

1. You may copy and distribute verbatim copies of the Program's source code as you receive it, in any medium, provided that you conspicuously and appropriately publish on each copy an appropriate copyright notice and disclaimer of warranty; keep intact all the notices that refer to this License and to the absence of any warranty; and give any other recipients of the Program a copy of this License along with the Program.

   You may charge a fee for the physical act of transferring a copy, and you may at your option offer warranty protection in exchange for a fee.

2. You may modify your copy or copies of the Program or any portion of it, thus forming a work based on the Program, and copy and distribute such modifications or work under the terms of Section 1 above, provided that you also meet all of these conditions:

   a) You must cause the modified files to carry prominent notices stating that you changed the files and the date of any change.

   b) You must cause any work that you distribute or publish, that in whole or in part contains or is derived from the Program or any part thereof, to be licensed as a whole at no charge to all third parties under the terms of this License.

   c) If the modified program normally reads commands interactively when run, you must cause it, when started running for such interactive use in the most ordinary way, to print or display an announcement including an appropriate copyright notice and a notice that there is no warranty (or else, saying that you provide a warranty) and that users may redistribute the program under these conditions, and telling the user how to view a copy of this License. (Exception: if the Program itself is interactive but does not normally print such an announcement, your work based on the Program is not required to print an announcement.)

   These requirements apply to the modified work as a whole. If identifiable sections of that work are not derived from the Program, and can be reasonably considered independent and separate works in themselves, then this License, and its terms, do not apply to those sections when you distribute them as separate works. But when you distribute the same sections as part of a whole which is a work based on the Program, the distribution of the whole must be on the terms of this License, whose permissions for other licensees extend to the entire whole, and thus to each and every part regardless of who wrote it.

Thus, it is not the intent of this section to claim rights or contest your rights to work written entirely by you; rather, the intent is to exercise the right to control the distribution of derivative or collective works based on the Program. In addition, mere aggregation of another work not based on the Program with the Program (or with a work based on the Program) on a volume of a storage or distribution medium does not bring the other work under the scope of this License.

3. You may copy and distribute the Program (or a work based on it, under Section 2) in object code or executable form under the terms of Sections 1 and 2 above provided that you also do one of the following:

a) Accompany it with the complete corresponding machine-readable source code, which must be distributed under the terms of Sections 1 and 2 above on a medium customarily used for software interchange; or,

b) Accompany it with a written offer, valid for at least three years, to give any third party, for a charge no more than your cost of physically performing source distribution, a complete machine-readable copy of the corresponding source code, to be distributed under the terms of Sections 1 and 2 above on a medium customarily used for software interchange; or,

c) Accompany it with the information you received as to the offer to distribute corresponding source code. (This alternative is allowed only for noncommercial distribution and only if you received the program in object code or executable form with such an offer, in accord with Subsection b above.)

The source code for a work means the preferred form of the work for making modifications to it. For an executable work, complete source code means all the source code for all modules it contains, plus any associated interface definition files, plus the scripts used to control compilation and installation of the executable. However, as a special exception, the source code distributed need not include anything that is normally distributed (in either source or binary form) with the major components (compiler, kernel, and so on) of the operating system on which the executable runs, unless that component itself accompanies the executable.

If distribution of executable or object code is made by offering access to copy from a designated place, then offering equivalent access to copy the source code from the same place counts as distribution of the source code, even though third parties are not compelled to copy the source along with the object code.

4. You may not copy, modify, sublicense, or distribute the Program except as expressly provided under this License. Any attempt otherwise to copy, modify, sublicense or distribute the Program is void, and will automatically terminate your rights under this License. However, parties who have received copies, or rights, from you under this License will not have their licenses terminated so long as such parties remain in full compliance.

5. You are not required to accept this License, since you have not signed it. However, nothing else grants you permission to modify or distribute the Program or its derivative works. These actions are prohibited by law if you do not accept this License. Therefore, by modifying or distributing the Program (or any work based on the Program), you indicate your acceptance of this License to do so, and all its terms and conditions for copying, distributing or modifying the Program or works based on it.

6. Each time you redistribute the Program (or any work based on the Program), the recipient automatically receives a license from the original licensor to copy, distribute or modify the Program subject to these terms and conditions. You may not impose any further restrictions on the recipients' exercise of the rights granted herein. You are not responsible for enforcing compliance by third parties to this License.

7. If, as a consequence of a court judgment or allegation of patent infringement or for any other reason (not limited to patent issues), conditions are imposed on you (whether by court order, agreement or otherwise) that contradict the conditions of this License, they do not excuse you from the conditions of this License. If you cannot distribute so as to satisfy simultaneously your obligations under this License and any other pertinent obligations, then as a consequence you may not distribute the Program at all. For example, if a patent license would not permit royalty-free redistribution of the Program by all those who receive copies directly or indirectly through you, then the only way you could satisfy both it and this License would be to refrain entirely from distribution of the Program.

    If any portion of this section is held invalid or unenforceable under any particular circumstance, the balance of the section is intended to apply and the section as a whole is intended to apply in other circumstances.

    It is not the purpose of this section to induce you to infringe any patents or other property right claims or to contest validity of any such claims; this section has the sole purpose of protecting the integrity of the free software distribution system, which is implemented by public license practices. Many people have made generous contributions to the wide range of software distributed through that system in reliance on consistent application of that system; it is up to the author/donor to decide if he or she is willing to distribute software through any other system and a licensee cannot impose that choice.

    This section is intended to make thoroughly clear what is believed to be a consequence of the rest of this License.

8. If the distribution and/or use of the Program is restricted in certain countries either by patents or by copyrighted interfaces, the original copyright holder who places the Program under this License may add an explicit geographical distribution limitation excluding those countries, so that distribution is permitted only in or among countries not thus excluded. In such case, this License incorporates the limitation as if written in the body of this License.

9. The Free Software Foundation may publish revised and/or new versions of the General Public License from time to time. Such new versions will be similar in spirit to the present version, but may differ in detail to address new problems or concerns.

    Each version is given a distinguishing version number. If the Program specifies a version number of this License which applies to it and "any later version", you have the option of following the terms and conditions either of that version or of any later version published by the Free Software Foundation. If the Program does not specify a version number of this License, you may choose any version ever published by the Free Software Foundation.

10. If you wish to incorporate parts of the Program into other free programs whose distribution conditions are different, write to the author to ask for permission. For software which is copyrighted by the Free Software Foundation, write to the Free Software Foundation; we sometimes make exceptions for this. Our decision will be guided by the two goals of preserving the free status of all derivatives of our free software and of promoting the sharing and reuse of software generally.

NO WARRANTY

11. BECAUSE THE PROGRAM IS LICENSED FREE OF CHARGE, THERE IS NO WARRANTY FOR THE PROGRAM, TO THE EXTENT PERMITTED BY APPLICABLE LAW. EXCEPT WHEN OTHERWISE STATED IN WRITING THE COPYRIGHT HOLDERS AND/OR OTHER PARTIES PROVIDE THE PROGRAM "AS IS" WITHOUT WARRANTY OF ANY KIND, EITHER EXPRESSED OR IMPLIED, INCLUDING, BUT NOT LIMITED TO, THE IMPLIED WARRANTIES OF MERCHANTABILITY AND FITNESS FOR A PARTICULAR PURPOSE. THE ENTIRE RISK AS TO THE QUALITY AND PERFORMANCE OF THE PROGRAM IS WITH YOU. SHOULD THE PROGRAM PROVE DEFECTIVE, YOU ASSUME THE COST OF ALL NECESSARY SERVICING, REPAIR OR CORRECTION.

12. IN NO EVENT UNLESS REQUIRED BY APPLICABLE LAW OR AGREED TO IN WRITING WILL ANY COPYRIGHT HOLDER, OR ANY OTHER PARTY WHO MAY MODIFY AND/OR REDISTRIBUTE THE PROGRAM AS PERMITTED ABOVE, BE LIABLE TO YOU FOR DAMAGES, INCLUDING ANY GENERAL, SPECIAL, INCIDENTAL OR CONSEQUENTIAL DAMAGES ARISING OUT OF THE USE OR INABILITY TO USE THE PROGRAM (INCLUDING BUT NOT LIMITED TO LOSS OF DATA OR DATA BEING RENDERED INACCURATE OR LOSSES SUSTAINED BY YOU OR THIRD PARTIES OR A FAILURE OF THE PROGRAM TO OPERATE WITH ANY OTHER PROGRAMS), EVEN IF SUCH HOLDER OR OTHER PARTY HAS BEEN ADVISED OF THE POSSIBILITY OF SUCH DAMAGES.

END OF TERMS AND CONDITIONS

Installation Instructions

The *Red Hat Linux 7 For Dummies* CDs offer valuable information that you won't want to miss. To install Red Hat Linux from the CDs to your hard drive, follow these steps.

1. **Insert CD1 into your computer's CD-ROM drive.**

2. **Double-click the CD icon to show the CD's contents.**

3. **Double-click the Read Me First icon.**

   The Read Me First text file contains information about the CD's programs and any last-minute instructions you may need in order to correctly install them.

4. **Other programs come with installer programs — with these, you simply open the program's folder on the CD and then double-click the icon with the words "Install" or "Installer."**

   Sometimes the installers are actually self extracting archives, which just means that the program files have been bundled up into an archive, and this self extractor unbundles the files and places them on your hard drive. This kind of program is often called an .sea. Double click anything with .sea in the title, and it will run just like an installer.

   After you have installed the programs you want, you can eject the CD. Carefully place it back in the plastic jacket of the book for safekeeping.

For more information, see the "About the CD" appendix.

Limited Warranty

Hungry Minds, Inc. (hereafter HMI) warrants that the Software and Software Media are free from defects in materials and workmanship under normal use for a period of sixty (60) days from the date of purchase of this Book. If HMI receives notification within the warranty period of defects in materials or workmanship, HMI will replace the defective Software Media.

HMI AND THE AUTHOR OF THE BOOK DISCLAIM ALL OTHER WARRANTIES, EXPRESS OR IMPLIED, INCLUDING WITHOUT LIMITATION IMPLIED WARRANTIES OF MERCHANTABILITY AND FITNESS FOR A PARTICULAR PURPOSE, WITH RESPECT TO THE SOFTWARE, THE PROGRAMS, THE SOURCE CODE CONTAINED THEREIN, AND/OR THE TECHNIQUES DESCRIBED IN THIS BOOK. HMI DOES NOT WARRANT THAT THE FUNCTIONS CONTAINED IN THE SOFTWARE WILL MEET YOUR REQUIREMENTS OR THAT THE OPERATION OF THE SOFTWARE WILL BE ERROR FREE.

This limited warranty gives you specific legal rights, and you may have other rights that vary from jurisdiction to jurisdiction.

FOR DUMMIES
BOOK REGISTRATION

We want to hear from you!

Visit **dummies.c** ~~register this book and~~ ll us how you liked it!

- Get entered i

- Give us feedl ~~~~ ~~hat you like best,
  what you like ~~~~ e to ask the author
  and us to change!

- Let us know any other *For Dummies* topics that interest you.

Your feedback helps us determine what books to publish, tells us what coverage to add as we revise our books, and lets us know whether we're meeting your needs as a *For Dummies* reader. You're our most valuable resource, and what you have to say is important to us!

Not on the Web yet? It's easy to get started with *Dummies 101: The Internet For Windows 98* or *The Internet For Dummies* at local retailers everywhere.

Or let us know what you think by sending us a letter at the following address:

For Dummies Book Registration
Dummies Press
10475 Crosspoint Blvd.
Indianapolis, IN 46256

...FOR DUMMIES™

BESTSELLING
BOOK SERIES